Bloom's Modern Critical Views

Bloom's Modern Critical Views

THE BRONTËS
New Edition

Edited and with an introduction by
Harold Bloom
Sterling Professor of the Humanities
Yale University

BLOOM'S
LITERARY CRITICISM
An imprint of Infobase Publishing

Editorial Consultant, Susan Carlson

Bloom's Modern Critical Views: The Brontës—New Edition

Copyright ©2009 by Infobase Publishing

Introduction ©2009 by Harold Bloom

All rights reserved. No part of this publication may be reproduced or utilized in any form or by any means, electronic or mechanical, including photocopying, recording, or by any information storage or retrieval systems, without permission in writing from the publisher. For more information contact:

Bloom's Literary Criticism
An imprint of Infobase Publishing
132 West 31st Street
New York NY 10001

Library of Congress Cataloging-in-Publication Data

The Brontës / edited and with an introduction by Harold Bloom.—New ed.
    p. cm.—(Blooms's modern critical views)
Includes bibliographical references (p.   ) and index.
ISBN 978-1-4381-1280-0 (alk. paper)
1. Brontë family. 2. English fiction—19th century—History and criticism. I. Bloom, Harold.

PR4169.B77 2008b
823'.809—dc22
                                        2008032550

Contents

Editor's Note

My Introduction considers *Jane Eyre* and *Wuthering Heights* as northern romances, each obsessed with the myth and personality of George Gordon, Lord Byron.

Humphrey Gawthrop rather problematically traces what he regards as the displaced theme of black slavery in Emily and Charlotte Brontë, after which Alexandra Leach reflects on the justly neglected poetry of Anne Brontë.

The strange religious imagery of *Jane Eyre*'s close is studied by Joshua Essaka, while Rebecca Fraser praised the effect of her Belgian teacher, Heger, upon the young Charlotte Brontë.

James Reamy takes us back to the Gothic element in the childhood writings of the Brontës, after which Meghan Bullock and later Joan Bellamy examine Anne's best novel, *The Tenant of Wildfell Hall*.

Shakespearean allusions in the Brontës are analyzed by Paul Edmondson, while the question of love in Charlotte Brontë is contrasted with its treatment by Jane Austen by Susan Ostrov Weisser.

In this volume's final essay, Patsy Stevenson interestingly considers the effects of Shelley's life and poetry upon *Wuthering Heights*.

HAROLD BLOOM

Introduction

THE BRONTËS

I

The three Brontë sisters—Charlotte, Emily Jane, and Anne—are unique literary artists whose works resemble one another's far more than they do the works of writers before or since. Charlotte's compelling novel *Jane Eyre* and her three lesser yet strong narratives—*The Professor, Shirley, Villette*—form the most extensive achievement of the sisters, but critics and common readers alike set even higher the one novel of Emily Jane's, *Wuthering Heights*, and a handful of her lyrical poems. Anne's two novels—*Agnes Grey* and *The Tenant of Wildfell Hall*—remain highly readable, although dwarfed by *Jane Eyre* and the authentically sublime *Wuthering Heights*.

Between them, the Brontës can be said to have invented a relatively new genre, a kind of northern romance, deeply influenced both by Byron's poetry and by his myth and personality, but going back also, more remotely yet as definitely, to the Gothic novel and to the Elizabethan drama. In a definite, if difficult to establish sense, the heirs of the Brontës include Thomas Hardy and D.H. Lawrence. There is a harsh vitalism in the Brontës that finds its match in the Lawrence of *The Rainbow* and *Women in Love*, though the comparison is rendered problematic by Lawrence's moral zeal, enchantingly absent from the Brontës' literary cosmos.

The aesthetic puzzle of the Brontës has less to do with the mature transformations of their vision of Byron into Rochester and Heathcliff, than with their earlier fantasy-life and its literature, and the relation of that life and literature to its hero and precursor, George Gordon, Lord

1

Byron. At his rare worst and silliest, Byron has nothing like this scene from Charlotte Brontë's "Caroline Vernon," where Caroline confronts the Byronic Duke of Zamorna:

> The Duke spoke again in a single blunt and almost coarse sentence, compressing what remained to be said, "If I were a bearded Turk, Caroline, I would take you to my harem." His deep voice as he uttered this, his high featured face, and dark, large eye burning bright with a spark from the depths of Gehenna, struck Caroline Vernon with a thrill of nameless dread. Here he was, the man Montmorency had described to her. All at once she knew him. Her guardian was gone, something terrible sat in his place.

Byron died his more-or-less heroic death at Missolonghi in Greece on April 19, 1824, aged thirty-six years and three months, after having set an impossible paradigm for authors that has become what the late Nelson Algren called "Hemingway all the way," in a mode later exploited by Norman Mailer, Gore Vidal, and some of their peers. Charlotte was eight, Emily Jane six, and Anne four when the Noble Lord died and when his cult gorgeously flowered, dominating their girlhood and their young womanhood. Byron's passive-aggressive sexuality—at once sadomasochistic, homoerotic, incestuous, and ambivalently narcissistic—clearly sets the pattern for the ambiguously erotic universes of *Jane Eyre* and *Wuthering Heights*. What Schopenhauer named (and deplored) as the Will to Live, and Freud subsequently posited as the domain of the drives, is the cosmos of the Brontës, as it would come to be of Hardy and Lawrence. Byron rather than Schopenhauer is the source of the Brontës' vision of the Will to Live, but the Brontës add to Byron what his inverted Calvinism only partly accepted, the Protestant will proper, a heroic zest to assert one's own election, one's place in the hierarchy of souls.

Jane Eyre and Catherine Earnshaw do not fit into the grand array of heroines of the Protestant will that commences with Richardson's Clarissa Harlowe and goes through Austen's Emma Woodhouse and Fanny Price to triumph in George Eliot's Dorothea Brooke and Henry James's Isabel Archer. They are simply too wild and Byronic, too High Romantic, to keep such company. But we can see them with Hardy's Tess and, even more, his Eustacia Vye, and with Lawrence's Gudrun and Ursula. Their version of the Protestant will stems from the Romantic reading of Milton, but largely in its Byronic dramatization, rather than its more dialectical and subtle analyses in Blake and Shelley, and its more normative condemnation in Coleridge and in the Wordsworth of *The Borderers*.

JANE EYRE

The Byronism of Rochester in *Jane Eyre* is enhanced because the narrative is related in the first person by Jane Eyre herself, who is very much an overt surrogate for Charlotte Brontë. As Rochester remarks, Jane is indomitable; as Jane says, she is altogether "a free human being with an independent will." That will is fiercest in its passion for Rochester, undoubtedly because the passion for her crucial precursor is doubly ambivalent; Byron is both the literary father to a strong daughter, and the idealized object of her erotic drive. To Jane, Rochester's first appearance is associated not only with the animal intensities of his horse and dog, but with the first of his maimings. When Jane reclaims him at the novel's conclusion, he is left partly blinded and partly crippled. I do not think that we are to apply the Freudian reduction that Rochester has been somehow castrated, even symbolically, nor need we think of him as a sacrificed Samson figure, despite the author's allusions to Milton's *Samson Agonistes*. But certainly he has been rendered dependent upon Jane, and he has been tamed into domestic virtue and pious sentiment, in what I am afraid must be regarded as Charlotte Brontë's vengeance upon Byron. Even as Jane Eyre cannot countenance a sense of being in any way inferior to anyone whatsoever, Charlotte Brontë could not allow Byron to be forever beyond her. She could acknowledge, with fine generosity, "that I regard Mr. Thackeray as the first of modern masters, and as the legitimate high priest of Truth; I study him accordingly with reverence." But *Vanity Fair* is hardly the seedbed of *Jane Eyre*, and the amiable and urbane Thackeray was not exactly a prototype for Rochester.

Charlotte Brontë, having properly disciplined Rochester, forgave him his Byronic past, as in some comments upon him in one of her letters (to W. S. Williams, August 14, 1848):

> Mr. Rochester has a thoughtful nature and a very feeling heart; he is neither selfish nor self-indulgent; he is ill-educated, misguided; errs, when he does err, through rashness and inexperience: he lives for a time as too many other men live, but being radically better than most men, he does not like that degraded life, and is never happy in it. He is taught the severe lessons of experience and has sense to learn wisdom from them. Years improve him; the effervescence of youth foamed away, what is really good in him still remains. His nature is like wine of a good vintage, time cannot sour, but only mellows him. Such at least was the character I meant to portray.

Poor Rochester! If that constituted an accurate critical summary, then who would want to read the novel? It will hardly endear me to feminist critics if I observe that much of the literary power of *Jane Eyre* results from its authentic sadism in representing the very masculine Rochester as a victim of Charlotte Brontë's will-to-power over the beautiful Lord Byron. I partly dissent, with respect, from the judgment in this regard of our best feminist critics, Sandra M. Gilbert and Susan Gubar:

> It seems not to have been primarily the coarseness and sexuality of *Jane Eyre* which shocked Victorian reviewers . . . but . . . its "anti-Christian" refusal to accept the forms, customs, and standards of society—in short, its rebellious feminism. They were disturbed not so much by the proud Byronic sexual energy of Rochester as by the Byronic pride and passion of Jane herself.

Byronic passion, being an ambiguous entity, is legitimately present in Jane herself as a psychosexual aggressivity turned both against the self and against others. Charlotte Brontë, in a mode between those of Schopenhauer and Freud, knows implicitly that Jane Eyre's drive to acknowledge no superior to herself is precisely on the frontier between the psychical and the physical. Rochester is the outward realm that must be internalized, and Jane's introjection of him does not leave him wholly intact. Gilbert and Gubar shrewdly observe that Rochester's extensive sexual experience is almost the final respect in which Jane is not his equal, but they doubtless would agree that Jane's sexual imagination overmatches his, at least implicitly. After all, she has every advantage, because she tells the story, and very aggressively indeed. Few novels match this one in the author's will-to-power over her reader. "Reader!" Jane keeps crying out, and then she exuberantly cudgels that reader into the way things are, as far as she is concerned. Is that battered reader a man or a woman?

I tend to agree with Sylvère Monod's judgment that "Charlotte Brontë is thus led to bully her reader because she distrusts him ... he is a vapid, conventional creature, clearly deserving no more than he is given." Certainly he is less deserving than the charmingly wicked and Byronic Rochester, who is given a lot more punishment than he deserves. I verge upon saying that Charlotte Brontë exploits the masochism of her male readers, and I may as well say it, because much of *Jane Eyre's* rather nasty power as a novel depends upon its author's attitude towards men, which is nobly sadistic as befits a disciple of Byron.

"But what about female readers?" someone might object, and they might add: "What about Rochester's own rather nasty power? Surely he could not have gotten away with his behavior had he not been a man and well-financed to boot?" But is Rochester a man? Does he not share in the full ambiguity of Byron's multivalent sexual identities? And is Jane Eyre a woman? Is Byron's

Don Juan a man? The nuances of gender, within literary representation, are more bewildering even than they are in the bedroom. If Freud was right when he reminded us that there are never two in a bed, but a motley crowd of forebears as well, how much truer this becomes in literary romance than in family romance.

Jane Eyre, like *Wuthering Heights*, is after all a romance, however northern, and not a novel, properly speaking. Its standards of representation have more to do with Jacobean melodrama and Gothic fiction than with George Eliot and Thackeray, and more even with Byron's *Lara* and *Manfred* than with any other works. Rochester is no Heathcliff; he lives in a social reality in which Heathcliff would be an intruder even if Heathcliff cared for social realities except as fields in which to take revenge. Yet there is a daemon in Rochester. Heathcliff is almost nothing but daemonic, and Rochester has enough of the daemonic to call into question any current feminist reading of *Jane Eyre*. Consider the pragmatic close of the book, which is Jane's extraordinary account of her wedded bliss:

> I have now been married ten years. I know what it is to live entirely for and with what I love best on earth. I hold myself supremely blest—blest beyond what language can express; because I am my husband's life as fully as he is mine. No woman was ever nearer to her mate than I am; ever more absolutely bone of his bone and flesh of his flesh.
>
> I know no weariness of my Edward's society: he knows none of mine, any more than we each do of the pulsation of the heart that beats in our separate bosoms; consequently, we are ever together. To be together is for us to be at once as free as in solitude, as gay as in company. We talk, I believe, all day long: to talk to each other is but a more animated and an audible thinking. All my confidence is bestowed on him, all his confidence is devoted to me; we are precisely suited in character—perfect concord is the result.
>
> Mr. Rochester continued blind the first two years of our union: perhaps it was that circumstance that drew us so very near—that knit us so very close! for I was then his vision, as I am still his right hand. Literally, I was (what he often called me) the apple of his eye. He saw nature—he saw books through me; and never did I weary of gazing for his behalf, and of putting into words the effect of field, tree, town, river, cloud, sunbeam—of the landscape before us; of the weather round us—and impressing by sound on his ear what light could no longer stamp on his eye. Never did I weary of reading to him: never did I weary of conducting him where he wished to go: of doing for him what he wished to be done. And there was a pleasure in my services, most full, most exquisite, even though

sad—because he claimed these services without painful shame or damping humiliation. He loved me so truly that he knew no reluctance in profiting by my attendance: he felt I loved him so fondly that to yield that attendance was to indulge my sweetest wishes.

What are we to make of Charlotte Brontë's strenuous literalization of Gen. 2:23, her astonishing "ever more absolutely bone of his bone and flesh of his flesh"? Is *that* feminism? And what precisely is that "pleasure in my services, most full, most exquisite, even though sad"? In her "Farewell to Angria" (the world of her early fantasies), Charlotte Brontë asserted that "the mind would cease from excitement and turn now to a cooler region." Perhaps that cooler region was found in *Shirley* or in *Villette*, but fortunately it was not discovered in *Jane Eyre*. In the romance of Jane and Rochester, or of Charlotte Brontë and George Gordon, Lord Byron, we are still in Angria, "that burning clime where we have sojourned too long—its skies flame—the glow of sunset is always upon it—."

WUTHERING HEIGHTS

Wuthering Heights is as unique and idiosyncratic a narrative as *Moby-Dick*, and like Melville's masterwork breaks all the confines of genre. Its sources, like the writings of the other Brontës, are in the fantasy literature of a very young woman, in the poems that made up Emily Brontë's Gondal saga or cycle. Many of those poems, while deeply felt, simply string together Byronic commonplaces. A few of them are extraordinarily strong and match *Wuthering Heights* in sublimity, as in the famous lyric dated January 2, 1846:

> No coward soul is mine
> No trembler in the world's storm-troubled sphere
> I see Heaven's glories shine
> And Faith shines equal arming me from Fear
>
> O God within my breast
> Almighty ever-present Deity
> Life, that in me hast rest
> As I Undying Life, have power in Thee
>
> Vain are the thousand creeds
> That move men's hearts, unutterably vain,
> Worthless as withered weeds
> Or idlest froth amid the boundless main

To waken doubt in one
Holding so fast by thy infinity
So surely anchored on
The steadfast rock of Immortality

With wide-embracing love
Thy spirit animates eternal years
Pervades and broods above,
Changes, sustains, dissolves, creates and rears

Though Earth and moon were gone
And suns and universes ceased to be
And thou wert left alone
Every Existence would exist in thee

There is not room for Death
Nor atom that his might could render void
Since thou art Being and Breath
And what thou art may never be destroyed.

We could hardly envision Catherine Earnshaw, let alone Heathcliff, chanting these stanzas. The voice is that of Emily Jane Brontë addressing the God within her own breast, a God who certainly has nothing in common with the one worshipped by the Reverend Patrick Brontë. I do not hear in this poem, despite all its Protestant resonances, any nuance of Byron's inverted Miltonisms. *Wuthering Heights* seems to me a triumphant revision of Byron's *Manfred*, with the revisionary swerve taking Emily Brontë into what I would call an original gnosis, a kind of poetic faith, like Blake's or Emerson's, that resembles some aspects (but not others) of ancient Gnosticism without in any way actually deriving from Gnostic texts. "No coward soul is mine" also emerges from an original gnosis, from the poet's knowing that her *pneuma* or breath-soul, as compared to her less ontological psyche, is no part of the created world, since that world fell even as it was created. Indeed the creation, whether heights or valley, appears in *Wuthering Heights* as what the ancient Gnostics called the *kenoma*, a cosmological emptiness into which *we have been thrown*, a trope that Catherine Earnshaw originates for herself. A more overt Victorian Gnostic, Dante Gabriel Rossetti, made the best (if anti-feminist) observation on the setting of *Wuthering Heights*, a book whose "power and sound style" he greatly admired:

It is a fiend of a book, an incredible monster, combining all the stronger female tendencies from Mrs. Browning to Mrs. Brownrigg. The action is laid in Hell,—only it seems places and people have English names there.

Mrs. Brownrigg was a notorious eighteenth-century sadistic and murderous midwife, and Rossetti rather nastily imputed to *Wuthering Heights* a considerable female sadism. The book's violence is astonishing but appropriate, and appealed darkly both to Rossetti and to his close friend, the even more sadomasochistic Swinburne. Certainly the psychodynamics of the relationship between Heathcliff and Catherine go well beyond the domain of the pleasure principle. Gilbert and Gubar may stress too much that Heathcliff is Catherine's whip, the answer to her most profound fantasies, but the suggestion was Emily Brontë's before it became so fully developed by her best feminist critics.

Walter Pater remarked that the precise use of the term *romantic* did not apply to Sir Walter Scott, but rather:

> Much later, in a Yorkshire village, the spirit of romanticism bore a more really characteristic fruit in the work of a young girl, Emily Brontë, the romance of *Wuthering Heights*; the figures of Hareton Earnshaw, of Catherine Linton, and of Heathcliff—tearing open Catherine's grave, removing one side of her coffin, that he may really lie beside her in death—figures so passionate, yet woven on a background of delicately beautiful, moorland scenery, being typical examples of that spirit.

I always have wondered why Pater found the Romantic spirit more in Hareton and the younger Catherine than in Catherine Earnshaw, but I think now that Pater's implicit judgment was characteristically shrewd. The elder Catherine is the problematical figure in the book; she alone belongs to both orders of representation, that of social reality and that of otherness, of the Romantic Sublime. After she and the Lintons, Edgar and Isabella, are dead, then we are wholly in Heathcliff's world for the last half year of his life, and it is in that world that Hareton and the younger Catherine are portrayed for us. They are—as Heathcliff obscurely senses—the true heirs to whatever societally possible relationship Heathcliff and the first Catherine could have had.

Emily Brontë died less than half a year after her thirtieth birthday, having finished *Wuthering Heights* when she was twenty-eight. Even Charlotte, the family survivor, died before she turned thirty-nine, and the world of *Wuthering Heights* reflects the Brontë reality: the first Catherine dies at eighteen, Hindley at twenty-seven, Heathcliff's son Linton at seventeen, Isabella at thirty-one, Edgar at thirty-nine, and Heathcliff at thirty-seven or thirty-eight. It is a world where you marry early, because you will not live long. Hindley is twenty when he marries Frances, while Catherine Earnshaw is seventeen when she marries the twenty-one-year old Edgar Linton. Heathcliff is nineteen when he makes his hellish marriage to poor Isabella, who is eighteen at the time. The only happy lovers, Hareton and the second Catherine, are twenty-four and eighteen, respectively, when they marry. Both patterns—early marriage and early death— are thoroughly High Romantic, and emerge from the legacy of Shelley, dead at twenty-nine, and of Byron, martyred to the cause of Greek independence at thirty-six.

The passions of Gondal are scarcely moderated in *Wuthering Heights*, nor could they be; Emily Brontë's religion is essentially erotic, and her vision of triumphant sexuality is so mingled with death that we can imagine no consummation for the love of Heathcliff and Catherine Earnshaw except death. I find it difficult therefore to accept Gilbert and Gubar's reading in which *Wuthering Heights* becomes a Romantic feminist critique of *Paradise Lost*, akin to Mary Shelley's *Frankenstein*. Emily Brontë is no more interested in refuting Milton than in sustaining him. What Gilbert and Gubar uncover in *Wuthering Heights* that is antithetical to *Paradise Lost* comes directly from Byron's *Manfred*, which certainly is a Romantic critique of *Paradise Lost*. *Wuthering Heights* is *Manfred* converted to prose romance, and Heathcliff is more like Manfred, Lara, and Byron himself than is Charlotte Brontë's Rochester.

Byronic incest—the crime of Manfred and Astarte—is no crime for Emily Brontë, since Heathcliff and Catherine Earnshaw are more truly brother and sister than are Hindley and Catherine. Whatever inverted morality—a curious blend of Catholicism and Calvinism—Byron enjoyed, Emily Brontë herself repudiates, so that *Wuthering Heights* becomes a critique of *Manfred*, though hardly from a conventional feminist perspective. The furious energy that is loosed in *Wuthering Heights* is precisely Gnostic; its aim is to get back to the original Abyss, before the creation-fall. Like Blake, Emily Brontë identifies her imagination with the Abyss, and her *pneuma* or breath-soul with the Alien God, who is antithetical to the God of the creeds. The heroic rhetoric of Catherine Earnshaw is beyond every ideology, every merely social formulation, beyond even the dream of justice or of a better life, because it is beyond this cosmos, "this shattered prison":

"Oh, you see, Nelly! he would not relent a moment, to keep me out of the grave! *That* is how I'm loved! Well, never mind! That is not my Heathcliff. I shall love mine yet; and take him with me — he's in my soul. And," added she, musingly, "the thing that irks me most is this shattered prison, after all. I'm tired, tired of being enclosed here. I'm wearying to escape into that glorious world, and to be always there; not seeing it dimly through tears, and yearning for it through the walls of an aching heart; but really with it, and in it. Nelly, you think you are better and more fortunate than I; in full health and strength. You are sorry for me—very soon that will be altered. I shall be sorry for *you*. I shall be incomparably beyond and above you all. I *wonder* he won't be near me!" She went on to herself. "I thought he wished it. Heathcliff, dear! you should not be sullen now. Do come to me, Heathcliff."

Whatever we are to call the mutual passion of Catherine and Heathcliff, it has no societal aspect and neither seeks nor needs societal sanction. Romantic love has no fiercer representation in all of literature. But "love" seems an inadequate term for the connection between Catherine and Heathcliff. There are no elements of transference in that relation, nor can we call the attachment involved either narcissistic or anaclitic. If Freud is not applicable, then neither is Plato. These extraordinary vitalists, Catherine and Heathcliff, do not desire in one another that which each does not possess, do not lean themselves against one another, and do not even find and thus augment their own selves. They *are* one another, which is neither sane nor possible, and which does not support any doctrine of liberation whatsoever. Only that most extreme of visions, Gnosticism, could accommodate them, for, like the Gnostic adepts, Catherine and Heathcliff can only enter the *pleroma* or fullness together, as presumably they have done after Heathcliff 's self-induced death by starvation.

Blake may have promised us the Bible of Hell; Emily Brontë seems to have disdained Heaven and Hell alike. Her finest poem (for which we have no manuscript, but it is inconceivable that it could have been written by Charlotte) rejects every feeling save her own inborn "first feelings" and every world except a vision of earth consonant with those inaugural emotions:

Often rebuked, yet always back returning
To those first feelings that were born with me,
And leaving busy chase of wealth and learning
For idle dreams of things which cannot be:

To-day, I will seek not the shadowy region;
Its unsustaining vastness waxes drear;
And visions rising, legion after legion,
Bring the unreal world too strangely near.

I'll walk, but not in old heroic traces,
And not in paths of high morality,
And not among the half-distinguished faces,
The clouded forms of long-past history.

I'll walk where any own nature would be leading:
It vexes me to choose another guide:
Where the gray flocks in ferny glens are feeding;
Where the wild wind blows on the mountain side.

What have those lonely mountains worth revealing?
More glory and more grief than I can tell:
The earth that wakes *one* human heart to feeling
Can centre both the worlds of Heaven and Hell.

Whatever that centering is, it is purely individual, and as beyond gender as it is beyond creed or "high morality." It is the voice of Catherine Earnshaw, celebrating her awakening from the dream of heaven:

> "I was only going to say that heaven did not seem to be my home; and I broke my heart with weeping to come back to earth; and the angels were so angry that they flung me out, into the middle of the heath on the top of Wuthering Heights; where I woke sobbing for joy."

HUMPHREY GAWTHROP

Slavery: Idée Fixe *of Emily and Charlotte Brontë*

Slavery is a subject common to both Charlotte Brontë's novel Jane Eyre *and Emily Brontë's* Wuthering Heights. *Even where a direct West Indian or African connection is absent, slavery-related themes such as brutality, exploitation, and deprivation are present. This article considers the background to the Brontë family's knowledge of slavery, and how it manifests itself in their work.*

May Sinclair, in *The Three Brontës*, writes of Charlotte Brontë being 'woken up' by her reading of *Wuthering Heights:*

> Charlotte, I think, said to herself, 'That is what I ought to have done. That is what I will do next time.' And next time she did it . . . if you must have an influence to account for Jane Eyre, there is no need to go abroad to look for it . . . the strongest spirit, which was Emily's, prevailed . . . Charlotte's genius must have quickened in her when her nerves thrilled to the shock of Wuthering Heights.[1]

The two novels may be linked by a common but malevolent theme — Carribean (Indian) slavery — with Emily the forerunner. *Jane Eyre* was begun in August 1846, a few months after *Wuthering Heights* was completed. Heathcliff's

Brontë Studies, Volume 28, Number 2 (July 2001): pp. 113–121. © The Brontë Society 2001.

mother is referred to by Emily as an 'Indian Queen'.[2] Was this only in jest, or is it a clue to ancestry? Rochester calls Bertha, his wife, his 'Indian Messalina'.[3] I suggest that the shared use of the word 'Indian' is no accident. The sisters read their work aloud to each other. Both may be bent on creating story lines with overtones of slavery in order to wash out and make clean the stained handkerchief that was Brotosh colonial oppression. The drift underscoring both novels may be the redemption of slaves and consequent comeuppance of slave-masters. The conclusion to this study spotlights the target. Both novels can lead us to believe that Emily and Charlotte were impeaching systems that allowed, not only white domination of black, but, in a figurative, and lesser, sense, male domination of female, and adult domination of child.

Rochester tells Jane Eyre that his father knew 'Mr. Mason, a West India planter and merchant . . . his possessions were real and vast.' Bertha, of Creole ancestry, is shipped to England to be locked in a third-storey room at Thornfield. Her Creole mother would be somebody born West Indian or Latin American, but of European, especially Spanish, descent. Antoinetta, the mother, sounds Spanish, but could equally be English. The whole background of Bertha Mason and Heathcliff, two violent, unbridled characters, is highly suggestive of brutality born out of slavery, which was the biggest issue of the time. In chapter 11 of *Wuthering Heights* Heathcliff addresses Catherine with:

> I seek no revenge on you . . . That's not the plan. The tyrant grinds
> down his slaves and they don't turn against him: they crush those
> beneath them.

Heathcliff crushed those beneath him. Slaves were mostly identified by single names, and Heathcliff has one. We must look to the novels to see to what extent Afro-Caribbean slavery may have gained a foothold in both, and examine the sources of knowledge available to Emily and Charlotte, of Africa (see Appendix A for sources that first aroused the imaginations of the young Brontës) and, at this juncture, the Caribbean.

Midnight, 31 July 1838, is recorded as the time and date on which full freedom came to slaves in the British colonies. A slave in the Jamaican capital of Spanish Town recorded his thanks 'to Almighty God and next the English nation, whose laws have relieved us from the bondage in which we have been held. God bless and grant long life to our Queen Victoria'.[4] Black freedom at last, granted by the white hand of England, that had itself been selling blacks into slavery for over two hundred years prior to their final emancipation. The date would not have passed unnoticed in the Brontë household. British history was heavily discoloured by Britain's major role in the slave trade up to 1838, but even after emancipation Britain was showing signs of imperialism towards India. As Susan Meyer puts it:

> Perhaps the eight years since emancipation provided enough historical distance for Brontë (that is Charlotte) to make a serious and public, though implicit, critique of British slavery and British imperialism in the West Indies.[5]

Meyer's article deals with Charlotte only, but this comment would seem to apply to Emily, with liberty the breath of her nostrils, even more.

The Reverend Patrick Brontë had connections with the great abolitionist William Wilberforce, 'the African's Friend',[6] having been sponsored by him through St John's College, Cambridge, and having sent his daughters to the Clergy Daughters' School at Cowan Bridge, of which Wilberforce was a patron.[7] Wilberforce visited Keighley and Theodore Dury in July 1827, as Juliet Barker has recorded. She points out that it seems more than likely that Patrick would have been invited to Keighley to meet Wilberforce.[8] With Wilberforce a Member of Parliament for a Yorkshire seat (Hull), and Patrick having doubtless read *A Letter on the Abolition of the Slave Trade addressed to the Freeholders and other Inhabitants of Yorkshire* (1807), and followed the various reports of public meetings and subsequent petitions to Parliament (312 from England and Wales, 187 from Scotland),[9] the evidence points to the Haworth parsonage fairly humming with passion and indignation at the injustice of slavery. The nearby Ponden House library had copies of John Tuffman's *Island of Antigua, Brief Account of* (1787) and Daniel McKinnan's *A Tour through British West Indies* (1804), so Charlotte and Emily would have had the opportunity to read these in addition to first-hand knowledge from their father of the slave trade, and Wilberforce and his campaign to end it. The general debate about black freedom would also reach the parsonage through various papers and periodicals, and any article about Wilberforce and his disciples would have been keenly mulled over. In 1838 the *Quarterly Review* included a review of the *Life of William Wilberforce*. Branwell, too, would bring his sisters information about Liverpool (the premier port in the slave trade after Bristol, and where Heathcliff was found[10]) after his visits of 1839 and 1845.[11] Branwell's 1845 drawing of the boxers Bendigo and Caunt shows them delineated as black silhouettes, though neither was, in fact, black. That they are shown to be black and semi-naked, with the figure on the left holding a chain, is highly suggestive of a slavery setting.[12]

There are other sources of Caribbean knowledge to be mentioned. In 1838 John Gibson Lockhart's *Life of Sir Walter Scott*, Bart, his father-in-law, first appeared. As F. B. Pinion has written,[13] it can be assumed that Charlotte and her sisters read Lockhart as soon as they could after its appearance.

Margaret Smith is of the same opinion.[14] Lockhart records that in August 1825, John Wilson (of *Blackwood's Magazine*), staged a regatta in honour of Canning, attended by Scott, Wordsworth, Southey, and others, the venue being John Bolton's Storrs Hall on Lake Windermere:

> A large company had been assembled there in honour of the min-
> ister . . . It has not, I suppose, often happened to a plain English
> merchant, wholly the architect of his own fortunes, to entertain at
> one time a party embracing so many illustrious names . . . .[15]

G. Bernard Wood has written of historical notes in the vestibule of the modern Storrs Hall, an hotel, which state that Bolton owned slaves. Slaves carried to the West Indies might fetch as much as £44; the trade was not at that time illegal.[16]

On the 15 June 1839, in a letter to Ellen Nussey, Charlotte wrote of her stay at Swarcliffe Hall, near Harrogate, the summer residence of John Greenwood, brother of Mrs John Benson Sidgwick, to whose children Charlotte was presently governess. In their article on Jane Eyre and the Greenwood family, Sarah Fermi and Robin Greenwood mention that Frederick Greenwood would also have been present at this summer gathering and that Frederick Greenwood's wife was the daughter of Samuel Staniforth, a Liverpool merchant who inherited a large fortune made in whaling and the slave trade.[17] Her brother, the Reverend Thomas Staniforth, the son and heir of Samuel Staniforth, was afterwards to inherit Storrs Hall, the home of his uncle John Bolton. The article poses the question — could Thomas have visited his sister and her husband Frederick Greenwood while they were at Swarcliffe Hall, so that conversation could have turned on the West Indies and Spanish Town in Jamaica, to be overhead by Charlotte? She and Emily may have heard the same name — John Bolton — mentioned by Branwell, who had been resident in the Lakes as tutor to the Postlethwaite boys in 1840 and, no doubt, spent free time in the local inns and picked up gossip. We know the cause of Branwell's dismissal as tutor — 'visibly the worse for drink'.[18]

Another Caribbean fragment is mentioned in a letter Charlotte wrote to Monsieur Heger on 24 October 1844: 'I have just had bound all the books you gave me when I was at Brussels. I take delight in contemplating them; they make quite a little library. To begin with, there are the complete works of Bernardin de St. Pierre — the Penses de Pascal . . .'. In St. Pierre's romance *Paul et Virginie,* published in 1787, the heroine perishes in a shipwreck on her way back to Paul, a Creole from the Caribbean. Charlotte would read it some time after 1843. She included ships with the names *Paul et Virginie* and *Antigua* in *Villette.*[19] *Antigua* may have come from Tuffman's account of the island of that name in the Ponden House library.

We should now consider how, and to what extent, Charlotte and Emily used their gleanings from these sources (including those in Appendix A) in *Jane Eyre* and *Wuthering Heights*. (Already in her first novel, *The Professor*, Charlotte had made tentative slave allusions with her 'parting her lips, as full as those of a hot-blooded Maroon' and 'when she stole about me with the soft step of a slave — I felt at once barbarous and sensual as a pasha'.[20])

Emily, the stronger spirit, was the likely precursor in sowing the seed of slavery and then by inference damning it. We shall consider her first. Her crosscurrent of slavery seems even more deeply and deliberately submerged than the other components, themes, and ideas found by the commentators in *Wuthering Heights:* love and loss of love, morality, duplicity, revenge, inheritance, education, nature and culture, and so on. Slavery may be there too. It ties in with ideas of inheritance and revenge certainly, and does nothing to disturb or displace the poetic, Gondal, origins of the characters depicted. The immediate and most obvious clue to slavery as a theme which Emily first gives us is Heathcliff's single name. She does not mean to imply thereby that Heathcliff is a slave, but that he may be descended from a slave. From chapter 4 of *Wuthering Heights* we gather that Mr Earnshaw christened Heathcliff after a son that had died in childhood. Herbert Dingle has suggested he was the elder Earnshaw's illegitimate son.[21] The name Heathcliff attaches to the boy as both Christian and surname. He is never Heathcliff Earnshaw. By analogy, in the long history of the slave trade, the moment slaves were landed from the slave ships they were given new names, to change identity, to subjugate them even further and confirm the white power in whose vice-like grip they were held. Simple Christian names recurred time and again.[22] Books are full of instances from the lives of individual slaves, thus we can point to Hamlet (slave), Jupiter (slave), Jamaica (slave), Fedon (slave leader), Hannibal (slave), Moses (slave), Mingo (slave), Quamina (slave leader and black deacon) — the list never ends.[23] All the characters in *Wuthering Heights* have first and second names or titles, except Heathcliff. (Ellen Dean calls him 'Mr Heathcliff' when addressing him, but by that time he has returned to the Heights after an absence of three years.) To the list of single names we can add Joseph and Zilah who, as servants, were slaves in a sense.

Add to Heathcliff's single name his stated attributes, and the idea that Emily is adding a slave component to her story takes a firmer hold. Edward Chitham suggests that Emily had thought about the situation of ex-slaves and half-castes.[24] Page 1 of *Wuthering Heights* refers to Heathcliff's 'black eyes,' and chapter 4 to his black hair, his skin 'as dark almost as if it came from the devil'. In chapter 6 of the novel he is 'a little Lascar, or an American Spanish castaway.' In chapter 7, Heathcliff says to Nelly 'I wish I had light hair and a fair skin.' Nelly says to Heathcliff 'A good heart will help you to a bonny face, my lad, if you were a regular black.' Again, 'your mother an Indian Queen,' and '. . . you were kidnapped by wicked sailors and brought to England' (which is a slave ship in reverse, in effect). In the same chapter 7, however, there is a reference to Heathcliff's 'elegant locks,' hardly suggestive of pure negroid hair, but Emily never implies that Heathcliff is totally black. In chapter 17, when Heathcliff breaks into the Heights and fights with Hindley, Emily describes his 'sharp cannibal teeth.' This strongly suggests that Africa is somehow buried deep in Heathcliff's ancestry. If that is accepted, it follows that Emily may also be hinting at inter-breeding in Heathcliff's relationships. Stevie Davies considers Catherine's 'I *am* Heathcliff' to be one of the most unforgettable gestures of bonding in literature.[25] Is Emily implying by those three words that Catherine and Heathcliff are not only a spiritual, but also a physical, amalgam? She is even stronger on innuendo with the consummate marriage of Heathcliff and Isabella Linton (which produces Linton Heathcliff).

Violence is a strong ingredient in *Wuthering Heights*. All slave-masters and their slaves knew that the relationship was forged by and secured in violence. Whipping played a central role in maintaining slavery and defined the relationship between white master and black slave.[26] Thus Hindley treats Heathcliff with violence: Heathcliff is 'hardened . . . to ill-treatment: he would stand Hindley's blows without winking or shedding a tear.' Hindley, in chapter 6, is now master of the Heights, denies Heathcliff education, makes him work out of doors and says he must sleep with the servants. In chapter 7, Hindley's treatment of Heathcliff was 'enough to make a fiend of a saint.'

Is the story of Heathcliff that of the risen slave? Heathcliff, descended from slave stock, survives and returns to claim the Heights. Does he become, in his turn, successor to Hindley in terms of cruelty? In chapter 14 Heathcliff, having cruelly belittled Isabella his wife, and thrust her from the room, says to Ellen Dean:

> I have no pity! I have no pity! The more the worms writhe, the more I yearn to crush out their entrails! It is a moral teething; and I grind with greater energy, in proportion to the increase of pain'.

In chapter 21, Heathcliff says of Hareton:

> 'I can sympathise with all his feelings, having felt them myself. I know what he suffers now, for instance, exactly; it is merely a beginning of what he shall suffer, though . . . I've got him faster than his scoundrel of a father secured me, and lower . . .'

The cruelty builds in chapter 27: '. . . my father threatened me,' gasped the boy [Linton Heathcliff] . . . 'and I dread him — I dread him!' This is the terror of a victim, and the worse for being Heathcliff's own son. Linton 'wakes and shrieks in the night, by the hour ...' after Heathcliff has brutalized him (chapter 29). Cathy is not spared either, being on the receiving end of 'a shower of terrific slaps on both sides of the head' and Cathy shows Linton "her cheek cut on the inside, against her teeth and her mouth filling with blood' (chapter 28). She is threatened with having to marry Linton immediately, or remain a prisoner at Wuthering Heights until her father is dead. Ellen is imprisoned at the Heights five nights and four days. Finally, Heathcliff removes Cathy from the grange by force and hurries her to the Heights — his prisoner — where she is consigned to eat her meals in the kitchen with Joseph.

There are some of the worst scenes of violence in literature, reminiscent, in a different context, of the worst excesses of slavery. Utter control was the code, and if any sign of rebellion appeared, punitive violence erupted. Linton and Cathy are constantly harried and punished for stepping out of line; a slave's deviation from the code would be met with even worse horrors such as face-branding, mutilation, and amputation.[27] (Rochester's wealth, we should note, was derived from slave labour, and Charlotte makes him suffer similar slave punishments at the hands of Bertha — burning, blinding, and maiming.) Heathcliff is pitiless in the pursuit of his goal — the accretion of property by the use of power: this is no different from a ruthless slave-owner accruing wealth on the backs of his slaves.

These three clues, Heathcliff's single name, his characteristic features, and his violence, seem to point to a consistent theme of slavery in *Wuthering Heights*. Heathcliff is bred out of slavery and, having usurped Hindley, is himself tainted by his birthright to adopt Hindley's own power-lust. He comes to own Wuthering Heights and Thrushcross Grange and the descendants of both owning families are totally in his power. But suddenly, by making him see Catherine's ghost, Emily strips Heathcliff of his property and power, as if in celebration of the final, and real, emancipation of slaves from 1838. The storm of slavery that had been blowing over the West Indies for two hundred years was now finally blown out. The heredity of slavery was over, order established once more. Cathy and Hareton become children of freedom.

In the final chapter, Nelly muses:

'But where did he come from, the little dark thing, harboured by a good man to his bane?' muttered superstition, as I dozed into unconsciousness. And I began, half dreaming, to weary myself with imaging some fit parentage for him ... I tracked his existence over again, with grim variations; at last, picturing his death and funeral: of which, all I can remember is, being exceedingly vexed at having the task of dictating an inscription for his monument, and consulting the sexton about it; and, as he had no surname, and we could not tell his age, we were obliged to content ourselves with the single word, 'Heathcliff.'[28]

We have reached the end, but are still, apparently, expected to be as uncommitted as Emily was about Heathcliff's genesis. Ellen Dean has no idea where he was born, or who were his parents.[29] In spite of her guideposts, Emily does not point us in a specific direction. But we may notice that all the births, deaths, and marriages in the novel take place approximately within the last fifty years of the slave trade, 1757 to 1803. While slaves had to wait until 1838 for full freedom, the trade itself was outlawed in 1807, four years after the marriage of Cathy and Hareton in 1803.

Charlotte (awakened by *Wuthering Heights*, according to May Sinclair) may be following, in the creation of Bertha, the same evocative ancestral trail taken by Emily with Heathcliff, yet far more explicitly. She too, gives out only pointers at first: 'I presently gathered that the new-comer was called Mr. Mason ... Presently the words Jamaica, Kingston, Spanish Town, indicated the West Indies as his residence'.[30] And then that low laugh from a locked room. The tension builds with Rochester's awareness of Mason's presence at Thornfield: 'Mason! — the West Indies!' and Charlotte makes him repeat the words three times, growing 'whiter than ashes'.[31] We sense a watershed approaching, and in chapter 26 we go over the edge. Charlotte delivers a series of hammer blows to the reader's senses, Bertha comes from Creole stock, she rises up like a 'clothed hyena on its hind feet'. The analogy with one of the most savage animals on the plains of Africa is very vivid. Bertha depicted as a hyena suggests her descent from the same continent. The hyena's laugh and Bertha's laugh seem to match each other with a grisly sameness. Both have a vicious bite. Bertha is mad, and her mother both a madwoman and a drunkard. Charlotte could have made Rochester's wife, for whom various 'Yorkshire attic' models have been suggested, pure French — say Adèle's mother Celine Varens, at one time Rochester's mistress. Charlotte chose instead the Caribbean for her parentage, and the whole spectrum of planters, slaves, and the Afro-Atlantic trade suddenly comes into view. It is a brilliant stroke, this *coup de foudre*, with its implication not only of slavery, but bigamy too. Whilst a Creole can be born free, that is free of African descent, Charlotte conjures up the possibility that Bertha Mason's ancestors might have included slaves, with all that that implies: a voyage of months on a slave ship, in conditions of the greatest adversity, storms at sea, in chains, prone to the spread of disease (smallpox, dysentery), open to sexual harassment, and finally the new name and the new pidgin language (creole).[32] Wilberforce's colleague, Thomas Clarkson, on a fact-finding mission, saw in the windows of a Liverpool shop leg-shackles, hand-cuffs, thumb-screws, and mouth-openers for force-feeding used on board the slavers.[33]

These mixtures of pigmentation in the history of Charlotte's Creole gave the novel a very dramatic and topical background. Rochester's marriage to a woman with black antecedents bears some resemblance to the shock to earlier readers and audiences of Othello's alliance with Desdemona. Charlotte must have intended this. The inference is strong that Charlotte and Emily must have discussed the idea of miscegenation. As *Wuthering Heights* was being shaped and written before Charlotte began writing *Jane Eyre*, it does seem possible that Charlotte borrowed the idea of Bertha's mixed ancestry from Emily and Heathcliff.

Allegorically, both novels may be using a sub-text and condemning other forms of slavery apart from black subjection to white, namely female to male (governesses not least) and child to adult. In Chapter 27, when he is telling Jane of his mistresses, Rochester says:

> Hiring a mistress is the next worse thing to buying a slave: both are often by nature, and always by position, inferior: and to live familiarly with inferiors is degrading. I now hate the recollection of the time I passed with Celine, Giacinta, and Clara.

Lowood School and, earlier, Mrs Reed, are examples of child slavery. Rochester pays a heavy price for his symbolic domination of women as well as his amassing of colonial wealth. Heathcliff pays the ultimate price for his cruelty, and his acquisition of property does not help him in the long run either. Emily and Charlotte stamp their libertarian authority on both novels and strike a dual blow for freedom.

Before leaving the sisters it is perhaps worth noting one or two facts about Jamaica that were in place before their birth. It was settled by the British in 1665. By 1768 there were 17,000 whites to 167,000 slaves, and by 1809 the figures were 30,000 and 300,000 respectively. In the decade 1783–1793, Liverpool ships made nearly nine hundred round trips and disposed of slaves to a value of £15,186,850.[34] By 1800 1.5 million Africans had been landed in the British Islands. Between 1775 and 1824 half the region's sugar came from Jamaica. The single most important crop — the biggest volume of exports, the most lucrative produce, and the crop which devoured the labours of ever-increasing gangs of slaves — was sugar. By 1800 the British consumption of sugar had increased 2500 per cent in 150 years, all this the work of slaves.[35]

Notes

1. May Sinclair, *The Three Brontës* (London: Hutchinson & Co., 1914).
2. Emily Brontë, *Wuthering Heights* (The World's Classics, Oxford University Press, 1947), chapter 7.
3. Charlotte Brontë, *Jane Eyre* (The World's Classics, Oxford University Press, 1991), chapter 27.
4. W. L. Burn, *Emancipation and Apprenticeship in the British West Indies* (London, 1937), p. 360.

5. Susan L. Meyer, *Imperialism at Home: Race in Victorian Women's Fiction* (Ithaca, NY, 1996), pp. 60–95.

6. Juliet Barker, *The Brontës* (Weidenfeld & Nicolson, 1994), p. 145.

7. Barker, p. 119.

8. Barker, p. 145.

9. Oliver Warner, *William Wilberforce and his Times* (London: B. T. Batsford Ltd., 1962), pp. 64, 104.

10. *Wuthering Heights*, chapter 4.

11. Barker, pp. 313, 469–470.

12. Christine Alexander and Jane Sellars, *The Art of the Brontës* (Cambridge: Cambridge University Press, 1995), p. 348.

13. F. B. Pinion, Scott and Wuthering Heights, *Brontë Society Transactions*, 21.7 (1996), p. 313.

14. Margaret Smith, *Letters of Charlotte Brontë*, vol. 2 (Oxford: Clarendon Press, 2000), p. 432, n. 1.

15. J. G. Lockhart, *Memoirs of the Life of Sir Walter Scott, Bart*, abridged version in one volume, p. 529.

16. G. Bernard Wood, *A Negro Trail in the North of England* (Country Life Annual, 1967).

17. Sarah Fermi and Robin Greenwood, 'Jane Eyre and the Greenwood Family', *Brontë Society Transactions*, 22 (1997), p. 47.

18. Barker, p. 333.

19. Charlotte Brontë, *Villette* (Oxford University Press, 1984), Notes, p. 536.

20. Both extracts are quoted in Robert B. Heilman, 'Charlotte Brontë's 'New Gothic', in *From Austen to Conrad*, ed. by R. C. Rathburn and M. Steinmann (Minneapolis, Minn.: University of Minnesota Press, 1958), pp. 118–132. A Maroon was a black Jamaican runaway slave; they formed bands and threatened white supremacy.

21. Herbert Dingle, 'The Origin of Heathcliff', *Brontë Society Transactions*, 16.2 (1972), pp. 131–138.

22. James Walvin, *Black Ivory, Slavery in the British Empire*, 2nd edition (Blackwell, 2001), p. 56.

23. Walvin's Index, and his numerous sources, contain these names. Quamina appears on p. 237 of his text. This name may be compared with 'Quashia Quamina', quoted, for example, in Winifred Gerin's *Branwell Brontë* (Thomas Nelson & Sons Ltd., 1961), Appendix A, p. 314: '. . . Branwell, as well as Charlotte and Emily, had from childhood written and romanced about a black changeling child, "Quashia Quamina" . . .'.

24. Edward Chitham, *The Birth of Wuthering Heights* (Macmillan, 1998), p. 119.

25. Stevie Davies, *Emily Brontë, Heretic* (Women's Press, 1994), p. 199.

26. Walvin, *Black Ivory*, p. 206.

27. Walvin, p. 212.

28. *Wuthering Heights*, chapter 34.

29. *Wuthering Heights*, chapter 34.

30. *Jane Eyre*, chapter 18.

31. *Jane Eyre*, chapter 19.

32. Walvin, *Black Ivory*, p. 57.

33. Oliver Warner, *William Wilberforce and his Times*, p. 48.

34. Warner, p. 19.
35. Walvin, *Black Ivory*, p. 5.

Appendix A

Mungo Park (1771–1806), African explorer, was known to, and is mentioned in, Lockhart's *Life of Scott* (see note 15) at p. 109. Park wrote *Travels in the Interior of Africa* (1799). The Catalogue of Books in the Library of Keighley Mechanics Institute includes under 'Geography, Voyages, Travels, & c.' Campbell's 'Parke's (sic) travels in Africa,' Lander's 'Records of Captain Clapperton's Last Expedition to Africa' and 33 volumes of 'Modern Traveller' of which Africa comprises volumes 20, 21, and 22. The West Coast of Africa was re-created by Charlotte and Branwell as their imaginary kingdom of Angria. Tom Winnifirth's Biographical Note to his edition of Branwell's poems (New York University Press, 1983) explains that Mungo Park's explorations and articles in *Blackwood's Magazine* gave them background information on Africa. The modern Ashanti, in Ghana, is recalled by Rebecca Fraser's reference to 1834 seeing the expansion of Glass Town with the foundation of Angria, 'given to Zamorna in recognition of his labours in the Ashantee wars'; see p. 88 of her *Charlotte Brontë*.

Appendix B

There is an interesting factual footnote to record concerning Emily, who may have based her pseudonym Ellis (Bell) on George Ellis (1753–1815), whom she found in Lockhart's *Life of Scott*. Ellis was born in the West Indies. Ellis's father, also George, had been a planter on Jamaica (obviously using slave labour), and his maternal grandfather, Samuel Long, member of the Council of Jamaica, was the father of Edward Long, a Jamaican writer and planter, who employed some 300 slaves at Lucky Valley plantation in Clarendon, Jamaica. Edward Long was the author of a *History of Jamaica* in 1774, as Walvin records (p. 124). Lockhart is silent on the slavery connections of the Ellis and Long families. Nevertheless, Emily may have assumed they existed, and we should not forget Charlotte's comment that 'Liberty was the breath of Emily's nostrils; without it she perished.' To this extent Heathcliff's struggle may represent, as part of the story, Emily's tribute to the final victory of liberty over bondage which was marked by the year 1838.

Appendix C

Dominica, birthplace of Jean Rhys, author of the Brontë-related novel, *Wide Sargasso Sea,* was granted to Britain by the Peace of Paris. Her mother was a Creole. The novel fills in the missing story in *Jane Eyre*. Rochester, on honeymoon in the Caribbean, receives a letter from Daniel Cosway. 'You have been shamefully deceived by the Mason family. They tell you perhaps that your wife's name is Cosway, the English gentleman Mr. Mason being her stepfather only, but they don't tell you what sort of people were these Cosways. Wicked and detestable slave-owners since generations — yes everybody hate them in Jamaica. Wickedness is not the worst. There is madness in that family . . . I am your wife's brother by another lady, half-way house as we say. Her father and mine was a shameless man and of all his illegitimates I am the most unfortunate and poverty stricken . . . ask that devil of a man Richard Mason three questions and make him answer you. Is your wife's mother shut away, a raging lunatic and worse besides? Was your wife's brother an idiot from birth, though God mercifully take him early on? Is your wife herself going the same way as her mother and all knowing it? (*Wide Sargasso Sea* (London: Deutsch, 1996: later editions)).

ALEXANDRA LEACH

"Escaping the body's gaol":
The Poetry of Anne Bronte

"She thought not of the grave, for that is but the
body's gaol, but of all that is beyond it."

Ellen Nussey (Gaskell 297)

A well-known and still ubiquitous twentieth-century reference source
dismisses Anne Bronte as "the youngest and least gifted of the celebrated
Bronte sisters," and "writer of a few negligible poems" (de Ford 73). Often
side-stepped by critics and underrated by Charlotte Bronte herself, Anne
Bronte's work sheds light on the intriguing Bronte family, but more importantly it reveals the inner thoughts of an early Victorian woman struggling
to find an authentic voice. I believe that Bronte's poems chart her progress
from derivative copyist at the side of Emily Bronte, her sister and early literary twin, through an increasing self-awareness arising from her experiences
as a governess, to a fully-realized expression of her mature views and beliefs.
Anne Bronte uses images of confinement and loneliness and metaphors of
prisons and tombs throughout this journey. Instead of outgrowing this conventional Romantic vocabulary that has been bequeathed and taught her,
she learns to reuse it as a language that describes her own understanding of
life's boundaries.

Victorian Newsletter, Volume 101 (22 March 2002): pp. 27–31. © 2002 Ward Hellstrom
Publishing.

Anne Bronte does not fit the mold created by Charlotte, Emily, and Branwell Bronte and their later mythmakers. As a poet she works much more in the tradition of earlier hymn writers and poets such as Cowper and Moore, and is much closer to Wordsworth, among Romantic writers, than the Byron and Shelley favored by her siblings. Anne Bronte's poetry emphasizes the faculty of reason, specifically reason aided by conscience. Emotions are not inconsequential in her work, but they hold a subservient position to the discipline of the intellect. Her most mature works lead her to positions that at first may be seen as conventional or overly pious. In fact Anne Bronte's views on a generous and forgiving deity and on universal salvation are not common, but represent a philosophy reached on her own through both logical analysis and much soul-searching.

Bronte's preferred methodology is a self-reflexive examination of her own personal experiences. Apart from the Gondal poems, which are based on the imaginary land and characters of Gondal that she invented and shared with Emily, all of Bronte's poetry arises from personal experience. She tries to make sense of her life by subjecting these experiences to intellectual scrutiny and challenge by other views. She does not shy away from examining difficult issues; and Anne Bronte's life experiences were difficult. Apart from the relatively stable years between her two older sisters' deaths when she was five until she went away to school at age fifteen, she was either away from home and homesick, or back in her father's parsonage becoming increasingly alienated from other family members. Still she worked successfully as a governess for five years, published two novels, two poems in magazines, and a joint volume of poetry with Charlotte and Emily, all before her death at age twenty-nine. She was sent to school at all only because Emily was unable to adjust to life away from Haworth and could not finish out her term; Charlotte, who taught at the school, barely mentions her youngest sister in her abundant correspondence from this period. When Charlotte and Emily traveled to Brussels to prepare themselves to open a girls' school, Anne Bronte was not invited to go. The major joys of her life were the yearly visits to the sea at Scarborough while she was employed by the Robinson family. After her resignation, probably as a result of Branwell's indiscretions with Mrs. Robinson, those trips came to an end. It is not believed that she was ever offered an opportunity to marry.

Many of Bronte's poems use words that express confinement: cages, tombs, prisons, dungeons, chains. This device is not unexpected since the poetry and novels by women of this era are permeated by what Sandra Gilbert and Susan Gubar have called an "oppressive imagery of confinement that reveals that the female artist feels trapped and sickened by suffocating alternatives, and by the culture that created them" (64). What is strikingly unique is that Anne Bronte finds alternative meanings for metaphors that typically express disappointment, bereavement, loneliness, and homesickness.

Her early poems become scaffolds for the later poems, with the topography of the early years showing little resemblance to that of the final ones.[1] An examination of the early Gondal poems, the middle poems written mainly while she was a governess, and the late poems written back home in the Haworth parsonage demonstrates this progression.

Most of the Gondal poems were written between 1836 and 1840, in Haworth. Ada Harrison and Derek Stanford have called these the "imaginary" poems because they are by a woman who has not yet been bruised by hard experience (172). They are also the imaginary poems because they are infected by Emily's "torrid" Byronic heroes (Harrison and Stanford 175). It is especially illuminating to think of them, however, as the inauthentic poems since they are so heavily influenced by Emily. But even in these imitative, fledgling poems, Bronte asserts her own views of life that do not share Emily's themes of revenge, rebellion, and scorn.

In "A Voice from the Dungeon," the prisoner, Marina Sabia, speaks in a resigned voice:

> I'm buried now; I've done with life;
> I've done with hate, revenge and strife;
> I've done with joy, and hope and love
> And all the bustling world above.
>
> Long have I dwelt forgotten here
> In pining woe and dull despair;
> This place of solitude and gloom
> Must be my dungeon and my tomb. (3: 1–9)

The dungeon and the tomb are virtually the same since to be imprisoned and forgotten is a living death. Near the poem's end, Marina Sabia utters "one long piercing shriek," which rouses her from her one consoling dream of child and lover:

> I looked around in wild despair,
> I called them, but they were not there;
> The father and the child are gone,
> And I must live and die alone. (3: 51–54)

After this melodramatic episode the poem returns to its resigned misery. "A Voice from the Dungeon" is a highly derivative poem and has even been mistaken for Emily's work (Bronte 167). Bronte's heroines are not usually given to making piercing shrieks, but the joy that the dreaming Marina Sabia feels in being reunited with her darling child is purely Anne Bronte. Neither

Charlotte nor Emily seems particularly interested in children and neither expresses the yearning for a child that their sister voices.

"The Captive's Dream" is similar to "A Voice from the Dungeon" in that an imprisoned woman, Alexandrina Zenobia, who lies wasting in a dungeon, dreams of her lover. The Byronic influence is clear in his description: "his hollow wandering eyes," "his marble brow." And as Alexandrina Zenobia tries to reach him:

> I struggled wildly but it was in vain,
> I could not rise from my dark dungeon floor,
> And the dear name I vainly strove to speak,
> Died in a voiceless whisper on my tongue, ... [2] (4: 18–21)

Bronte transfers the emphasis from Alexandrina' s suffering to her concern for the man who "bleeds and breaks" for her. She could stoically bear her imprisonment if only it did not bring suffering upon her beloved. Bronte's personality emerges in these lines, in her disquiet over another's grief, even when she speaks in the voices of stock characters and locates them in the Gothic settings of earlier Romantic poetry.[3]

Both of these poems were written before Anne Bronte assumed her first position as governess in April 1840. Then the imaginary world of Gondal became largely silent and Bronte's experiences as a paid employee in a busy household began to supply the material for her verses. It was also at this time that an attentive man, her father's curate, William Weightman, entered her life. His death, at the age of twenty-eight, in 1842 almost certainly inspired Anne's lines on a dead lover. Her work as a governess ended in 1845 and her brief career as a published writer began.

The poem, "The Captive Dove," clearly represents a woman yearning for freedom. A bird in a cage is a common image of a trapped individual, a yearning soul, or a woman with limited opportunities. The caged bird is also a particularly appropriate metaphor for the Victorian governess, since a governess is an educated lady who is required to work, trapped essentially, within the homes of other people. The employment of a governess acts as a testimony to the economic power of the Victorian middle-class father and an indication of his wife's leisure and ornamental status (Peterson 5); it is also living proof that the woman's own family and home have failed her. A governess lives in exile from her own family, yet resides outside the circle of her employer's family and apart from the lower world of the household servants.

In "The Captive Dove" Anne Bronte evokes the image of the gentle bird with its haunting call. The scene is so heartbreaking that it has the power to turn the speaker from her own loneliness:

Poor restless Dove, I pity thee,
And when I hear thy plaintive moan
I'll mourn for thy captivity
And in thy woes forget mine own. (24: 1–4)

In vain! In vain! Thou canst not rise—
Thy prison roof confines thee there;
Its slender wires delude thine eyes,
And quench thy longing with despair. (24: 9–12)

A prison no longer has to have heavy stone walls or to be a cold, damp dungeon since invisible wires serve to confine the prisoner. Although the image is more subtle, the airy cage still represents incarceration. But Bronte does not have escape in mind:

Yet hadst thou one gentle mate
Thy little drooping heart to cheer
And share with thee thy captive state,
Thou couldst be happy even there. (24: 17–20)

It is not the captivity that is so hard to bear; it is the loneliness and neglect. Bronte recognizes that relationship is crucial to her emotional health; to be condemned to live without a soul mate is almost unbearable (Gilligan 8). William Weightman's early death prevents him from ever rescuing her from her captive state, but his very real spiritual presence in her mind inspires new metaphors of separation and loneliness.

In the first two stanzas of "Yes Thou Art Gone," Anne Bronte describes the physicality of her lover's tomb:

Yes, thou art gone and never more
Thy sunny smile shall gladden me;
But I may pass the old church door
And pace the floor that covers thee;

May stand upon the cold damp stone
And think that frozen lies below
The lightest heart that I have known,
The kindest I shall ever know. (31: 1–8)

Placing the burial under the church floor strongly identifies with Weightman's tomb in Haworth's village church. He is doubly entombed: frozen below the floor and shut up within the building itself, and he is doubly dead: lifeless as well as frozen. The speaker's pacing movements further emphasize the narrow, captive space. The poem's mood however is not bleak; it concludes by reflecting on the sweetness of the lover's transient existence and its lasting impression upon the poet.

"Mirth and Mourning," and its companion poem, originally published as "Weep Not Too Much, My Darling," are some of the last of the Gondal poetry. Written a year after Bronte's return to Haworth, and at a time that it appears Emily had stopped writing poetry, this pair of verses demonstrates that the themes of Gondal are merging with the themes of Bronte's experiential verses, and that Gondal's dungeons no longer serve to contain her thoughts. In the first poem Zerona argues with another speaker who implores her to cast away her sorrow. But Zerona cannot be joyful when her lover is still imprisoned:

> For, in the brightest noontide glow,
> The dungeon's light is dim;
> Though freshest winds around us blow,
> No breath can visit him. (50: 17–20)

This poem may be an internal dialogue that takes place in the mind of Zerona. A mental duel such as this is consistent with Bronte's increasing use of dialogue and rational argument as a way to refine ideas and present satisfactory conclusions. The technique reaches its maturity in her last poems.

Striking similarities exist in the description of Zerona's prisoner-lover to the dead lover of Bronte's bereavement poems. The lines, "What waste of youth, what hopes destroyed," and "If he must sit in twilight gloom" could easily refer to Weightman. In the answering poem, the imprisoned lover responds, begging Zerona to enjoy nature for his sake:

> When through the prison grating
> The holy moonbeams shine,
> And I am wildly longing
> To see the orb divine
> Not crossed, deformed, and sullied
> By those relentless bars
> That will not show the crescent moon,
> And scarce the twinkling stars.
>
> It is my only comfort
> To think, that unto thee
> The sight is not forbidden—
> The face of heaven is free. . . . (51: 17–28)

The anguished lament raised by the first poem is not left unchallenged. Bronte does not realize her purpose until she provides a convincing counter-argument that offers comfort in a seemingly hopeless situation.

In "Severed and Gone," Bronte is still reconciling herself to a lost love. Again, she unflinchingly surveys death's abode:

> I know that in the narrow tomb
> The form I loved was buried deep,
> And left, in silence and in gloom,
> To slumber out its dreamless sleep.
>
> I know the corner, where it lies,
> Is but a dreary place of rest:
> The charnel moisture never dries
> From the dark flagstones o'er its breast. (55: 5–12)

Bronte does not dwell upon the corrupting body. Instead, within her silent bedchamber she prays that Heaven will grant her a vision of her loved one, glorious in the afterlife. Bronte craves a visit from such a spiritual visitor, for as long as she can remember him she can keep his memory fresh. She firmly believes the earthly tomb can be transcended and replaced by "the more distant residence of the spirit" (Harrison and Stanford 186). Bronte is increasingly understanding herself to be the one in exile, far from her eternal home of Heaven.

Four poems survive from the late summer of 1847 until shortly before Bronte's death in May 1849. These are her most authentic poems and although though they contain some conventional didactic elements, to dismiss them as such is to miss their individuality; for Anne Bronte's s didacticism is not commonplace, but is "of a passionate kind" (Ewbank 52), and the pupil she is most concerned with examining is herself. She is rarely adamant; her religion is "a quest, a patient sifting and internal discussion" (Chitham, "Religion" 133). An examination of the extensive revisions and word listings on Bronte's manuscripts reveals that she sifts not only religious ideas but words in her efforts to achieve a clearer and simpler vocabulary. Her choice of hymn and ballad forms also allows the most musical of the Bronte clan comfortable boundaries within which to create. These are contours that many writers before her have used, providing comfortable familiarity in their economical rhymes and traditional rhythms (Scott 61).

"Self-Communion" is her longest poem—a dialogue between the poet and an immortal speaker, perhaps Wisdom or Reason. It is a poem so autobiographical in nature that Edward Chitham has placed it among primary sources for understanding Anne Bronte's personality (Bronte 3). The questioner asks the poet to look back on her life and search her memory, a step that will provide her with the guidance she seeks. Bronte insists that even as a child she strove "to find the narrow way" but her childish prayers and artless cries were scorned by those around her. In time, the child (it) grew wiser than her teachers in seeking the path to Heaven:

> It asked for light, and it is heard;
> God grants that struggling soul repose;
> And, guided by his holy word,
> It wiser than its teachers grows.
> It gains the upward path at length,
> And passes on from strength to strength. . . . (57: 115–120)

One of Bronte's chief fears is that her experiences and reflections are chilling and hardening her heart. She laments the loss of an early friendship, someone who was her "sun by day and moon by night." Critics widely believe that Bronte is referring to an increasing estrangement from Emily, whose early literary partnership had brought her so much delight.[4] Emily's scorn of her sister's crystallizing religious faith becomes a source of deep anguish for Anne Bronte: the poet chooses to hide her concerns and discoveries from those closest to her, further constricting the shell of silence that she inhabits. In "Self-Communion," the first speaker (echoing Bronte's own conscience) assures her:

> Could I but hear my Saviour say,—
> "I know thy patience and thy love;
> How thou has held the narrow way,
> For my sake laboured night and day,
> And watched, and striven with them that strove;
> And still hast borne, and didst not faint,"—
> Oh, this would be reward indeed! (57: 326–332)

The second of the two poems that Bronte saw published during her lifetime is entitled, significantly, "The Narrow Way."[5] Using archetypal images of the Christian pilgrim (Duthie 85), it is a rousing foursquare evangelical hymn filled with admonishments, encouragement, and assurances of God's rewards:

> Believe not those who say
> The upward path is smooth,
> Lest thou shouldst stumble in the way
> And faint before the truth.

It is the only road
Unto the realms of joy;
But he who seeks that blest abode
Must all his powers employ. (58: 1–8)

The "narrow way" has now evolved into a major theme in Anne Bronte's last poems, and she is no longer interested in exhuming its Romantic ancestors, damp dungeons or silent tombs, to express it. These metaphors have merged with a well-known phrase in Christian theology, the "straight and narrow" path.[6] Anne Bronte's belief in the end is that life indeed is filled with sorrow and loneliness. And when even her dearly loved home is no longer a place of refuge, with Emily alienated, Charlotte pursuing her own ambitious goals, and Branwell wallowing in self-abuse and defeat, she can still envision a path that will lead her to her final destination of Heavenly reward and reunion with loved ones. She affirms a constricted life of disappointments and absent opportunities by transforming it into a pathway that if followed carefully and faithfully will lead to a reconciling God. That which was a language of failed expectations and estrangement now expresses a firm conviction that a life lived within narrow borders can ultimately lead Home.

NOTES

1. Teddi Lynn Chicester draws the opposite conclusion for Emily Bronte's poems.

2. Both Elizabeth Hollis Berry and Maria Frawley provide in-depth discussions of silence and voicelessness in Bronte's poems and novels.

3. The name Alexandrina Zenobia is notable. Emily has nothing to say about this Gondal character in her poems, although Charlotte includes a Zenobia in her juvenile writings. The historical Zenobia was the third century C.E. Queen of Palmyra who was captured and paraded through Rome in golden chains. It would have been typical of Bronte to derive her character from a real person rather than create her entirely as a fiction.

4. See Mary Summer's article for an exploration of this issue.

5. Desmond Pacey reported in the *Times Literary Supplement* his discovery that this poem had appeared in the December 1848 issue of *Fraser's Magazine*; many works on Anne Bronte do not include this information.

6. "Because strait is the gate, and narrow is the way, which leadeth unto life, and few there be that find it" (Matt. 7: 13–14).

WORKS CITED

Berry, Elizabeth Hollis. *Anne Bronte's Radical Vision: Structures of Consciousness.* Victoria, BC: University of Victoria, 1994.

Bronte, Anne. *The Poems of Anne Bronte: A New Text and Commentary.* Edited by Edward Chitham. London: Macmillan, 1979.

Chichester, Teddi Lynn. "Evading 'Earth's Dungeon's Tomb': Emily Bronte A.G.A., and the Fatally Feminine." *Victorian Poetry*, 29 (1991): pp. 1–15.

Chitham, Edward. *A Life of Anne Bronte*. Oxford: Blackwell, 1991.

———. "Religion, Nature and Art in the Work of Anne Bronte," *Bronte Society Transactions*, 24 (1999): pp. 129–145.

de Ford, Miriam A. "Bronte, Anne." *British Authors of the Nineteenth Century*. Edited by Stanley J. Kunitz. New York: Wilson, 1936: pp. 73–74.

Duthie, Enid L. *The Bronte's and Nature*. New York: St. Martin's Press, 1986.

Ewbank, Inga-Stina. *Their Proper Sphere: A Study of the Bronte Sisters as Early-Victorian Female Novelists*. Cambridge: Harvard University Press, 1966.

Fawley, Maria H. *Anne Bronte*. New York: Twayne, 1996.

Gilbert, Sandra M., and Susan Gubar. *The Madwoman in the Attic: The Woman Writer and the Nineteenth-Century Literary Imagination*. New Haven: Yale University Press, 1979.

Gaskell, Elizabeth. *The Life of Charlotte Bronte*. London: Smith, Elder, 1900.

Gilligan, Carol. *In a Different Voice: Psychological Theory and Women's Development*. Cambridge: Harvard University Press, 1982.

Harrison, Ada, and Derek Stanford. *Anne Bronte: Her Life and Work*. London: Methuen, 1959.

Pacey, Desmond. "'The Narrow Way.'" *Times Literary Supplement*, 18 Aug 1966, p. 743.

Peterson, M. J. "The Victorian Governess: Status Incongruence in Family and Society." *Suffer and Be Still: Women in the Victorian Age*. Edited by Martha Vicinus. Bloomington: Indiana University Press, 1973: pp. 3–19.

Scott, P. J. M. *Anne Bronte: A New Critical Assessment*. London: Vision, 1983.

Summer, Mary. "Anne Bronte's Religion: First Signs of Breakdown in Relations with Emily." *Bronte Society Transactions*, 25 (2000): pp. 18–30.

ESSAKA JOSHUA

"Almost my hope of heaven": *Idolatry and Messianic Symbolism in Charlotte Brontë's* Jane Eyre

"My Master," he says, "has forewarned me. Daily he announces more distinctly,—'Surely I come quickly;' and hourly I more eagerly respond,—'Amen; even so come, Lord Jesus!'"[1]

The ending of *Jane Eyre*, with its mysterious citation of the book of Revelation and anticipation of the martyr's death of St. John Rivers, has long struck critics as problematic. Marianne Thormählen, for instance, suggests that the shift from "the happy domesticity of the Rochesters to the dying missionary has puzzled readers for generations."[2] Attempts at understanding this shift have centered on the enigmatic characterization and purpose of St. John Rivers.[3] Thormählen, who writes the most sustained account of the problem, argues that *Jane Eyre* "seems to transmit a profoundly contradictory picture" of St. John Rivers.[4] Thormählen holds that St. John acts in an inconsistent manner: he saves Jane from certain death after she has crossed the moor in her escape from Edward Rochester, yet he is also her oppressor in attempting, forcefully, to persuade her to submit to a loveless marriage and a possible early death as a Christian missionary in India. Judith Williams likewise points out the inconsistency, suggesting that St. John cannot be seen as truly charitable, even though he is an exponent of "evangelical charity," as Jane describes him.[5] The significance, for Williams, lies in St. John's demise. St. John anticipates his sainthood, rather than achieves it. His lack

Philological Quarterly, Volume 81, Number 1 (Winter 2002): pp. 81–107.

of love, then, may play a part in his possible shortfall.[6] On the other hand,
Pollard and Gordon suggest more simply that there is no difficulty, as St.
John's virtuous withdrawal from worldly pleasures is part of his saintly jour-
ney.[7] The central theological question concerning his character seems to be:
Is St. John without fault and therefore entitled to sainthood?

Thormählen resolves the problem of St. John's charitable yet destructive
nature by proposing that he has different attitudes to strangers and loved ones.
He is charitable to the former but less indulgent to those who have come
into his fold. Thormählen is, nevertheless, of the opinion that, as St. John
is devoid of sympathy for his fellow creatures and takes pride in advocating
reason above passion, he is at fault. The Christian religion highlights the
importance of love, but St. John denies this. Moreover, Thormählen suggests,
St. John is guilty of the sin of spiritual pride. As this would effectively debar
St. John from sainthood, Thormählen considers a range of solutions aimed
at understanding his character. Following Jerome Beaty, Thormählen states
that Jane and Edward have acted correctly in having sought and received
Divine guidance.[8] Their union is, therefore, validated by God and is as close to
perfection as any earthly relationship can be: "The interrelationship of human
and Divine love is a central factor in the Brontë fiction as a whole and never
more so than in *Jane Eyre*."[9] The novel, then presents a difficulty, Thormählen
says: "if love is the answer, what about St. John?"[10] Thormählen's argument up
to this point has been that "love for God and Jesus is lacking in his [St. John's]
religion as Jane conceives it at Morton, to say nothing of love for mankind."[11]
Thormählen thus is forced to focus on the question of whether anything has
changed in St. John's character by the time he reaches the end of his life, and
she acknowledges that the novel does not ascribe a change in character to St.
John in order to make him worthy of sainthood. She, therefore, argues for a
reconsideration of St. John's character at the end of the novel on the basis of
the words of his closing letter (quoted in part above): St. John's

> plea expresses an eager yearning for Christ as well as that unques-
> tioning acquiescence in God's will which is the peculiar charac-
> teristic of saved souls. The Christian it seems, has finally got the
> better of the man; he is ambiguous still, but his old relentlessness,
> the "fever in his vitals" (III. iv. 361), is gone. Like Rochester,
> so different from him in so many ways, he has submitted to the
> Divine order, and now he is preparing to meet his true love, Jesus
> Christ. . . . The ending of *Jane Eyre* is not a closure so much as a
> balancing of the book, which leaves the reader to contemplate two
> very dissimilar patterns of human endeavour under the Heaven to
> which both assign ultimate power. It does not seem necessary to
> prefer one to the other or to pronounce a verdict on either.[12]

Thormählen's solution is to keep separate the religious paths taken by Edward (and Jane) on the one hand and St. John on the other, arguing that Brontë does not choose between them. There is, in my estimation, however, enough evidence in the novel to suggest that Brontë does make a choice, and that the final sentence of the novel encapsulates its fundamental theme.

The central religious theme of the novel is the renouncing of idolatry, for which St. John acts as a symbol. St. John is problematic, however, because a secondary theme of the novel is that rejecting idolatry does not require a rejection of human relationships. Indeed, part of the point seems to be that renouncing idolatry is necessary for good human relationships. Brontë approves Jane's "pattern of human endeavour," not St. John's. In this article I shall try to demonstrate that the ending, far from creating problems for our understanding of the novel, is in fact part of a sustained account of the role of Jesus, the Christian Messiah, in human relationships, and that if read in the way that I shall suggest, *Jane Eyre* is, despite some of the ways in which it has been presented in the critical literature, a deeply religious novel, and indeed a novel with an orthodox and unexceptionable Christian message. The novel's idolaters make false gods of other characters; they do this by treating these other characters as if they had Messianic status, or could somehow supplant the Christian Messiah. Much of the evidence for this resides in the Biblical references in the novel, upon which there has, as yet, been little sustained comment. If we look closely at the implicit and explicit Biblical references, it is striking how many of these references overtly or covertly ascribe Messianic status to the various characters in the novel. The novel frequently does this by applying specific Christological verses. This association between Messianic symbolism and fictional characters is wholly eschewed at the end of the novel, to be replaced by an unequivocal focus on Christ. I shall argue that one of the novel's purposes—or at least one of the narrator's purposes—is to show that human relationships are successful only if the partners in the relationship avoid the dangers of idolizing each other. Salvation, as it were, comes not from human relationships and the human beloved, but from Christ, the heavenly beloved. While it is not my main purpose to give an account of the enigmatic role of St. John Rivers in the novel, I shall try to show too that my reading of the religious aspects of *Jane Eyre* can provide a solution to the cryptic conclusion of the novel, which is, of course, a quotation from a Messianic text.

I shall begin by examining the various Biblical and theological references in the novel, largely in the order in which they appear, highlighting the development of these allusions. I shall not look at all such references, but focus on those that have specific Messianic context, or at least that relate to the general theme of idolatry—the worship of the creature. At the same time, I shall show how the narrative includes contrary images and cautions the reader that these Messianic identifications and pretensions are *disordered*. Almost all of the passages where characters in the novel are associated with Messianic imagery and texts are *negative* in their general message and effect. Characters assume the aspect of *false* Messiahs: their actions are consequently dysfunctional, and the effects of these actions disruptive. But this is not so in every case, and I shall consider the exceptions secondly. On the basis of this examination, I shall try to come to some preliminary conclusions about the Christian message found in the novel, a message which is explicitly found in contemporary religious literature that, variously, either was or may well have been known to Charlotte Brontë. I shall finally relate my conclusion to the novel's problematic ending, associated with St. John Rivers.

2

Jane Eyre displays a clear progression in the ascription of Messianic status. To begin with the protagonists: Edward Rochester implicitly thinks of *Jane Eyre* as his Messiah from an early stage in their encounter; Jane takes rather longer to think of Edward in this way. A hint of what is to appear later in full-blown form is seen during the second meeting of Jane and Edward—the first meeting when each is aware of the other's identity. Edward commands Jane to "Go into the library," but immediately excuses his peremptory manner: "— I mean, if you please. — (Excuse my tone of command; I am used to say 'Do this,' and it is done: I cannot alter my customary habits for one new inmate)."[13] In at least two respects, this passage represents Edward placing himself in a weak position relative to Jane. Obviously, despite his commanding manner, he is immediately forced to apologize and excuse himself. But the words of his excuse are taken from an episode that occurs in the Gospels of Matthew and Luke: the healing of the centurion's servant. The centurion asks for Jesus' help in a way that explicitly links the centurion's authority with his unworthiness:

> The centurion answered and said, Lord, I am not worthy that thou shouldest come under my roof: but speak the word only, and my servant shall be healed. For I am a man under authority, having soldiers under me: and I say to this man, Go, and he goeth; and to another, Come, and he cometh; and to my servant, Do this, and he doeth it.[14]

The episode holds the centurion as an example of a gentile who is more deserving of Jesus' help because it is more difficult for him to have faith. Edward's description to Jane of his own authority is, then, suffused with ambiguity and qualification. But addressing Jane in the terms used by the centurion to address Jesus anticipates Edward's later attitude: Jane is indeed, as he sees it, his Messiah.

The next time Edward makes Messianic allusions is again in relation to his own actions and status. He attempts to justify his proposed bigamy by arguing that his love for Jane is sufficient to atone for the wrongdoing, in the way that Christians understand Christ's atoning work to be an expiation for human sin:

> Again and again he said, "Are you happy, Jane?" And again and again I answered, "Yes." After which he murmured, "It will atone—it will atone. Have I not found her friendless, and cold, and comfortless? Will I not guard, and cherish, and solace her? Is there not love in my heart and constancy in my resolves? It will expiate at God's tribunal. I know my Maker sanctions what I do. For the world's judgment—I wash my hands thereof. For man's opinion—I defy it."[15]

This picture of Edward atoning for sin through his love for Jane is clearly an attempt to recast the sin he is committing as a Messianic act of self-sacrifice. Edward believes his actions to be sanctioned by God, asserting that Jane's happiness will be adequate reparation for bigamy. He justifies the importance of his role in Jane's life by echoing John's gospel: "I will not leave you comfortless: I will come to you."[16] Here Jesus asks the disciples to believe in him, listing the benefits of doing so. Throughout this speech Edward presents himself as the saint who has his eyes firmly fixed on Heaven, rejecting earthly reputation in favor of the salvation he can bring to Jane. This is, nevertheless, a disordered image of a Messianic mission: the committing of a sin in order to atone for a wrong. In justifying bigamy in this way, Edward displays spiritual pride. In washing his hands of the "world's judgment," he echoes Pilate's self-absolution and complicity in the crucifixion in Matt. 27:24.

Edward's general inclination is to identify Jane as his Messiah, rather than present himself as Messianic. Jane, his "angel" and "comforter," causes him to be "healed and cleansed,"[17] just as Jesus heals and cleanses the sick as a metaphor for his healing and cleansing the human race of its sin.[18] Yet Jane never accepts Edward's description of her as Messianic: "Mr. Rochester, you must neither except nor exact anything celestial of me, — for you will not get it, any more than I shall get it of you; which I not at all anticipate."[19] In spite of her reluctance to accept the role of Edward's Savior, in this conversation Jane uses a phrase highly reminiscent of Jesus talking of the nature of his relationship to his disciples in John's Gospel: "For *a little while* you will perhaps be as you are now,—a very *little while;* and then you will turn cool."[20] Compare with John's Gospel:

Then said Jesus unto them, Yet a *little while* am I with you, and
then I go unto him that sent me. . . . A *little while,* and ye shall not
see me: and again, a *little while,* and ye shall see me, because I go
to the Father. Then said some of his disciples among themselves,
What is this that he saith unto us, A *little while,* and ye shall not
see me: and again, a *little while,* and ye shall see me: and, Because
I go to the Father? They said therefore, What is this that he saith,
A *little while?* We cannot tell what he saith. Now Jesus knew that
they were desirous to ask him, and said unto them, Do ye enquire
among yourselves of that I said, A *little while,* and ye shall not see
me: and again, a *little while,* and ye shall see me?[21]

These are similarities that could hardly have been missed by readers from a
Biblically literate culture. Perhaps the echo of John's Gospel indicates that
on some level Jane accepts Edward's worship of her as his Savior, but Jane
ostensibly distances herself from Edward's misunderstanding of her role.
Later, after the aborted wedding and Jane is in flight, she is tempted for a
moment to think herself into this role as Edward's Savior: "I could go back
and be his comforter—his pride; his redeemer from misery; perhaps from
ruin."[22] But Jane rejects this and continues her journey. Redeeming is obviously a Messianic function; but so too is comforting according to John 14:18
"I [Jesus] will not leave you comfortless; I will come to you."[23]

Jane, too, begins to see Edward in a God-like role:

My future husband was becoming to me my whole world; and more
than the world: almost my hope of heaven. He stood between me
and every thought of religion, as an eclipse intervenes between
man and the broad sun. I could not, in those days, see God for his
creature: of whom I had made an idol.[24]

This is precisely the dysfunction that the novel urges its readers against. The
passage marks a crucial change in Jane's view of Edward. Just as Edward has
inclined to view Jane in Messianic terms, he is now her Messiah, her God,
and, as Jane realizes but is powerless to avoid, he has replaced her Christian
belief with, indeed, something altogether more "pagan."[25]

The novel provides several other hints that the developing love between
Jane and Edward is in conflict with sound religion, irrespective of the bigamy
that any marriage would involve. One theme that runs through the scenes
between Edward and Jane in volume 2 is that of the Fall: as the relationship
between Edward and Jane develops, the narrator brings in imagery of the
Garden of Eden, and reports Edward as likening Jane to Eve. Most strikingly,
Edward's proposal of marriage takes place in a metaphorical Eden, complete

with fruit. Jane describes the scene in great detail. It begins with an opulent mid-summer sun setting at the "sweetest hour of the twenty-four," "burning with the light of a red jewel."[26] Jane walks into the garden at Thornfield and, as the change in tense indicates, she becomes absorbed in her memory of her encounter with Edward:

> I went apart into the orchard. No nook in the grounds was more sheltered and more *Eden-like;* it was full of trees, it bloomed with flowers: a very high wall shut it out from the court. . . . I look round and I listen. I see trees laden with ripening fruit. I hear a nightingale warbling in a wood half a mile off; no moving form is visible, no coming step audible; but that perfume increases: I must flee. I make for the wicket leading to the shrubbery, and I see Mr. Rochester entering. . . . He strolls on, now lifting the gooseberry-tree branches to look at the fruit, large as plums, with which they are laden; now taking a *ripe cherry* from the wall; now stooping towards a knot of flowers, either to inhale their fragrance or to admire the dew-beads on their petals. A great *moth* goes humming by me; it alights on a plant at Mr. Rochester's foot: he sees it, and bends to examine it.[27]

It is not hard to see the point here. The scene takes place in Eden, and Edward has already eaten the fruit. The month, which makes a further appearance later in the scene, is used frequently in the Bible to indicate destruction: "Lay not up for yourselves treasures upon earth, where moth and rust doth corrupt, and where thieves break through and steal, but lay up for yourselves treasures in heaven, where neither moth nor rust doth corrupt, and where thieves do not break through nor steal"; "Sell that ye have, and give alms; provide yourselves bags which wax not old, a treasure in the heavens that faileth not, where no thief approacheth, neither moth corrupteth."[28] There are perhaps echoes, in the passage quoted, of the Song of Solomon 4:12–15, 5, a feature that may be relevant given the long Christian identification of the male lover in this poem with Christ: perhaps another instance of Jane's implied idolization of Edward. The honey, fruit, flowers, fragrance, enclosed garden and latched door are present in both.

Representing Thornfield as Eden alludes to the post-lapsarian nature of Edward and Jane. When Adam and Eve are cast out from paradise they live amongst thorns: "thorns also and thistles shall it bring forth to thee; and thou shalt eat the herb of the field."[29] Edward is a kind of Eve, tempting Jane; he also sees Jane as Eve. Edward's proposal of marriage addresses Jane in terms reminiscent of the language used to describe Eve in Genesis: "I ask you to pass through life at my side—to be my second self, and my best earthly companion"; "I love you as my own flesh."[30] Compare Genesis:

And the Lord God said, It is not good that the man should be alone; I will make him an help meet for him. And Adam said, This is now bone of my bones, and flesh of my flesh: she shall be called Woman, because she was taken out of Man. . . . Therefore shall a man leave his father and his mother, and shall cleave unto his wife: and they shall be one flesh.[31]

A little later, Edward ironically speculates that Jane wants half of his estate. His advice against this warns her not to be an Eve, a poisoner of their good relations; Jane playfully replies in a way that makes it clear that she is, or could be, not only this but something more: Edward's tempter, and someone who can vanquish him:

"You are welcome to all of my confidence that is worth having, Jane: but for God's sake, don't desire a useless burden! Don't long for poison — don't turn out a downright Eve on my hands!"

"Why not, sir? You have just been telling me how much you like to be conquered, and, how pleasant overpersuasion is to you. Don't you think I had better take advantage of the confession, and begin and coax, and entreat—even cry and be sulky if necessary—for the sake of a mere essay of my power?"[32]

Both of them, of course, are too late: Jane has, albeit unwittingly, tempted Edward, and he has already eaten the fruit.

The novel's suggestions that the whole marriage proposal and the relationship that develops are like the Fall of mankind are paralleled by another equally disturbing set of images at this point: that Jane is a witch, an image that its itself carefully grounded in Biblical texts. The story of Samson is alluded to, with Jane explicitly likening herself to Delilah:

". . . The conquest I undergo has a witchery beyond any triumph I can win. Why do you smile, Jane? What does that inexplicable, that uncanny turn of countenance mean?"

"I was thinking, sir (you will excuse the idea; it was involuntary), I was thinking of Hercules and Samson with their charmers—"

"You were, you little, elfish—"[33]

And a little later Jane reports, "He said I was a capricious witch."[34] Witches place charms and spells on their victims, and in this case the charm is entirely to make Jane into a goddess.

The most curious Messianic allusion, very different from the sort of reference that I have been considering so far, occurs during the night-time visit of Edward's mad wife to Jane's bedroom on the night before the marriage ceremony:

> . . . Presently she took my veil from its place; she held it up, gazed at it long, and then she threw it over her own head, and turned to the mirror.
> . . . It removed my veil from its gaunt head, rent it in two parts, and flinging both on the floor, trampled on them.[35]

The reference here is to Jane's wedding veil, but the whole passage is reminiscent of the tearing of the Veil of the Temple that according to the Gospels was torn either just before or during Jesus' death: "The veil of the temple was rent in twain from the top to the bottom."[36] For Christians, this symbolizes the end of the Old Law, the Law that St. Paul identifies as leading to sin and deserved condemnation. The destruction of the wedding veil symbolizes and anticipates very neatly the narrator's subsequent assessment of this sinful, bigamous marriage: it is only when both the marriage and the disordered relationship between Jane and Edward are abandoned that both characters can order their affections in such a way that they can form a successful bond.

The events immediately after the interrupted marriage ceremony include several relevant Biblical references. Most interesting are the quotations from Psalms 22 and 69 that Jane makes immediately after the failed wedding ceremony:

> "Be not far from me, for trouble is near: there is none to help."[37]
> In truth "the waters came into my soul; I sank in deep mire: I felt no standing; I came into deep waters; the floods overflowed me."[38]

The quotations from these psalms are placed at the end of volume 2, emphasizing their significance as a watershed. The first verse of Psalm 22, "My God, my God, why hast thou forsaken me," is one of Jesus' "last words" on the Cross, and the whole psalm is traditionally understood as Christological—indeed, as specifically related to Christ's crucifixion.[39] Psalm 22:18 is alluded to at other points in the Passion narratives.[40] Psalm 69 is also twice alluded to in the Passion narratives.[41] Again, these allusions have led Christians standardly to want to interpret Psalm 69 christologically, and specifically as related to Christ's Passion. Given this, it is striking that Jane's only scriptural allusions immediately after the humiliation of the wedding ceremony are to these two psalms, so closely associated with Christ's passion and death. Furthermore, Jane refers to Psalm 69 indirectly at this point in the narrative:

"I seemed to have laid me down in the dried-up bed of a great river; I heard a flood loosened in remote mountains, and felt the torrent come: to rise I had no will, to flee I had no strength. I lay faint; longing to be dead."[42] Clearly, these are strong descriptions of affliction and powerlessness in the face of the adversity Jane is confronting.

The first page of volume 3, a dialogue internal to Jane, contains another reference to Psalm 22:1 that in turn leads to a further Messianic allusion:

> "Let me be torn way, then!" I cried. "Let another help me!"
>
> "No; you shall tear yourself away; none shall help you: you shall, yourself, pluck out your right eye; yourself cut off your right hand: your heart shall be the victim; and you, the priest, to transfix it."[43]

Here, Jane is, like Christ, priest and victim. Compare for example the Epistle to the Hebrews:

> But Christ being come an high priest . . . by his own blood he entered in once into the holy place, having obtained eternal redemption for us. . . . Christ . . . through the eternal Spirit offered himself without spot to God.[44]

Jane is to follow Christ's command according to Matt. 5:

> Ye have heard that it was said by them of old time, Thou shalt not commit adultery: But I say unto you, That whosoever looketh on a woman to lust after her hath committed adultery with her already in his heart. *And if thy right eye offend thee, pluck it out, and cast it from thee:* for it is profitable for thee that one of thy members should perish, and not that thy whole body should be cast into hell. *And if thy right hand offend thee, cut it off, and cast it from thee:* for it is profitable for thee that one of thy members should perish, and not that thy whole body should be cast into hell. It hath been said, Whosoever shall put away his wife, let him give her a writing of divorcement: But I say unto you, That whosoever shall put away his wife, saving for the cause of fornication, causeth her to commit adultery: and whosoever shall marry her that is divorced committeth adultery.[45]

It is significant that Jane's potentially adulterous relationship with Edward is alluded to here. Margaret Smith notes that "the exhortation to purify by self-mutilation occurs elsewhere in the gospels, but significantly it is in this particular passage that it is associated with condemnation of adultery."[46]

Joseph Prescott understands "the verses as a commentary on the intended adultery, and actual maiming of Rochester."[47] Jane tears herself from the man who loves her "as [his] own flesh."[48]

Reading these passages from *Jane Eyre* is difficult. On the one hand, the close association of Jane with these Messianic texts could lead the reader to suppose that she is still being portrayed in a fundamentally negative light. Jane's departure, for instance, is linked to Edward's redemption.[49] On the other hand, it is quite clear that the references alluded to are associated with the beginning of Jane's "redemption": her immediate departure from Thornfield and her subsequent suffering. Presumably, the point is that Jane already perceives that the correct course of action is not to be Edward's Messiah. It is, rather, to be Christ-like in a theologically acceptable way: to "take up her cross and follow [Christ]."[50] As we shall see below, this is precisely how St. John Rivers, in his final letter from the mission-field, presents to Jane the Christian's duty, and in spite of St. John's defects, it is quite clear that this is how the narrator leads us to understand his mission too.

During these developments in Jane's religious personality, Edward fails to change in any way. He twice alludes to himself as damned. During the wedding ceremony itself, he notes that his attempted bigamy sends him to Hell:

> Mr. Rochester continued, hardily and recklessly: "Bigamy is an ugly word!—I meant, however, to be a bigamist: but fate has out-manœuvred me; or Providence has checked me,—perhaps the last. I am little better than a devil at this moment; and, as my pastor there would tell me, deserve no doubt the sternest judgments of God,—even to the quenchless fire and deathless worm."[51]

Edward sees himself as lost. Jane's morally prudent decision to leave leads to earthly wretchedness for him, and his own actions have led to his spiritual damnation. Jane attempts to redirect him: "Do as I do: trust in God and yourself. Believe in heaven. Hope to meet again there."[52] Edward rejects this heavenly goal, accusing Jane directly: "You condemn me to live wretched, and to die accursed. . . . You snatch love and innocence from me? You fling me back on lust for a passion—vice for an occupation?"[53] Jane's presence, then, is seen by Edward as sufficient to save him from Hell and to guide him aright. But this is, in Christianity, the role of Christ alone: Jane is still understood by Edward in Messianic terms. Jane, contrariwise, has realized that the only cure for their malaise is the renouncement of idolatry:

> I was experiencing an ordeal: a hand of fiery iron grasped my vitals. Terrible moment: full of struggle, blackness, burning! Not a human being that ever lived could wish to be loved better than

I was loved; and him who thus loved me I absolutely worshipped: and I must renounce love and idol. One drear word compromised my intolerable duty—"Depart!"[54]

The passage precisely parallels Jane's comments on page 277, the moment when she notes that she has made Edward her "idol": the solution to their disordered, potentially bigamous relationship, is to renounce this idolatry. Jane counsels Edward accordingly: "I advise you to live sinless; and I wish you to die tranquil."[55] Jane, from a Christian point of view (and thus, as I shall argue, from the novel's central point of view), does not fall into idolatry as rapidly as Edward, and begins to escape from it more quickly.

Almost immediately after Jane's initial abandonment of this idolatrous attitude, she feels an assurance of Edward's well-being too, an assurance that originates not from her own idolatrous worship of Edward, but from her well-ordered worship of God. Jane discovers this as she wanders across the moor.

Worn out with this torture of thought, I rose to my knees. Night was come, and her planets were risen: a safe, still night; too serene for the companionship of fear. We know that God is everywhere; but certainly we feel His presence most when His works are on the grandest scale spread before us: and it is in the unclouded night-sky, where His worlds wheel their silent course, that we read clearest His infinitude, His omnipotence, His omnipresence. I had risen to my knees to pray for Mr. Rochester. Looking up, I, with tear-dimmed eyes, saw the mighty milky-way. Remembering what it was—what countless systems there swept space like a soft trace of light—I felt the might and strength of God. Sure was I of His efficiency to save what He had made: convinced I grew that neither earth should perish, nor one of the souls it reassured. I turned my prayer to thanksgiving: the Source of Life was also the Saviour of Spirits. Mr. Rochester was safe: he was God's and by God would he be guarded.[56]

The block between Jane and God that Edward had become is now removed: precisely as the result of Jane's disavowal of her idolatry. The right ordering of her relationship to God has as its consequence the well-being of Edward, and thus perhaps the inchoate possibility of a right relationship with Edward too. Jane cannot be Edward's Savior; but God can. In this wilderness, Jane takes on the role of John the Baptist, rather than that of Christ who is tempted by Satan in the wilderness.

Behold, I send my messenger before thy face, which shall prepare thy way before thee. The voice of one crying in the wilderness,

Prepare ye the way of the Lord, make his paths straight. John did baptize in the wilderness, and preach the baptism of repentance for the remission of sins.[57]

Making Biblical allusions, Jane calls the moor as a "wilderness" and a "golden desert."[58] John feeds on locusts and wild honey, whereas Jane eats wild "bilberries."[59] Jane's own healing takes time: even when she has explicitly abandoned her idolatry, she, like St. John Rivers (who is presented physically as a potential idol with his "Greek face"[60]), has further religious development to undergo:

I was sure St. John Rivers—pure-lived, conscientious, zealous as he was—had not yet found that peace of God which passeth all understanding: he had no more found it, I thought, than had I; with my concealed and racking regrets for *my broken idol* and lost elysium—regrets to which I have latterly avoided referring; but which possessed me and tyrannized over me ruthlessly.[61]

Jane's renunciation of idolatry is more complete than her renunciation of the idol and the false heaven that he has promised.

But Edward is not the only idol that Jane is in danger of worshiping. The powerful influence of St. John Rivers presents itself to her as a further, serious temptation to idolatry, and it is only after *this* idolatry is resisted that Jane's relationship with Edward is restored. I will discuss St. John's troubled role in the novel in the final section below. But it needs to be made clear that one of the reasons for the problematic status of St. John is Jane's disordered attitude towards him, an attitude that he has encouraged as much as Edward caused her earlier idolatry.

Jane begins by equating St. John's physical beauty with his spiritual beauty, understanding her relationship to her idol in these terms. In taking on St. John as her mentor, Jane tries to emulate him. Jane's inability to become beautiful is seen by her as a metaphor for her inability to achieve the physical and spiritual perfection that St. John stands for:

He wanted to train me to an elevation I could never reach: it racked me hourly to aspire the standard he uplifted. The thing was as impossible as to mould my irregular features to his correct and classic pattern, to give my changeable green eyes the sea blue tint and solemn lustre of his own.[62]

St. John's role as an idol is perhaps emphasized more so even than Edward's, in that it is an overtly religious choice that Jane is making. Marriage to St.

John is presented to her as a spiritual decision. At this point in her troubled relationship with this pseudo-Messianic figure, St. John dominates Jane in the same way that Edward manages to, and this is highlighted in the repetition of the reference to the healing of the centurion's servant. St. John uses Matt. 8:9 (= Luke 7:7–8), as Edward has done previously: "When he said 'go,' I went; 'come,' I came; 'do this,' I did it."[63] Jane is confused when confronted with this degree of authority. In presenting herself as the sick servant, and St. John as the centurion, Jane hints that she is aware that St. John should not stand in place of the Messiah. Nevertheless, Jane is battling with the confusion that the religious element of his authority presents. Even though Jane hints here that she is waiting for the real Messiah to heal her, realizing that St. John, in spite of his authority, is not to be seen as a Messianic figure, she is tempted to make an idol of him, as the following passage confirms:

> By straining to satisfy St. John till my sinews ache, I *shall* satisfy him—to the finest central point and farthest outward circle of his expectations. If I *do* go with him—if I—*do* make the sacrifice he urges, I will make it absolutely: I will throw all on the altar—heart, vitals, the entire victim. He will never love me; but he shall approve me.[64]

The language here is of sacrifice: a sacrifice not *on behalf of* St. John, but *to* him; it is an attempt to earn his approval. But the offering of sacrifices to creatures is the paradigm case of idolatry in the Old Testament.[65]

Indeed, St. John himself equates Jane's refusal of him with her damnation, as if he himself is not just one possible route to the salvific work of Christ, but that work itself. On the night before St. John's departure for Cambridge, he begins family prayers by reading Rev. 21:7-8:

> "He that overcometh shall inherit all things; and I will be his God, and he shall be my son. But," was slowly, distinctly read, "the fearful, the unbelieving, & c., shall have their part in the lake which burneth with fire and brimstone, which is the second death."
> Henceforward, I knew what fate St. John feared for me.[66]

The next morning, St. John leaves Jane a note that explicitly identifies marriage to him, and the subsequent missionary work, with salvation: "You left me too suddenly last night. Had you stayed longer, you would have laid your hand on the Christian's cross and the angel's crown."[67] Jane rejects St. John's offer because she rightly perceives that his understanding of *human* love is deficient: "I scorn your idea of love"[68]—partly because it is insufficiently emotional, but, more importantly, because it fails to value Jane as the distinct human being that she is:

> There would be recesses in my mind which would be only mine, to which he never came; and sentiments growing there fresh and sheltered, which his austerity could never blight, nor his measured warrior-march trample down: but as his wife—at his side always, and always restrained, and always checked—forced to keep the fire of my nature continually low, to compel it to burn inwardly and never utter a cry, though the imprisoned flame consumed vital after vital—*this* would be unendurable.[69]

St. John accepts only one part of Jesus' two-fold love commandment: he loves God, but not his neighbor. This notion of love is almost as disordered as that of the idolatrous characters earlier in the novel. Equally, Jane's refusal of St. John marks her final salvation from the dangers of idolatry.

The night before St. John's departure, Jane hears Edward's voice calling from afar, and experiences a Mighty Spirit: not Edward (though she hears his voice too) but God himself, and from this point in the novel all relationships are rightly ordered: all idolatry has been definitively forsaken, but not at the expense of well-ordered human relationships:

> I seemed to penetrate very near a Mighty Spirit; and my soul rushed out in gratitude at His feet. I rose from the thanksgiving—took a resolve—and lay down, unscared, enlightened—eager but for the daylight.[70]

The experience is indeed redemptive. Jane is as if liberated from prison:

> The wondrous shock of feeling had come like the earthquake which shook the foundations of Paul and Silas's prison: it had opened the doors of the soul's cell, and loosed its bands—it had wakened it out of its sleep, whence it sprang trembling, listening, aghast.[71]

This redemption coincides completely with Edward's repentance, his explicit acceptance of God and God's justice. His blindness symbolizes the abandonment of idolatry, and is thus not emasculation or castration, as has been suggested elsewhere, but a positive symbol for his religious well-being. Edward describes his conversion:

> "He [God] sees not as man sees, but far clearer: judges not as man judges, but far more wisely. I did wrong: I would have sullied

> my innocent flower—breathed guilt on its purity: the Omnipotent
> snatched it from me. I, in my stiff-necked rebellion, almost cursed
> the dispensation: instead of bending to the decree, I defied it. Divine
> justice pursued its course; disasters came thick on me: I was forced to
> pass through the valley of the shadow of death.—*His* chastisements
> are mighty; and one smote me which has humbled me for ever.... Of
> late, Jane—only of late—I began to see and acknowledge the hand
> of God in my doom. I began to experience remorse, repentance; the
> wish for reconciliation to my Maker. I began sometimes to pray: very
> brief prayers they were, but very sincere."[72]

The valley of death provides no comfort here, unlike that of Psalm 23; God's
staff provides no comfort to Edward, only punishment ("Yea, though I walk
through the valley of the shadow of death, I will fear no evil: for thou art
with me; thy rod and thy staff they comfort me").[73] Nevertheless, the rhetoric
is thoroughly Christian—indeed the stress on the divine dispensation and
decree is characteristic of orthodox Calvinism. The scene ends with fragments of Edward's thoroughly traditional prayer:

> "I thank my Maker, that in the midst of judgment he has remem-
> bered mercy. I humbly entreat my Redeemer to give me strength to
> lead henceforth a purer life than I have done hitherto!"[74]

One curious feature of this scene is the narrator's comparison of herself to the
Virgin Mary, quoting Mary's words: "I kept these things ... and pondered them
in my heart."[75] Perhaps we are to think of Jane as ultimately the person whose
actions lead Edward back to orthodox religion and non-idolatrous human relationships? We should recall too Jane's role as mediator between Edward and the
world during his blindness: "I was then his vision, as I am still his right hand."[76]
Immediately after this scene, the final chapter opens with Jane's famous summary of subsequent events: "Reader, I married him."[77] So the abandonment of
idolatry, the refusal to treat other human beings as though they have any sort
of Messianic function, leads to the resolution of the plot.

Central to this analysis is the identification of Edward, St. John,
and Jane as false Messiahs. Other characters, including Jane as a child,
occasionally receive something like Messianic status in ways that lack
negative implications. The very young Jane suffers in a way that is likened
to the sufferings of Jesus. The elder Jane—the narrator of the story—
comments about her treatment at the hand of her guardian, Mrs Reed: "I
ought to forgive you, for you knew not what you did: while rending my
heart-strings, you thought you were only up-rooting my bad propensities."[78]
"Father forgive them; for they know not what they do" is said by Jesus on

the Cross.[79] Jane's comment apparently ascribes to herself a Messianic role. But this comment is from the older Jane, from someone who, like the first Christian martyr, Stephen, can use Christ's words from the cross merely as a way of following the example of Jesus.[80] There is no idolatry here, merely the practice of Christian virtue.

The only real exception is the remarkable Helen Burns. Helen Burns is identified as a Christ-like figure by means of some implicit scriptural quotation found in Jane's first conversation with her, a conversation that takes place on the same day that she has seen Helen flogged. Jane is puzzled that Helen does not want to retaliate. Helen immediately cites Jesus' teaching: "The Bible bids us return 'good for evil,'"[81] and implicitly places herself in the role of recounting Jesus' teachings: "Learn from me," she exhorts Jane, just as Christ exhorts his disciples "learn of me."[82] Helen proceeds to teach Jane the message of forgiveness, distancing herself from being perceived as Messianic:

> "Read the New Testament, and observe what Christ says, and how he acts—make his word your rule, and his conduct your example."
> "What does he say?"
> "Love your enemies; bless them that curse you; do good to them that hate you and despitefully use you."[83]

Charles I, too, one of the subjects of the conversation, is presented by Helen as a type of Christ, a "murdered king," whose "enemies were the worst: they shed blood they had no right to shed."[84] The words Helen uses to describe the martyrdom of Charles I echoes those used for Jesus, whose enemies are described as shedding innocent blood. Pilate says "I have sinned in that I have betrayed the innocent blood."[85] This is a way of further presenting Helen in the role of someone who reports Jesus' teachings. Why is Helen Burns not a false Messiah? Helen is not a substitute for Christ in the sense of being an idolized object of adoration. She merely takes on Christ's teaching role, and can represent Christ in this way without thereby becoming the object of an idolatrous and dysfunctional devotion—the very problem exhibited by the other Christ-like characters.

3

Jane Eyre presents idolatry as sinful, and the eradication of this kind of worship as necessary for well-ordered human relationships. The novel does not, however, counsel that human relationships should be abandoned altogether; it suggests that relationships should not stand in the way of the worship that is due to God. If this is the message of the novel, then it is a

standard orthodox Christian one which was readily available to Charlotte
Brontë herself.

A similar message can be found, for example, in Isaac Watts's volume,
Discourses of the Love of God (1729). This has a section on "Rules to moderate
excessive Love to Creatures":

> Set up the Love of God supreme in your Heart, and keep it so.
> This Principle of divine Love will grow jealous if any meaner Love
> rise too high, and become its Rival, or make too near Approaches
> to its Seat and Throne. A sovereign Love to God will limit and
> moderate all inferior Love. . . . Remember that excessive Love to
> the Creatures hath often provoked a jealous God to embitter them
> to us terribly by remarkable Providences, or to cut them off sud-
> denly in his Anger. The way to keep our Comforts, is to love them
> with Moderation.[86]

Watts's work was well-known to the Brontës.[87] Watts preaches not
that human relationships are wrong, but that they are liable to fail if
they are pursued at the expense of love for God. The doctrine can also
be found in an interesting collection of sermons by the anti-Calvinist
G. W. Woodhouse, published in 1839 and owned by Patrick Brontë (and
thus readily accessible to Charlotte at Haworth). The subject of Sermon
IV ("The Gracious Permission. Col. 3.2") is salvation, and Woodhouse's
point is that a person's salvation depends on his or her truly "prefer[ring]
the anticipation of heavenly joy to all the passing pleasures and promises
of the present life."[88]

> If it were possible to believe that all of us were saved, the hope of
> the future would be a glorious hope. If, without any misgiving or
> uncertainty, we were assured, that as we have often met together
> in peace in this house of prayer, so hereafter we should all meet
> together in peace in the presence of God, joyful indeed would be
> to us the prospect of eternity. In that case we should have little
> difficulty in complying with the admonition of the text [Col. 3.2:
> "Set your affection on things above, not on things on the earth"],
> and setting our affection on things above. Our prayer would then
> be the expression of our heart's sincere desire, when we said, "Thy
> kingdom come": "Come, Lord Jesus, come quickly."[89]

Woodhouse avers that human relationships are good in themselves, and
that it is a good thing to value them. He does not believe, however, that
they should take the place of the Christian's primary relationship with God.

He quotes, therefore, a passage emphasizing the centrality of Christ in Christian salvation history, specifically the second coming, the thematically crucial verse cited at the conclusion of *Jane Eyre*.[90] Woodhouse later in the same sermon makes the point about the centrality of Christ more explicit. Salvation depends on

> whether we seek for our good from the world, or seek it from God:
> whether we live holy lives, or live in carelessness: whether we set
> our affection of things above, or on things of the earth. It is but a
> little while, and everything that is bright in this world will have
> faded away. . . . If we lay up for ourselves treasures in heaven, and
> spend our time on earth in the service of God, then, when Christ,
> who is our life, shall appear, we shall appear with him in glory.[91]

It is, of course, precisely the combination of the polemic against idolatry in daily life with the expectation of Jesus' coming that marks out the Messianism of *Jane Eyre*.

The application of these sorts of insights to human relationships—even familial ones—is made more clearly in the letters of the Evangelical and moderate Calvinist Henry Venn, whose biography and selected letters were published in 1834. Venn believed Calvinism to be true, but unlike more extreme Calvinists was unwilling to condemn those who did not. A copy of Venn's extremely popular and well-known *Complete Duty of Man* (1763) was in the library at Ponden Hall, and thus possibly available to Charlotte.[92] Venn was the father of the Clapham Sect's pastor, John Venn, and was counted among those Evangelical clergyman admired by Patrick Brontë.[93] Venn's letters include insights that seem very close to the kind of view that *Jane Eyre* seems to defend. The newly married Venn writes to his wife, Eling, in the following terms:

> You will believe me, when I assure you it gives me great pleasure
> to find you love me so tenderly. But you have need to beware, lest
> I should stand in God's place; for your expressions, "that you know
> not how to be from me an hour without feeling the loss, & c." seem
> to imply something of this kind. My dearest E[ling], we must ever
> remember that word which God hath spoken from Heaven: "Then
> time is short: let those who have wives, be as if they had none; and
> those who rejoiced, as if they rejoiced not." Both for myself and
> you, I would always pray that God may be so much dearer to us,
> than we are to each other, that our souls in His love may "delight
> themselves in fatness," and feel He is an all-sufficient God. By this
> means we shall most likely to continue together, and not provoke

the stroke of separation by an idolatrous love to one another. But this means *we shall love one another in God and for God.*[94]

Venn's point is that the avoidance of idolatry in human relationships is necessary for Christian love, and that such love should always be subordinated to love for God.

Furthermore, the Christian redirection of human relationships is counseled in *The Maid of Killarney* (1818), written by Brontë's father, Patrick. Here, conventional anti-Catholic polemic leads to a stress on the sole mediatorship of Christ, and thus a rejection of the Catholic mistake that would allegedly make Christ-like intermediaries of mere humans (i.e., priests). Nanny, the Catholic servant, in Patrick Brontë's tale, is tended by the Protestant Mr. MacFarsin; while on her death-bed, she comes to a new (and Protestant) understanding of the importance of Christ as the sole intermediary:

> "But tell me, Nanny," said Mr. MacFarsin, looking sorrowfully, "do you hope that these things [viz. "the Priest . . . the wafer, that is . . . the body and blood of the blessed *Jasus*"] will save you? Do you expect they will take you to heaven?"
>
> Nanny, recovering herself a little, and speaking louder and with greater emphasis, cried — "Ah! No—ah? No—nothing can save me but Christ! Ah? No—nothing can save me but Christ! In myself I am all sin, but Christ is good; and I believe in him, and love him, and so God loves me, and makes me good."[95]

If my reading of these theological references in *Jane Eyre* is correct, a central religious message of the novel is that earthly attachments cannot substitute for loving God. This is a commonplace of Christian theology. Brontë suggests, further, that love relationships are dysfunctional without a correct love for Christ, but that in this context proper love for fellow creatures is possible and wholly appropriate. St. John's path is rejected by Jane, not because he places too much emphasis on the role of Christ, but because he overlooks the fact that prioritizing Christ does not entail refusing to allow a secondary place for human affection too. Jane and Edward are able to "love one another in God and for God."[96] St. John rightly exhorts Jane to value Christ above all else. But he fails to see that this unconditional love of God does not require the abandonment of earthly attachments. St. John's love for Jane is non-idolatrous; but it is not thereby well-ordered. St. John's battle with idolatry parallels that of Jane. Both reject it, but St. John rejects human love as well. The extremity of St. John's suppression of love is seen when he observes Rosamond Oliver:

I saw his solemn eye melt with sudden fire, and flicker with resistless emotion. . . . His chest heaved once, as if his large heart, weary of despotic constriction, had expanded, despite the will, and made a vigorous bound for the attainment of liberty. But he curbed it, I think, as a resolute rider would curb a rearing steed.[97]

St. John curbs his emotions like a despotic ruler, but they are not easily kept in check. Jane understands St. John to have made a choice between loving Rosamond and loving God, and presents what she imagines is St. John's internal monologue as an explication of his decision to renounce his love for Rosamond:

"I love you, and I know you prefer me. It is not despair of success that keeps me dumb. If I offered my heart, I believe you would accept it. But that heart is already laid on a sacred altar: the fire is arranged round it. It will soon be no more than a sacrifice consumed."[98]

The likeness Jane paints of Rosamond offers a further temptation to St. John. He gazes at the picture like an idolatrous Pygmalion, and as he admires it the picture seems as if it comes to life: "It smiles!" he says.[99] Jane discomfits St. John by offering to paint him a copy to take with him on his mission, asking:

". . . would it be a consolation to have that memento in your possession; or would the sight of it bring recollections calculated to enervate and distress?"
He now furtively raised his eyes: he glanced at me irresolute, disturbed: he again surveyed the picture.
"That I should like to have it is certain: whether it would be judicious or wise is another question."[100]

Worshiping the picture symbolizes the worship of Rosamond and, like Jane, St. John struggles in his temptation by idolatrous love. This struggle is continued in his attempt to convert Hindus, whom he regards as idol worshipers.

St. John symbolizes merely a half of the novel's main religious teaching. His is, with regard to the relationship he proposes to undergo with Jane, an extreme example of non-idolatrous love, but it is not an example of a well-ordered love. St. John is unable to build a relationship with God's creatures into his relationship with God; he merely sees their usefulness. The novel is suggesting, through the Messianic symbolism, that a love relationship is wholly compatible with love for God, provided that it is non-idolatrous (i.e., one in which the participants "love one another in God and for God").

Renouncing idolatry does not involve renouncing deep human relationships. St. John is a symbol for the rejection of idolatry, but his thematic function extends no further. Without him, the reader may not realize the centrality of the polemic against idolatry. But his presence is not sufficient for the full understanding of the novel's religious significance. For this we need an understanding of the relationship between Jane and Edward. Brontë's allusion to scripture explicates the development of this relationship, enabling us to grasp the Christian significance of the characters and plot.

Jane reveals that St. John expects to stand before the throne of God without fault, but is he without fault?[101] His devaluing of his fellow creatures suggests that he is not. St. John's mission, Jane hints, is self-appointed; "He entered on the path he had marked for himself; he pursues it still."[102] She continues: "Himself has hitherto sufficed to the toil; and the toil draws near its close: his glorious sun hastens to its setting."[103] The unusual syntax (using "Himself" as the subject) draws attention to St. John's active role in his own martyrdom. Jane is conscious of St. John's spiritual pride: "His is the ambition of the high master-spirit, which aims to fill a place in the first rank of those who are redeemed from the earth."[104] No human stands between St. John and "his sure reward, his incorruptible crown," but *Jane Eyre* offers an alternative and better calling: marriage, provided there is no danger of idolatry.[105] St. John's fault is not his pride (though Jane is aware of his pride) but simply his inability to find a right love towards creatures.

Notes

1. *Charlotte Brontë, Jane Eyre*, edited by Jane Jack and Margaret Smith (Oxford: Clarendon Press, 1969): p. 579 (vol. 3, ch. 12 [38]). All citations from *Jane Eyre* are to this edition. Many of the Biblical references discussed here are noted in various editions.

2. Marianne Thormählen, *The Brontës and Religion* (Cambridge University Press, 1999): p. 217.

3. There are a few exceptions. As Hook and Tromly do not deal with the issue in relation to relevant theological concerns, I do not discuss them further. See Ruth Hook, "The Father of the Family," *Brontë Society Transactions*, 17 (1977): p. 107; Annette Tromly, *The Lover of the Mask: The Autobiographers in Charlotte Brontë's Fiction, English Literary Studies Monograph Series*, volume 26 (University of Victoria Press, 1982): pp. 60–61.

4. Thormählen, *The Brontës and Religion,* p. 205.

5. *Jane Eyre*, 444 (vol. 3, ch. 3 [29]).

6. Caroly Williams, "Closing the Book: The Intertextual End of *Jane Eyre*," in *Victorian Connections*, edited by Jerome McGann (University Press of Virginia, 1989): p. 83.

7. Felicia Gordon, *A Preface to the Brontës* (New York & London: Longman, 1989); Arthur Pollard, "The Brontës and Their Father's Faith," in *Essays and Stud-*

ies, edited by Raymond Chapman (London: John Murray; Atlantic Highlands, NJ: Humanities Press, 1984).

8. Jerome Beaty, *Misreading Jane Eyre: A Postformalist Paradigm* (Ohio State University Press, 1996): pp. 210–211.

9. Thormählen, *The Brontës and Religion*, p. 218.

10. Ibid.

11. Ibid.

12. Ibid., pp. 218–219.

13. *Jane Eyre*, p. 151 (vol. 1, ch. 13).

14. Matt. 8:8–9 = Luke 7:7–8. All references are to the King James Version.

15. *Jane Eyre*, pp. 321–322 (vol. 2, ch. 8 [23]).

16. John 14:18.

17. *Jane Eyre*, p. 327 (vol. 2, ch. 9 [24]).

18. Mark 1:42; Luke 7:22; 1 John 1:7; Rev. 1:5.

19. *Jane Eyre*, p. 327 (vol. 2, ch. 9 [24]).

20. Ibid., my italics.

21. John 7:33; John 16:16–19; my italics.

22. *Jane Eyre*, 410 (vol. 3, ch.1 [27]).

23. See too Isa. 61:2, generally understood as Messianic in the light of Jesus' use of part of the verse in Luke 4:19.

24. *Jane Eyre*, p. 346 (vol. 2, ch. 9 [24]).

25. Ibid., p. 344 (vol. 2, ch. 9 [24]).

26. Ibid., p. 311 (vol. 2, ch. 8 [23]).

27. Ibid., pp. 311–312 (vol. 2, ch. 8 [23]); my italics.

28. Matt. 6:19–20; Luke 12:33; see also Job 4:19, Job 13:28, Job 27:18, Ps. 39:11, Isa. 51:8, Hos. 5:12.

29. Gen. 3:18.

30. *Jane Eyre*, p. 319 (vol. 2, ch. 8 [23]); *Jane Eyre*, 320 (vol. 2, ch. 8 [23]).

31. Gen. 2:8; 23–24.

32. *Jane Eyre*, pp. 329–330 (vol. 2, ch. 9 [24]).

33. Ibid., p. 328 (vol. 2, ch. 9 [24]).

34. Ibid., p. 341 (vol. 2, ch. 9 [24]).

35. Ibid., p. 358 (vol. 2, ch. 10 [25]).

36. Mark 15:38; see too Matt. 27:51; Luke 23:43.

37. *Jane Eyre*, p. 374 (vol. 2, ch.11 [26]) and Ps. 22:11.

38. *Jane Eyre*, p. 375 (vol. 2, ch.11 [26]), adapted quotation of Ps. 69:1–2: "Save me, O God; for the waters are come in unto my soul. I sink in deep mire, where there is no standing: I am come into deep waters, where the floods overflow me."

39. Matt. 27:46; Mark 15:34.

40. See Matt. 27:35; Mark 15:23; Luke 23:34, and explicitly quoted at John 19:24.

41. See Ps. 69:21, alluded to at Matt. 27:48, Mark 15:23 and Luke 23:36; and Ps. 69:4, alluded to at John 15:25.

42. *Jane Eyre*, p. 374 (vol. 2, ch.11 [26]).

43. Ibid., p. 379 (vol. 3, ch. 1 [27]).

44. Heb. 9:11–12, 14.

45. Matt. 5:27–32; my italics.

46. *Charlotte Brontë, Jane Eyre*, edited by Margaret Smith, *The World's Classics* (Oxford University Press, 1975): pp. 468–469, note to p. 301.

47. Ibid.

48. *Jane Eyre,* p. 320 (vol. 2, ch. 8 [23]).

49. See John's Gospel: "Nevertheless I tell you the truth; It is expedient for you that I go away: for if I go not away, the Comforter will not come unto you; but if I depart, I will send him unto you" (John 16:7).

50. Mark 8:34.

51. *Jane Eyre,* p. 368 (vol. 2, ch. 9 [26]).

52. Ibid., p. 403 (vol. 3, ch. 1 [27]).

53. Ibid., pp. 403–404 (vol. 3, ch. 1 [27]).

54. Ibid., pp. 402–403 (vol. 3, ch. 1 [27]).

55. Ibid., p. 404 (vol. 3, ch. 1 [27]).

56. Ibid., p. 414 (vol. 3, ch. 2 [28]).

57. Mark 1:2–4.

58. *Jane Eyre,* p. 415 (vol. 3, ch. 2 [28]).

59. Ibid.

60. Ibid., p. 440 (vol. 3, ch. 3 [29]).

61. Ibid., pp. 449–450 (vol. 3, ch. 4 [30]); my italics.

62. Ibid., p. 509 (vol. 3, ch. 8 [34]).

63. Ibid., p. 508 (vol. 3, ch. 8 [34]).

64. Ibid., pp. 516–517 (vol. 3, ch. 8 [34]).

65. See Lev. 19:4, Lev. 26:1, Lev. 26:30, Deut. 29:17, 2 Kings 17:12, Isa. 2:8, Hab. 2:18.

66. *Jane Eyre,* p. 532 (vol. 3, ch. 9 [35]).

67. Ibid., p. 538 (vol. 3, ch. 10 [36]).

68. Ibid., p. 522 (vol. 3, ch. 8 [34]).

69. Ibid., pp. 520–521 (vol. 3, ch. 8 [34]).

70. Ibid., p. 537 (vol. 3, ch. 9 [35]).

71. Ibid., p. 539 (vol. 3, ch. 10 [36]).

72. Ibid., p. 571 (vol. 3, ch. 11 [37]).

73. Ps. 23:4.

74. *Jane Eyre,* p. 573 (vol. 3, ch. 11 [37]).

75. Ibid., p. 573 (vol. 3, ch. 11 [37]), quoting Luke 2:19.

76. Ibid., pp. 576–577 (vol. 3, ch. 12 [38]).

77. Ibid., p. 574 (vol. 3, ch. 12 [38]).

78. Ibid., p. 19 (vol. 1, ch. 3).

79. Luke 23:34; for "rending my heart-strings," see Joel 2:13.

80. See Acts 7:59 and Luke 23:46.

81. *Jane Eyre,* p. 63 (vol. 1, ch. 6).

82. Matt. 11:29.

83. *Jane Eyre,* p. 66 (vol. 1, ch. 6); quoting Matt. 5:44.

84. Ibid., p. 65 (vol. 1, ch. 6).

85. Matt. 27:4.

86. Isaac Watts, *Discourses of the Love of God and the Use and Abuse of the Passions in Religion* (London: J. Clark and R. Hatt; E. Matthews; R. Ford, 1729): pp. 70–71.

87. Thormählen, *The Brontës and Religion,* p. 53.

88. G. W. Woodhouse, *Practical Sermons* (London & Birmingham: J. G. and F. Rivington; H. C. Langbridge; Wolverhampton: T. Simpson, 1846): pp. 2:53.

89. Ibid., 2:49.

90. Ibid.

91. Ibid., 2:63–64.

92. On the extent of Charlotte Brontë's access to the library at Ponden Hall see Juliet Barker, *The Brontës* (London: Weidenfeld and Nicolson, 1994): pp. 147–148; Thormahlen, *The Brontës and Religion*, pp. 122 and 235, n. 6.

93. Thormählen, *The Brontës and Religion*, p. 16.

94. Henry Venn, *The Life and a Selection from the Letters of the Late Rev. Henry Venn, M. A.* (London: John Hatchard, 1834): p. 69; my italics.

95. Patrick Brontë, "The Maid of Killarney; or Albion and Flora: A Modern Tale in Which Are Interwoven Some Cursory Remarks on Religion and Politics," in *Brontëana: The Reverend Patrick Brontë's Collected Works,* edited by J. Horsfall Turner (Bingley: T. Harrison, 1898): p. 137.

96. Venn, *Life*, p. 69.

97. *Jane Eyre*, p. 465 (vol. 3, ch. 5 [31]).

98. Ibid., p. 469 (vol. 3, ch. 6 [32]).

99. Ibid., p. 474 (vol. 3, ch. 6 [32]).

100. Ibid., p. 474–475 (vol. 3, ch. 6 [32]).

101. Ibid., p. 578 (vol. 3, ch. 12 [38]).

102. Ibid.

103. Ibid.

104. Ibid.

105. Ibid.

K. C. BELLIAPPA

Macauley's "Imperishable Empire" and "Nelly, I Am Heathcliff" in Emily Bronte's Wuthering Heights[1]

Among the great moments in life, looking at the list provided by Professor CDN, I found that Macaulay's concept of the "imperishable empire" was not only worthy of discussion but also extremely relevant at this point of time. Macaulay occupies a singularly important place in the history of India, for it was he who clinched the debate in favour of the introduction of English education in India. It was again Macaulay who formulated the Indian Penal Code. Macaulay spoke of the imperishable empire in his address to the House of Commons when it was debating on the transfer of power from the East India Company to the Crown. I believe this address should be read along with his well-known Minute on Indian Education. The usual response to Macaulay is to valorize him as the man who gave us the Liberal English Education which paved the way for India's independence. I need not to have labour the point as far as the positive influence of English education on India is concerned. I would like to, for a change, look at the other side of the coin since, in my considered opinion, it is time we did this. In his passionate plea for English education in India, what strikes the reader is the strategy adopted by Macaulay. As a distinguished historian, he offers many historical parallels to plead for the study of English in India since the fund was set apart for the "intellectual improvement of the people of this country." He speaks of the inherent superiority of the European system of

Journal of Indian Writing in English, Volume 30, Number 1 (Winter 2002): pp. 38–41.

61

knowledge and makes his now infamous remark that "a single shelf of a good European library was worth the whole native literature of India and Arabia." There has perhaps never been a more glib and brazen dismissal of the orient by a Westerner. This reminds us of Salman Rushdie's dismissal of Indian Literature in our regional languages vis-a-vis Indian Literature in English made in a special number of *The New Yorker* in 1997. And how can one even forget Macaulay's strongly racist overtones in his plea for the creation of "a class of persons Indian in blood and colour, but English in taste, in opinions, in morals and in intellect." Macaulay was indeed pleading for the creation of a class of Brown/Black Sahibs to act as intermediaries between the rulers and the ruled. But the overriding emphasis in the minute is on the backwardness of India and her people. Macaulay offers English education as the sole panacea for all the ills of this "uncivilized" country. For a more Eurocentric view of India, one cannot think of a better document than Macaulay's minute.

In many ways, his address at the House of Commons anticipates his ideological position in the Minute. He remarks in a rather astounding fashion that he would "rather trade with free people than govern savages." Let me quote his concluding remarks from his address at the House of Commons:

> Are we to keep the people of India ignorant in order that we may keep tham submissive? Or do we think that we can give knowl-edge without awakening ambition'? Or do we mean to awaken ambition and to provide it with no legitimate vent'? . . . It may be that the public mind of India may expand under our system until it has outgrown that system, that by good government we may educate our subjects into a capacity for better government, that having become instructed in European knowledge they may in some future age, demand European institutions. Whether such a day will ever come, I know not. Whenever it comes, it will be the proudest day in English History. . . . The sceptre may pass away from us. Victory may be inconstant to our arms. But there are tri-umphs which is followed by no reverse. There is an empire exempt from all natural cause of decay. These triumphs are the pacific triumphs of reason over barbarism that empire is the imperish-able empire of *our* arts and *our* morals, *our* literature and *our* laws. (emphasis mine)

The imperishable empire he speaks of is of arts, of morals, of literature and of laws. One cannot overlook the fact that they are all theirs, that is of the English. No doubt we have gone beyond Macaulay's original intentions in that we have now perhaps realised the value of our arts, of our morals, of our literature and of our laws. But it is important to remember that the Indian Penal Code was essentially discriminatory in nature, in favour of the white man. It is indeed sad that the very same Penal Code still rules *the* roost in our courts of Law. We are only now waking up to the new realities and are in the process of bringing in several amendments to the Indian Penal Code.

The logic behind Macaulay's imperishable empire is not easy to miss when he speaks of "the triumphs of reason over barbarism!" More than 50 years have elapsed since the collapse of the British Empire in India. But how does one describe the present day scenario? we live today in a world where Macaulay's imperishable empire has taken not an altogether different form, where the buzzword is Globalisation. As a result what we now have is the alarming prospect of all of us thinking. living and behaving like citizens of the world. We have imbibed Western values in all spheres of our lives and tend to swear by them at every given opportunity. Whereas the need of the hour for us is to assert our identity more strongly than even before in order to prevent us from ending as faceless citizens of the world. We may think globally but we have got to act locally. My fear is that Macaulay's deeprooted empire is indeed imperishable even though it has taken the form of American Imperialism with institutions like the World Bank and the International Monetary Fund dictating how we should live over lives. This is, in my view, far more dangerous and insidious than the 200 years of colonial rule.

As for my great moment in Literature is concerned, it is the portrayal of Catherine-Heathcliff relationship in Emily Bronte's novel, *Wuthering Heights*. Man-Woman relationship has fascinated writers from Shakespeare to D. H. Lawrence. But most of these relationships are quite predictable in nature. It is Catherine-Heathcliff relationship which is unique in the annals of world literature, for it provides us with a disturbingly original and insightful interpretation of Man-Woman relationship. And *Wuthering Heights* as a novel is exceptional since it makes it difficult, if not impossible, to take a definite view of life. The novel demonstrates how life is inexplicable, uncertain and defies easy generalisation.

What is truly remarkable about Catherine-Heathcliff relationship is not just its passionate intensity but the fact that their love is elemental and enduring, always transcending the limits set by the social world. The extraordinary nature of their relationship is expressed in one of the most memorable passages in the novel:

> . . . This is for the sake of one who comprehends in his person my feelings to Edgar and myself. I cannot express it: but surely you and everybody have an notion that there is, or should be, an existence of yours beyond you. What were the use of my creation if I were entirely contained here? My great miseries in this world

have been Heathcliff's miseries, and I watched and felt each from the beginning. my great thought in living is himself. If all else perished. and *he* remained, I should still continue to be; and if all else remained, and he were annihilated. the universe would turn to a mighty stranger. I should not seem a part of it. My love for Linton is like the foliage in the woods. Time will change it, I'm well aware, as winter changes; the trees. My love for Heathcliff resembles the eternal rocks beneath– a source of little visible delight, but necessary. Nelly, I *am* Heathcliff — he's always, always in my mind — not as a pleasure, any more than I am always a pleasure to myself — but as my own being — so don't talk of our separation again — it is impracticable: and . . . . (Ch. IX).

It is evident from this confession that for Catherine her relationship with Heathcliff is something more than love, passion, commitment; it is a craving, a need of a more fundamental kind. It has clear metaphysical overtones in the suggestion that a human being yearns for a vivifying contact with another in order to achieve a sense of completeness. There is this sense of kinship and identity between them and hence her remark, "Nelly, I *am* Heathcliff."

In the light of this clear explication of the true nature of Catherine-Heathcliff relationship, it is not difficult to understand why Catherine chooses to marry Edgar. However, the general tendency among critics ranging from Arnold Kettle to Terry Eagleton is to offer social and economic factors as the major reasons for Catherine's decision to marry Edgar in preference to Heathcliff. They fail to realise that what makes Catherine an exceptional woman is her profound conviction that her marriage with Edgar would in no way affect her unique relationship with Heathcliff. Even a sensitive critic like Q. D. Leavis, rather simplistically likens this to one who wants to have her cake and eat it too. And in recent years, the Feminist approach to *Wuthering Heights* has given us diverse readings of the novel. A representative illustration of such a reading is found in *The Mad Woman in the Attic* by Sandra M. Gilbert and Susan Gubar. They regard the novel as a female version of the male *bildungsroman* and suggest that while "triumphant self-discovery" is the goal of the male hero, it is "anxious self-denial" which is the "ultimate product of female education." They go on to remark that "what Catherine, or any girl, must learn is that she does not know her own name, and therefore cannot know either who she is or whom she is destined to be." Such a sweepingly one-sided account of Catherine's femininity is hard to accept since she is aware, even if partially, of what constitutes her true identity. It is important to remember that *Wuthering Heights* can also be read as a metaphysical romance with serious mystical overtones especially in relation to Catherine-Heathcliff relationship. And this should make it apparent that this relationship clearly transcends societal barriers. What is truly fascinating in the novel is Emily Bronte's questioning the very idea of individual identity as expressed in unequivocal terms in Catherine's assertion that she *is* Heathcliff.

NOTE

1. Paper presented at the C. N. Sanjay Birth Anniversary Symposium on "Great Moments in Life and Literature" at Dhvanyaloka on 8–9 November, 2001.

REBECCA FRASER

Monsieur Heger: Critic or Catalyst in the Life of Charlotte Brontë?

Text of the lecture given to the Brontë Society on 5 April 2003, at the Beverly Arms Hotel, Beverley, Yorkshire.

At a time when Charlotte Brontë was out-growing her dependence on the imaginary world of Angria, the stimulation provided by her experience of Brussels and, particularly the discipline and challenges imposed by her teacher, M. Heger, were instrumental in forming the great literature she subsequently wrote. Evidence of this influence is manifest in all her novels.

At the one hundred and fiftieth anniversary of the publication of Charlotte Brontë's greatest book *Villette*, it seems an appropriate moment to think about Monsieur Heger's effect on her life. Was he critic or catalyst? Can one argue that without him there would not have been the books or the success? I do not go in for 'what might have beens' in history. Charlotte Brontë's drive and determination must have got her and her family's work published somehow. Nevertheless I think that we must accord to Monsieur Heger an importance he may secretly have allowed himself in the life of Charlotte Brontë — though we have no way of knowing that! Charlotte Brontë would correctly prophesy to Aunt Branwell when she pleaded for the financial help she needed to go to Brussels, 'I feel an absolute conviction that, if this advantage were allowed us, it would be the making of us for life'.

Brontë Studies, Volume 28, Number 3 (November 2003): pp. 185–194. © The Brontë Society 2001.

The ongoing success of the Brontë Society, which was founded as long ago as 1893, testifies to the enduring appeal of the Brontë family, whose home at Haworth is Britain's most visited literary shrine. For many, the Brontë's personify a particularly British genius. Perhaps I should say particularly Yorkshire genius. Despite their Cornish mother and Irish father, it is Haworth and the untamed wilderness of Yorkshire that we most associate with the name of the Brontës. For the Brontës Yorkshire qualities are not just to do with the physical facts of a life spent on the edge of the Moors. It is also to do with a certain freedom in the way that the Brontës wrote, which enchant us now, and amazed people then.

Nevertheless, despite the very profound sense of Yorkshire in Charlotte Brontë's work, I believe that one must add that there was one very unusual element in the cocktail of sensitive Celtic blood and Yorkshire soil. I am standing on the very Yorkshire soil today that, a century and a half ago, brought forth a family of rare genius. But, daringly, considering where I am, I want to look at the place of a stranger in Charlotte Brontë's life, of the effect of going to Brussels on Charlotte Brontë's writing. In my view, the foreign land of Brussels and her teacher Constantin Heger had life-transforming effects on Charlotte Brontë. They made the difference between success and greatness, between what she herself called obscurity and becoming the toast of the Victorian literary world.

Emily Brontë needed the profound isolation she sought for her writing to flourish, but in Charlotte's case it was different. Her writing, whose juvenilia Mrs. Gaskell famously described as 'creative power carried to the verge of insanity', needed something to peg her down to earth. The person who did that was Monsieur Constantin Heger. Now you might argue, and many of you have probably done so in the past, that Constantin Heger was simply a teacher in a small Belgian school. How could he have helped the Brontë genius flower? Let us look at what he was like and what he did for Charlotte Brontë. I have called this lecture critic or catalyst, and I first want to look at Monsieur Heger as Charlotte Brontë's critic.

Why Belgium, why Brussels in the first place? Who or what was Monsieur Heger, and what was the nature of the school destined to be immortalized by Charlotte Brontë? Why, by 1841, was Charlotte casting around to find some way of leaving her home for a while? Charlotte Brontë was a woman whom we know from her writing was full of passionate desires and impulses; who was highly intelligent and well read. Yet she was condemned to what to her and to us must seem a very limited life. Other than teaching in schools, governessing in private houses was really all that was on offer for women of intelligence in the first half of the nineteenth century. If Charlotte Brontë were living today, the most enormous variety of options would be open to her. She could have fled her small village and gone to London. If she had attended university there she would have met young people with the sort of ambitions she had. She might have acted in or put on plays, in short been part of a supportive literary community. In Charlotte's case, although she had a supportive background of dear friends in Yorkshire, they were so unlike her. The simply could not understand her mentality and that made her feel very alienated. Throughout her life, Charlotte Brontë suffered from periods of immense depression, which were quite physically prostrating. When she was teaching at Roe Head she suffered a serious illness brought on by a religious crisis and feelings of unworthiness.

Charlotte Brontë's alienation was three stranded — it came from being a woman, from being ambitious, and from having a secret world of writing which had been her retreat ever since she was tiny. That world was an addictive one, the depth of her attachment to which neither of her closest friends, Ellen Nussey and Mary Taylor, could really understand. Only her family, Emily, Anne, and Branwell, could empathize with it. But by 1841, Charlotte had come to recognize the dangers her escapist world posed to her. She had really set her back against Angria because she thought that it was consuming her. As she would say to Ellen Nussey, if only Ellen knew her thoughts, 'the dreams that absorb me; and the fiery imagination that at times eats up and makes me feel Society as it is, wretchedly insipid, you would pity and I dare say despise me'. In the past she had got through the more pedestrian passages of her life by going to what she called 'the world below'. We all know the grip *that* world had on her, how the Duke of Zamorna had been her 'mental king'.

Sadly, by that date Charlotte Brontë had had enough experience of the world to no longer have much faith that writing could ever be the stuff of her life, of a woman's life. She had been told so by the poet laureate himself, Robert Southey, which only underlined the advice constantly given her in childhood by her father, the Reverend Patrick Brontë. By 1840, although she was still interested enough in being a writer to have approached Hartley Coleridge for literary advice, she had, as she said, pretty well locked her manuscripts away. She had tried governessing and loathed it for the condescension with which governesses were treated. As was said at the time, governesses were 'neither fish, nor fowl nor good red herring', in that it was impossible for most Victorian households to decide whether they were to be treated as members of the family, or as servants.

Being a governess might not really have been an option in any case. The volatile nature of Victorian finance, the speculation in railways and banking, meant that bankruptcy was a constant spectre for the Victorian middle class. Governess posts were actually becoming few and far between by the late 1830s. Opening their own school at Haworth was going to be the answer for the Brontës. That was why Charlotte had begged Aunt Branwell to finance an expedition to the continent so that she and Emily could learn some German, master their French, and improve their Italian.

Why Brussels? Well there is a quick answer to that! It was because of the Taylors. They were that family of vigorous men and women who would so seem to represent the highest virtues of this country, its strength and its pride, that Charlotte Brontë would even call them the Yorkes in her novel *Shirley*. Mary Taylor was Charlotte's friend and had the sort of intellectual fire and brilliance that Charlotte herself possessed. A very articulate early feminist, Mary Taylor would not only awaken a reluctant Charlotte to the prison-like conditions middle class were living under in the 1840s; she would also write a feminist novel and even emigrate to New Zealand, where to seek a more active life did not seem like a derogation of class.

Mary Taylor's father, who for most of his life had been a very successful businessman with his own bank and the monopoly on army cloth manufacture in the district, was evidently a perceptive and unusual man. He recognized little Charlotte Brontë's thirst to expand her literary boundaries beyond what the Keighley Mechanics' Institute could provide. He loaded her down with bales of French novels, including the work of Georges Sand.

In the risky climate of the 1830s, where bankruptcy was a frequent hazard of venture capitalism, Mr Taylor's business collapsed. He died bankrupt, though having honorably repaid all his creditors. The Taylors had been sufficiently wealthy that attending school in Brussels was considered necessary to put the finishing touches to the Taylor girls. Although a finishing school was not an option for the daughters of a poor curate like the Reverend Patrick Brontë, through the Taylors' connection to Mrs Jenkins, the wife of the British Embassy Chaplain whose brother came from the West Riding, another school was found in the Rue d'Isabelle. Mrs Jenkins' brother-in-law, the Reverend David Jenkins, had many years before succeeded Patrick Brontë as curate of Dewsbury and knew both Patrick Brontë and Ellen Nussey. Mrs Jenkins had heard that the Pensionnat Heger was a superb school from an English ex-patriot acquaintance. She had been governess to the French Princess who married the first King of Belgium, King Leopold. Her granddaughter was currently being educated by the excellent Hegers, a young couple with a growing family who also ran a small boarding school, the Pensionnat Heger. Greatly in Brussels' favour too, as far as the Brontës were concerned, when every penny counted, was that Belgium was well known to be half the price of Paris to live in. Moreover, the Taylor sisters were there so all would not be strange.

So Charlotte, who as usual was the driving force behind all family ventures, wrote off to the Pensionnat des Demoiselles run by the thirty-eight year old Madame Heger to ask if she and Emily could be taken on as, what were in effect, mature students to polish up their French and German. Madame Heger's husband, Constantin, was a professor at the prestigious Brussels boys' grammar school, the Athenée Royale, but he sometimes gave lessons to the more promising pupils at his wife's school. His presence on the school premises of course made him the dominant figure there, particularly as everyone who knew him agreed that he had an imposing and dramatic personality which went with his dark Italianate looks. As Monsieur Heger would tell Mrs Gaskell, he and had been so impressed by the simple and earnest tone of Charlotte's application that they decided to do a sort of package deal for the Brontës, including all the extras in one specific sum.

What was Charlotte Brontë like when she arrived in Belgium? I think the first thing to say was that she was craving instruction. Despite her intellectual bent and wide reading, she was pretty well self-taught. What she had learnt at Roe Head School was the bare minimum. Though it had given her a strong moral grounding and a sense of discipline, which she had hitherto lacked in her rather chaotic home, Charlotte was also yearning for intellectual and aesthetic stimulus. Many of us might think of Brussels as rather mundane, full of chocolate shops and about as thrilling as Switzerland. But to Charlotte Brontë, whose response to painting and literature was so fervid and so feverish, so intense, Brussels, with its ancient buildings and old churches, seemed a sort of Promised Land. This was her response when Mary Taylor wrote her about Brussels:

> Mary's letter spoke of some of the pictures and cathedrals she had seen—pictures the most exquisite—and cathedrals the most venerable—I hardly know what swelled to my throat as I read her letter— . . . Such a strong wish for wings . . . such an urgent wish to see—to know—to learn—something internal seemed to expand boldly for a minute—I was tantalised with the consciousness of faculties unexercised—then all collapsed and I despaired.

When Charlotte arrived in Brussels, although she was twenty-six years old, in many ways her ideas and attitudes were those of a far younger person. She had led an extremely sheltered life at Haworth, and much of it in the company of imaginary beings! She was looking to learn and expand her horizons. She was ambitious, she wanted to rise in the world and having an excellent school seemed the way to do it. We can imagine the two Brontë sisters, after the long journey finally arriving at the Rue d'Isabelle. Despite the dressmaking that made the Parsonage busy for weeks, their clothing seemed quaint to those who met them at the school, and Monsieur Heger at first probably felt rather sorry for them both. Emily was silent, difficult, and apparently domineering, and the tiny Charlotte was very shy, although more outgoing as she began to settle in. But after a while both Monsieur Heger and Charlotte Brontë began increasingly to look forward to their lessons.

What was Monsieur Heger like, and who was he? Thirty-three years old and descended from a family of Viennese jewellers whose ancestors had moved to Germany two hundred years before, Heger had trained as a barrister before becoming a teacher. He had also had a personal tragedy in his life. His first wife and their only child had child had died during the cholera epidemic that swept Brussels in 1833. Even allowing for some exaggeration in his obituaries, it seems that Monsieur Heger was an extraordinary teacher commonly agreed to possess '*une sorte de magnetism intellectuel*'. Although that grand old man of Victorian letters Leslie Stephen, the father of Virginia Woolf, might dismiss him unkindly as an 'Aeolus of the duck pond', Monsieur Heger was rather unique. As well as being exceptionally charismatic, he had a passion for contemporary literature that he began to impart to his new pupils once he had realized what sort of students he was dealing with. For although the plan had been to drill *les soeurs* Brontës in grammar and vocabulary, he rapidly saw that they had the capacity to cope with important French writing and that it would not be enough for his wife to teach them. Thanks to the good luck of destiny of encountering Monsieur Heger Charlotte at last was subjected to strenuous interrogation by the intense Monsieur Heger as to what made a piece of prose work and what did not.

All her life, Charlotte Brontë had read widely and enthusiastically but without any real guidance. In Monsieur Heger she encountered the stern critic she needed to make her look at literature with an academic eye, as well as someone with beliefs as strong as her own. Like her father, Monsieur Heger was determined to help educate factory workers by giving them evening classes. As far as he was concerned, being a teacher was a real vocation. As a writer Charlotte Brontë was in desperate need of discipline, as she had become all too aware. Monsieur Heger supplied it and we can imagine lesson after lesson as the man Charlotte at first privately called 'an insane tom-cat' railed at her and her sister for not properly applying their minds to what they were reading. We also know from Charlotte's exercise books in the British Library of the very patient care that Monsieur Heger began to take over Charlotte's devoirs, so that he worked on her prose style with her and urged her to abandon the redundant. Monsieur Heger also exposed Charlotte to the best contemporary French literature. Thanks to him, Charlotte Brontë, who was totally in tune with the ideas of the French Romantics and who came to them with a sense of recognition, also learned from them. The way they handled language, the inversion of syntax, the use of metaphor to express meaning in a wholly new way, was peculiarly suited to her genius. As Enid Duthie put in, 'in French Romanticism' Charlotte Brontë 'found abundant confirmation of her inborn sense that the novelist may also be a poet'.

The tutelage of M. Heger produced a new awareness in Charlotte of the possibilities of prose style, and of the many effects one can make by varying rhythm and language. Such debt did Charlotte feel to Monsieur Heger that she would later say that she would like to write a book and dedicate it to him because he had been her 'Maitre de Literature'. He was the only master of literature she had ever had, she would write in an excess of gratitude and enthusiasm. Like the other two important male figures in her life, Monsieur Heger might have helped Charlotte with her writing but he too very much counselled her against becoming a writer. He might have helped refine her prose style but he was also highly critical of her literary ambitions when she eventually outlined them to him. His aim was that Charlotte Brontë should become a teacher, never a writer. His general attitude towards the capabilities of the female sex, though progressive in mid-nineteenth century terms, was not advanced enough to view women as anything other then appendages of their husbands and children.

In many ways, despite Monsieur Heger's appreciation of Charlotte's work, he was a critic in the sense that he was one more restraining voice added to the chorus of disapproval concerning her ambitions to be a writer. We know from the presence of some Angrian manuscripts which turned up on a stall in Brussels at the beginning of the twentieth century (Charlotte had obviously brought them from Haworth to show to Monsieur Heger), that those ambitions were not quite dead, even in Brussels. How could they ever be entirely?

I believe that, more importantly, Monsieur Heger was also a catalyst. I use the word advisedly. Monsieur Heger was like a chemical flung into the fermenting mixture of Charlotte Brontë's mind, which had an extraordinary effect. And of course if one was a scientist hypothesizing what the outcome of an experiment would be if one took a brilliant teacher and a passionate pupil, one might predict that the pupil would fall in love with the teacher. What happened was still more interesting. For somehow back in Yorkshire, deprived of Monsieur Heger's presence, an astonishing reaction took place in the rich and intense imagination of Charlotte Brontë, where that inner life compensated for the poverty of daily existence. Charlotte Brontë never wrote as honestly as she did in *The Professor*. 'Belgium! Name unromantic and unpoetic, yet name that whenever uttered has in my heart an echo, such as no other assemblage of syllables, however sweet and classic, can produce . . . Belgium . . . It stirs my world of the past like a summons to resurrection.'

From then onwards, Belgium and Monsieur Heger were dwelt on obsessively. As she would write, the physiognomy, the lineaments, of Belgium, and indeed the Rue d'Isabelle and Monsieur Heger, were burnt onto her memory. Indeed, before Belgian developers bulldozed the Pensionnat and destroyed a patch of literary history, earlier biographers armed with copies of either *The Professor* or *Villette* could find their way round the Pensionnat with ease. It was exactly the same. Although Charlotte's four personal letters to Monsieur Heger give some indication of her feelings after she reluctantly returned from Brussels, how much more so do the novels. *The Professor* and *Villette* are both set in Brussels at a slightly altered Pensionnat Heger, while *Shirley*'s hero is half Flemish.

In the atmosphere of that small Yorkshire parsonage where creativity was seemingly accelerated, something amazing happened. Monsieur Heger, who was charismatic and distinguished but still a provincial schoolteacher, was fused with Charlotte's Byronic alter ego Zamorna that she had worshipped for so long. Mr Rochester was born. Some critics have laughed at Mr Rochester. One said he talked like a governess. Yet it was not a governess he spoke like, but a *teacher*. For those members of the Brontë Society who have read those sad little letters written after Charlotte's return, begging for communication from Brussels, there is something almost too painful about the tender descriptions of Mr. Rochester in *Jane Eyre*. For he is really Monsieur Heger writ large. 'My only master', Charlotte Brontë called Monsieur Heger in her letters; 'my master', Jane Eyre addresses Mr. Rochester.

The letters to Monsieur Heger breathe a kind of enchantment, which their recipient must have had a heart of stone to resist. Yet resist he did — after all he was most definitely a married man, the father of no less than five children. And in response, Charlotte's imagination, something she often seemed to have believed almost had a life of its own, got to work and carried her away from her unhappiness. The Thornfield section in *Jane Eyre* does give the impression of being written in white heat. Monsieur Heger was transformed, transmogrified, made broader, squarer:" 'I knew my traveller', Charlotte Brontë wrote, 'with his broad and jetty eyebrows, his square forehead, made squarer by the horizontal sweep of his black hair. I recognized his decisive hose, more remarkable for character than beauty ... his grim mouth, chin and jaw—yes all three were very grim and no mistake'. The famous erotic scene in the garden at Thornfield—no cold English garden this—was the Pensionat's garden transplanted, made by Charlotte's lyrical writing into a sort of Paradise.

We know that Charlotte Brontë began writing *Jane Eyre* as she stayed in Manchester watching over her father after his eye operation. Her father had so many similar qualities to M. Heger; force and power like his. As she watched him apparently maimed, did something in her exult that in her imagination at least she could wound Monsieur Heger, for as Mr. Rochester he is blinded and wounded. I won't say emasculated, though some more hard-line feminist critics argue that that is what is going on.

Monsieur Heger is the catalyst in Charlotte Brontë's life, in her transformation into a great writer, but in a sense catalysts are small things in their own right. They simply precipitate a chemical reaction for which all the ingredients are already present. If *Jane Eyre* was just a sort of Cinderella tale it might have become a bestseller, but what makes it so passionately loved is the character of Jane Eyre herself. For, as was much criticized at the time, Jane Eyre was an absolute rebel. Although since the mid-nineteenth century Jane Eyre has become a paradigm of the feisty female character, in fact she broke the mould.

The dominant idea of Charlotte Brontë's day was that women's influence depended on their being a sort of living repository of higher moral qualities. That in itself led to what the philosopher John Stuart Mill in 1861 would angrily call the 'exaggerated self-abnegation which is the present artificial ideal of feminine character'. As it would hurt Charlotte Brontë greatly to discover, her brand of realism was found very alarming by the mid-nineteenth century world, a world in which the harder women struggled to assert themselves, the more their male relations struggled to suppress them. When we remember the way that suffragettes were arrested just for marching for the vote less than a hundred years ago, we must see Charlotte Brontë and her heroines as early pronotypes for those women. Who knows whether the Pankhursts of Emily Davison were not once thrilled by those wonderful words in *Jane Eyre:*

> Nobody knows how many rebellions besides political rebellions ferment in the masses of life which people earth. Women are supposed to be very calm generally: but women feel just as men feel; they need exercise for their faculties, and a field for their efforts as much as their brothers do; they suffer from too rigid a restraint, too absolute a stagnation, precisely as men would suffer; and it is narrow-minded in their more privileged fellow-creatures to say that they ought to confine themselves to making puddings and knitting stockings, to playing on the piano and embroidering bags. It is thoughtless to condemn them, or laugh at them, if they seek to do more or learn more than custom has pronounced necessary for their sex.

As Charlotte would write to the editor at Smith, Elder and Co., Mr Williams, when brickbats began to rain down with the bouquets on her and her sisters' heads, her whole life's work had been about dismissing female stereotypes. Whatever the criticisms of her work, she continued to hold that 'conventionality is not morality' and that 'self-righteousness was not religion', and that furthermore she must have her own way in the matter of writing. Even if she distressed men by confounding their ideas of women, she was determined to continue to write as she felt was truthful. That impulse of course found its greatest fulfillment in *Villette*, which was in many ways her frankest and most autobiographical novel.

It would give Monsieur Heger and Brussels less than their due if one did not admit their transforming effect on the mind of Charlotte Brontë. For in a sense, one of the miracles of Brussels was that it injected a note of down-to-earth reality into Charlotte's writing. Two years before she left for Brussels, Charlotte Brontë had made a formal renunciation of Angria. She had recognized, as she put it, the need 'to quit' for a while that burning clime where we have sojourned too long . . . the mind would cease from excitement and turn now to a cooler region where the dawn breaks grey and sober'. It took real life in Brussels to make her ready to almost completely forgo the Byronic world. In *The Professor*, her first book written after Brussels, Charlotte wrote, 'I said to myself that my hero should work his way through life as I had seen real living men work theirs — that he should never get a shilling he had not earned — that no sudden turns should lift him in a moment to wealth and high station'. For in Brussels, Charlotte at last found so many things to stimulate and fascinate her, from unfamiliar customs to foreign religion, that she finally seemed to have found the real world more intriguing than the world below. Of course the charm of *Jane Eyre*, or should I more accurately say the *magic* of *Jane Eyre*, depends to no small extent on the strange alchemy which is half the workday world, half the greatest romance.

It is when we arrive at *Villette* we see that ten years after Brussels, once again by the strange effect of what one can only call Charlotte Brontë's genius, the tiny stage of the Pensionnat Heger has become the backdrop to one of the greatest nineteenth-century novels about the female condition. *Jane Eyre*, like *Wuthering Heights*, will never be knocked off its place in the Pantheon of great books. Nevertheless, if we divorce the plot of *Jane Eyre* from Charlotte Brontë's lyrical gifts, it may be faintly preposterous. But when we come to *Villette*, there is nothing unbelievable about it. *Villette* is monumental, terrible and, one feels, all too truthful an account of what life was like for so many women one hundred and fifty years ago. As Tony Tanner wrote in his brilliant introduction to the Penguin edition of *Villette:*

> It is only in *Villette* that Charlotte Brontë found the most appro-
> priate female narrator to explore in a sufficiently complex way the
> tensions and alternations in her own inner and outer experience to
> produce one of the great fictional studies, not of self-and-society,
> but the self without society, in our literature.

And somehow, as Charlotte dwelt obsessively on Monsieur Heger, she began to come to what echoes through *Villette* as almost abstract conclusions, about the empty nature of life for women in the nineteenth-century world where they are forced to conceal their true natures for the sake of male-imposed propriety. That is the greatness of *Villette:* in language so strange and height-ened that female misery has never been more poignantly conveyed, Charlotte Brontë demonstrates the fate of women with any strong feelings that are not what custom has pronounced appropriate for her sex. They are permanently forced to keep their true nature hidden. Of course what is most interesting about *Villette* is that, despite its misery, we emerge from the novel feeling that Lucy Snow and Charlotte Brontë herself have triumphed. M. Paul Emmanuel has not made the mistake that Dr Graham Bretton has made of judging Lucy by her physique. He does not think of Lucy as 'inoffensive as a shadow'. He sees that there is a powerful fire within her. In the end, Lucy is finally able to reveal her true nature to M. Paul, and he does not flinch away.

The most important thing about *Villette* is that Lucy finds someone to whom she can 'talk in her own way', just as Lucy at last triumphs over the spectre of the nun. As she says when she rushes at the nun on her bed and realizes it is a dummy put there so that Ginevra Fanshawe may escape with her suave lover, 'all the movement was mine, so was all the life, the reality, the substance, the force'. That is the effort of Charlotte herself, sitting on those long afternoons at Haworth without brother or sisters: that is Charlotte determined to never give in to outside opinion.

It was leaving England and getting away from her beloved home that energized so much that was latent in Charlotte. We know that she detested all kinds of religious zealots, but in Brussels she was brought up against what she saw as an even more tyrannous way of life under the rule of the Roman Catholic Church. We know that despite the restrictions of Yorkshire life, Charlotte herself had a certain amount of freedom there, certainly at her Haworth home and in the company of the Taylors. In Brussels, Charlotte was amazed by the more conservative nature of Belgian society, where if we judge by M. Paul's behaviour, certain passages in literature were censored for not being appropriate for delicately reared young women. In my view, the combination of what appeared to Charlotte Brontë to be the tyranny of Roman Catholicism, with its falseness, and its effect on what is required of women, made her want to pick up her pen and pour out her anger, ten years after Brussels.

From a biographer's point of view, what is fascinating about *Villette* is the hold it suggests that, years later, Monsieur Heger retained over Charlotte Brontë's feelings. Just as we know that for a while George Smith exercised a considerable hold over Charlotte Brontë's all too impressionable heart, so Graham Bretton wins Lucy's — hence the slightly strange shape of *Villette*. If not quite one of Henry James' 'baggy monsters' — the writing is too wonderful for that — it sometimes approaches it.

Charlotte Brontë was briefly dazzled by her newfound literary London life with Mr. Smith, and the protective aegis of Mrs Smith, but when it became clear that she and George Smith viewed one another very differently, Charlotte reverted to the past. The Brettons begin the novel but then vanish for many pages and it becomes clear to a biographer that Monsieur Heger is stealing back into Charlotte Brontë's heart, just as M. Paul Emmanuel steals back into Lucy Snowe's. By that time, she had a real friend of the bosom in the shape of Mrs Gaskell, to whom she could confide and whose charming daughters helped inspire the portrait of Pauline de Basompierre. But judging by the evidence in *Villette*, Charlotte Brontë began to return obsessively to the figure with whom she believed she had a sort of natural affinity, who she felt had truly understood her.

The greatness of *Villette* is that it is more than just an acutely observed *Bildungrosman* set in Belgium, and this is why I believe we must think of Monsieur Heger mainly as a catalyst. Without Monsieur Heger there would certainly have been no *Villette*. There would have been no *Pensionnat des Demoiselles;* there would be no Madame Beck. Furthermore, Mr Rochester, arguably the prototype of all post-1847 Romantic heroes, might have taken a very different form. It is as a portrait of what it means to be a nineteenth-century woman, however, and the pain that existing in the cage entails, and the great language that Charlotte Brontë summons up from the depth of her unhappiness, that makes it endure. And that is the product of Yorkshire, and of long days alone. As Charlotte wrote to Mrs Smith, who asked her to come and stay in January 1852, 'the solitude of my life I have certainly felt very keenly this winter — but everyone has his own burden to bear — and where there is no available remedy, it is right to be patient and trust that Providence will in His own good time lighten the load'.

In recompense for the lack of activity, in memory Charlotte saw action. She returned to the bustle of the school in Brussels, and recreated it in the minutest detail, overlaid by the heightened atmosphere of her pain. Lucy Snowe still has some of Charlotte's fire buried in her, remnants perhaps of Jane Eyre's rebelliousness, but it is banked down beneath misery and hopelessness and an ominously grim religion. As one reviewer would write, 'her talk is of duty — her predilections lie with passion'. And it is from Yorkshire winters and her observation of the wild weather effects that comes the weather in Belgium, which I doubt is ever as dramatic as that described by Charlotte Brontë's pen. For in Charlotte Brontë's extraordinary hands, even the weather becomes apocalyptic. She wrote to Mrs Gaskell in November 1851 that

> for a month or six weeks about the equinox (autumnal and vernal) is a period of the year, which, I have noticed, strangely tries me. Sometimes the strain falls on the mental, sometimes on the physical part of me: I am ill with neuralgic headache, or I am ground to the dust with deep dejection of spirits . . . That weary time has, I think and trust, got over for this year. It was the anniversary of my poor brother's death, and of my sister's failing health: I need say no more.

It seems to me that one of the truths about Charlotte Brontë was that her strange upbringing, the hold that the infernal world had upon her imagination, however much resented, and the tragedy of her life, meant that any subject approached by her would be transformed into something more striking than they were. Thus a little school in most vivid places in literature. Charlotte Brontë's gift needed something to feed on. By getting herself to Brussels, she found the provender from which emerged two of the greatest novels in the English language.

JAMES REANEY

The Brontës: Gothic Transgressor as Cattle Drover

Article reprinted from Gothic Fictions: Prohibition, Trangression, *edited by Kenneth W. Graham (New York; AMS Press, 1989), pages 227–244, with kind permission of the author and publishers.*

Not that long ago, I had the chance, in Ontario, Texas, and Yorkshire, to spend some months slowly working my way through the greater part of the Brontë juvenilia. This, for the most part, means the youthful writings of Charlotte and Branwell, some of it published, some of it still in their microscopic hand printing, microscopic because the original readers consisted of their own toy soldiers and dolls, the original inspirers of what grew into a huge saga of interconnecting stories, prose fragments, and poems which Charlotte and Branwell were still dreaming about when long past their majorities. Mercifully, a great portion of this eye-challenging manuscript labyrinth has been transcribed by W. C. Hatfield, the editor of Emily Brontë's poems. His priceless typescripts are available at the Brontë Parsonage Museum, Haworth, Yorkshire, and to simplify reference in a field where Branwell manuscripts are still an editorial nightmare, I have made full use of them in this essay.

I had started this project with several possible aims in view: find the sources of *Wuthering Heights*, explain the archangel imagery in *Shirley*, have a try at establishing a Brontë canon, or even write a much needed book in defence

Brontë Studies, Volume 29, Number 1 (March 2004): pp. 27–35. © 2004 The Brontë Society.

of Branwell against critics who dismiss him as a 'second-rate Manfred'. One small, simple question did keep nagging me, though, and eventually seemed to be important enough to need in immediate answer. Why do both Branwell and Charlotte make one of their shared Gothic heroes a cattle drover? As late as 1840, Charlotte (*Mr. Ashworth & Son* — an incomplete romance) has the Percy Northangerland figure go bankrupt, then disappear, a wicked Byronic nobleman up until this point, and next bob up again in Yorkshire as a cattle drover with a good credit rating even if questionably earned. Branwell and Charlotte's Northangerland must be one of the very few Gothic heroes to hold down a job, although Branwell's descriptions of his hero's herding journeys always manage to suggest some son of secret mythical edge beyond the world of actual cowjobbing. As preparation for some sort of answer, the first thing to clear out of the way is — what is Branwell and Charlotte's youthful epic basically about, and how is it told? Part of the reason for the insouciance with which they make a nobleman twice as Byronic as Byron chase cows is related to absurdist-nihilist attitudes these young writers have with regard to any notion of a connection between a reality-principle and story-telling. Here is a necessarily simplified and brief outline.

Twelve toy soldiers which his father gave to Branwell on his tenth birthday in 1826 become Twelve Adventurers who, towards the end of the eighteenth century, fictionally leave England to found a colony on the west coast of Africa, a colony known as the Glasstown Confederacy ruled by the Duke of Wellington with the foundation of Angria a later reaction to constant rebellion by Quashia, the son of the previous black ruler of the land imperialized by the Twelve. In Percy Northangerland, the black rebels have a friend inside the Confederacy who either supports their outbreaks or, in the name of Democracy, constantly rebels on his own against both the Duke and his son, Charlotte's favorite, Arthur Zamorna. Branwell called his favorite toy soldier Buonaparte; Charlotte called her favorite, after Branwell had given her permission to play with it, Wellington. What then seems to happen, and this with many windings and turnings as more than ten years of story-development goes by, is that the Buonaparte soldier becomes Percy Northangerland — atheist, rebel, demagogue, sadistic trouble maker, and the Wellington soldier becomes Charlotte's Zamorna — constitutionalist, younger, and more humane than the satanic Percy Northangerland to whom, nevertheless, he retrains profoundly attached in a curious love-hate relationship. Connecting the radical electrode with the constitutionalist one, many, many feminine figures intertwine themselves about this pair of demons. There is, for example, Lady Zenobia Ellrington who loves Zamorna, but marries Percy Northangerland: in reply, Zamorna marries Percy's daughter Mary. Over and over again, Percy rebels, is exiled, returns, is forgiven; eventually he goes too far. He has a young son of Zamorna's mutilated and murdered, but, mind you, this is in retaliation for Zamorna's causing his daughter's death by suddenly deserting her. Of course, Zamorna did that to stop Percy from continuing his attempts to take over the kingdom of Angria.

As Charlotte and Branwell edge into their twenties, the saga begins to exhaust itself, or rather look around for some adult, plausible clothing. Charlotte's Angrian novelettes start showing signs of realism. *The Professor*, with secret feet in Angria, is on its way. Branwell's *And the Weary Are at Rest* (1845) has the magic drover and many of other strange Angrian people, but all toned down. Everyone knows that Percy should be hanged except that Zamorna feels he will probably suffer more if he is not put out of his misery. After 1845, Branwell begins to tell friends that he is Northangerland. Not for nothing did the Brontë children call their literary world 'the world below'. If Branwell died thinking that he was the Byronic demon he had developed out of a toy soldier, we do indeed receive a disturbing vision of Percy Northangerland as Erlkönig, monster reaching out of the microscopic manuscripts and pulling his boyish creator down into the hell of exhausted introversion that had for a long time tormented him.

The above attempt to sum up the thousands and thousands of words in a complex saga jointly dreamed up by two Genii (more of this soon) obviously must slice through some labyrinthine intricacies in order to provide the amount of scaffolding we need for examination of the Drover motif. Perhaps two more comments should be made.

First, since the children took the initial situation of writing for and about toy soldiers so very literally, they stumbled upon a literary fact which many readers and writers would never have thought of and that is this: from the toy soldiers' viewpoint, from the literary characters' outlook inside the story, the Brontë children must seem inexplicable and terrifying giants who exercise equally frightening powers over their hapless playthings. In this, the literary creator is like the Genii in *The Arabian Nights*. Therefore, Charlotte and Branwell called themselves and their sisters the four Genii, and so do those of their literary creations as live a sufficiently long life to think about the metaphysics of what is happening to them. To illustrate this, here is Charlotte in an early tale called *The Foundling* in which Wellington's son Zamorna has died, but is suddenly revived:

> They informed him that that morning, as they were walking in the grove of trees, a terrific peal of thunder had burst directly over their heads. On looking up they perceived the four chief Genii, who rule the destinies of our world, appearing through an opening in the sky. 'Mortals,' they cried, in a voice louder than the previous thunder, 'We, in our abundant mercy, have been moved to compassion by oft repeated and grievous lamentations. The cold

corpse in the grave shall breathe again the breath of life, provided you here lodge a solemn oath that neither he nor his relatives shall ever take revenge on those who slew him, for it is the mighty Branii's will to revivify both the murderers also'. 'We swear', said they without hesitation, 'that none shall injure one hair of their perjured heads'. No sooner were these words uttered than the Genii vanished amidst the roar of ten thousand thunders.[1]

How absolute is the power the young storytellers have over their characters, particularly if Branwell is in a good mood! The result of the Genii or 'unconcealed author' convention is that the stories in the juvenilia have a rather strange floating feeling. Anything can happen, and usually does. Much stranger things happen than even an aristocrat turning into a cowherd, and they often do so with a sort of odd probability.

Secondly, since the original choice was Charlotte/Wellington as good versus Branwell/Napoleon as bad, no matter how Byronized and Satanized both characters became the stories always work for a reader's sympathy with Zamorna and fascinated terror at Percy; consequently, Zamorna never gets to be drover. Somewhere along the line it must have been drummed into the Brontë children's heads that drovers made mistakes. How does that humble profession fit in with all this?

So far as I can see, this figure makes: its first appearance in one of Branwell's *Letters from an Englishman* (1831):

> For a long time the Marquis of Douro and myself continued gazing on the scene silently, forgetting in our excess of admiration that we were in a chariot, or were any other than stone, till we were startled out of our reveries by the noise and bellowing of an immense drove of mountain cattle which were going toward the city, the road which was a noble width being one hundred yards across was choked up with them to the distance of a quarter of a mile . . .

The Marquis explains to the Englishman, Branwell's persona here, that the drover of this immense herd is none other than Pigtail 'that celebrated champion of Frenchmen' who turns out to be 'nearly 9 feet high, lean, bony and ill built, yet bearing the marks of extreme strength'. Enquiries as to where the cattle come from meet with the reply that they are stolen; Charles Wellesley, the Marquis of Douro's twin brother and a favorite persona of Charlotte's, also adds:

> Yes and once I saw this Pigtail sell to my Father some of our own cattle and my Father, knowing they were his, did not say anything

but paid him a penny apiece for them — knowing that he would be quite content with that sum and thus he recovered the beasts at 3 pence while had he gone to law or arrested the brute he would have had to pay 30 or 40 [pounds] . . .[2]

Where would the Brontë children have got hold of the idea of an evil cattle drover? My feelings are that this is the result of stories about his Irish past told them by their father, Patrick Brontë. After all, there are Irish traditions about his grandfather having been a big cattle drover. Still, how I arrived at this hypothesis needs some more preparation. In the voluminous and dreamlike flow of the juvenilia, Pigtail soon fades, regrettably, from view, and two other characters, more Branwell's specializations than Charlotte's, take over Pigtail's cattle driving and other more sadistic responsibilities (he loves torturing children). These are Robert King, also known as S'death, and his master, the aforementioned Alexander Percy Northangerland, known in earlier stories as Rogue. The former, S'death, is steward, valet, assistant drover, and groom to the latter.

Early descriptions of S'death appear in *The Coronation of Adrian Augustus Wellesley, First King of Angria* (1834): 'a little scrappy old chief, in a long brown coat and drovers boots, with a hat such as tops many a potato field, who bestrode his gaunt grey nag,"[3] and in *A New Year's Story* (1836): 'unknown and unregarded as a Yorkshire drover well might be'.[4] Nearly always drunk, known, and deservedly so, as a jackal and a hoary bloodhound, this remarkable figure drives both cattle and human beings for both the Percys, the father, old Edward Percy, a wicked Northumbrian nobleman, and his son, Rogue (later known as Percy Northangerland), who is born in Africa after S'death persuades the father to leave England for greener pastures in the Glasstown Confederacy. On their way to Africa through Ireland, S'death kills the Duke of Mornington for his master: with the plunder thereby gained, old Edward Percy buys a sizeable estate in Senegambia. Some years later, when Alexander Percy Northangerland desperately desires to get hold of his avaricious old father's money, S'death obligingly polishes him off. Since his victims are often much larger than himself, and he is described as being so old and decrepit, the reader is not surprised to learn that Robert King or S'death has very special powers — he Is really a disguised version of his author, Branwell Brontë! Yes, S'death's deadly activities turn out to be a parody of the omnipotent author who, at any time he chooses, can kill off as many of his own creations as he chooses.

The twelfth letter of *Letters from an Englishman*, 1832, shows this concept of story management in an embryonic state; there, a certain Highlander, the Ape of the Hills, has a vision of 'a little old man with a red head' who tells him to meet him at the seashore: 'when he reached the seaside in Northumberland, he saw coming toward the shore a copper cauldron with the little old man in it whom he had seen in his dream'. In the copper cauldron, they both sail to Africa where the Highlander joins in helping Percy Northangerland in yet another uprising: 'This old man was the Genius Branni!'.[5] Later, by having S'death as a much more disguised 'Branwell', this young author will considerably improve on this earlier and more cumbersome method of showing the author guiding, with visions and magic cauldrons, the plot of a story. In 1833, the whole idea is given another twist in *The Pirate;* by this time, the 'little red old man' has become a dwarfish S'death.

Percy Northangerland is the pirate, and a very successful one. The only trouble is that after the execution of his victims, his valet, S'death, with disgusting sadism, insists on re-stabbing each and every corpse. Having had enough, Percy and the narrator (the very Englishman who earlier on met with the giant Pigtail) gang up on the old ruffian and try to kill him, that is, kill the very person who is writing them:

> The old dwarf was striving to strike his knife into Rogue's [Percy's] heart. Rogue was grappling with him. They were both on the floor. In my hurry I seized a poker, and, running up, dashed it at the head of S'death. This stunned him. Rogue then snatching up a pistol from the table clapped it to his head and fired. The skull was blown to pieces and the brains scattered round the room. Rogue without speaking motioned me to take hold of his feet, and, himself seizing his shoulders, we proceeded silently up the steps to the deck. Here Rogue crying: "I have done with thee, thou wretch," took the ugly heap of mortality and hurled it into the sea.

But, it is not as easy for characters to be without an author as they may have imagined:

> When it touched the water a bright flash of fire darted from it, changed it into a vast GENIUS of immeasurable and indefinable height and size, and, seizing hold of a huge cloud with his hand, he vaulted into it, crying: "And I've done with thee, thou fool!" and disappeared among the passing vapours. Ere he departed three vast flashes of fire came bursting round. They were the Chief Genii, Talli, Emii, and Anni. He that ere this was the little hideous old man was the chief genius, and BRANNI. I stood petrified with fear and astonishment.[6]

Although Charlotte (Chief Genius Talli) can provide a few, this must be the most mind-boggling moment in all of the youthful writings, even more so when the reader remembers that it is written by a fifteen year old, and that it antedates not only Monty Python, Tony Hancock, and the Goon Show, but also Borges, Nabokov, and the *nouvelle vague*.

At this point in my reading of the juvenilia, I used to wonder why on top of all this S'death also had to be a drover: I thought of how drovers drive their cattle to market after which their beasts will be slaughtered; how this is what happens to quite a few of Branwell's Characters, his merciful revival of the dead Zamorna being, after all, in a tale written by his sister, Charlotte, S'death, then, is Branwell's supreme drover herding both cattle and dramatis personae this way and that, his tyranny only interrupted Charlotte's rescue attempts in her parallel stories. Probably, there is something to this use of the drover image, for one of the distinctive feelings about the Glasstown and Angria sagas is their constant movement through time and space as their creators' lively minds impel their creations now through the southern savannahs of the Glasstown Confederacy, now through the moorlands on Angria's northern borders. The other solution I have hinted at took some time to develop, partly because I kept missing the reference to it in a story by Charlotte.

S'death's most notable kill, the death of Maria, Percy's wife, leads to a break in Percy Northangerland's character on the other side of which he himself becomes a drover. It happens thusly. Having borne him two sons, Edward and William, Maria Percy is about to present him with another child. With pre-Freudian undertones, Percy suddenly orders S'death to kill the boys because, since they are males, they do not resemble their mother sufficiently. S'death does disappear with the boys, but neglects to tell anybody that he has hidden them alive from their father's wrath ready for use later on by Charlotte in *The Professor*. After bearing a girl baby, Maria dies of grief — for her two sons who she feels have probably been murdered. In an ecstasy of grief and guilt, Percy again turns pirate. After a spell of this, so we learn from *A New Year's Story*, he orders his vessel home under S'death captaincy, and lands alone on the coast of Sidon, there to wander back to Senegambia appearing 'on a sudden at Percy Hall before his mother and his child, after an absence of six dark and bloody years'. And, at this point he too becomes a drover:

> First, Percy knew that he was such an one as, if seen, could not be unnoticed; so he determined upon being seen — but by whom? The Aristocracy could not be moved: they had no complaint. The Democracy could, for they were bold and reckless; so he laid out thousands of his gory gains in enormous stocks and set up an immense concern in horses and horned cattle. Travelling through different kingdoms of the Union, attending all the great Fairs, and carrying along with him his lieutenant, Old S'death, and a desperate, dissolute company of partners, the dregs of the Western Aris-

tocracy, his companions of the Rover, and men lost to kindred, country, and religion in riotous debauchery. With such a SOUL, Percy of course became King and Emperor among all the Drovers, Cow-jobbers, Cattle-dealers, pasturers and farmers of Africa. They could not tell what to make of him, but they worshipped him and wondered at him.

Among the thousands who attended the great fairs at Fidena, Denard, and Selden, in Sneachisland or Pequena, Rossendale, Freetown, and other such marts in the east and south, he was monarch in the market place and hotel, made speeches, instilled corrupt and revolutionary ideas, increased and confirmed adherents, and in four years time became an object of alarm and suspicion to the scarcely awakened Government.[7]

As the Western Drover, Percy's specialty is the downfall of ancient houses, rather as Heathcliff's is the destruction of both the families of Thrushcross Grange and Wuthering Heights. In the *Coronation of Adrian Augustus Wellesley,* a Colonel Hartford tells such a story to a Branwellian persona called Richton. Happening to pass the ruins of Hartford House as they proceed to the ceremonies at Adrianopolis, the new capital of Angria, the colonel remembers that when Percy's cattle came up the road they raised such a cloud of dust that a tramp thought 'it was the bottomless pit opening all its smoke before him'. Inviting this demon to stay as a house guest, Sir Edward Hartford soon finds himself entangled:

> He [Northangerland] pretended to affect a mighty regard for the baronet, and soon entered into some deep gambling with him I can tell you, by which atrocious piece of acting he brought the baronet in a fortnight's time head over heels into difficulties; then he humbugged him into some intricate juggle in cattle-dealing, affected to put him again into fair water, gave him a note of hand to an unlimited time, laughed at the thoughts of Sir Edward paying him his due, and swore he should directly be worth twice the sum of what he owed him. Now, Sir Edward had a son, young squire, friend of mine. Rogue had infatuated him I think, for he almost talked of going as one of Rogue's riders, only the arch-fiend one night so swore and sneered him down that I think it cured him of the thought. Hartford had a daughter too, the Honourable Miss Amelia Hartford. She was then nineteen . . .[8]

The upshot is that Sir Edward loses all his property to Percy who seduces his daughter. The son he murdered in a neighbouring wood.

Through with Hartford Hall, Percy, leaving his steward Steaton (S'death?) to receive rents, next attacks a farmhouse on the northern moors known as Darkwall. The manuscript, written in 1837, is untitled and begins: 'The season had advanced into the last week of November before the wheels of my travelling carriage once more rattled over their native pavements', continuing with a conventional Branwell persona telling of a visit with the Thurstons of Darkwall whose family had once been lords of a nearby manor. Readers of *Wuthering Heights* and *Jane Eyre* may note such details as 'a plantation of gloomy firs, one clump of which the oldest and the highest stretched their horizontal arms above one gable like the genii of that desolate scene', and the fact that the property is haunted by a Gytrash:

> The Darkwall Gytrash was known by the form of an old dwarf-ish and hideous man, as often seen without a head as with one, and moving, at dark, along the naked fields which spread round the aged house. Its visits were connected in all men's minds with the fortunes of the family he hovered round, and evil omens were always drawn on such occasion, and, if tradition spoke true, ful-filled upon them.[9]

The situation calls for an appearance of this ominous phantom since the narrator finds Mrs Thurston anxiously waiting for the return of her husband from Fidena while having to entertain his friend, Percy Northangerland. The Western Drover, with all his cattle and entourage, has come on ahead of his host for possibly a longer stay than the Thurstons had anticipated. The story is unfinished, but what seems to have happened is that Percy has murdered Mr Thurston and, as he once did at Hartford Hall, is about to lay siege to Darkwall with property and woman as prime objectives:

> While his gang was present he had appeared sour and impetuous, they were now gone; and while his hostess occupied a sofa by the fire he arose on a sudden and commenced a progress backwards and forwards through the room. His majestic figure, now light-ened, now shadowed, as he advanced to or receded from the fire, and his blue, wayward eyes enkindled and his expression each moment changing, while he poured forth on many a subject, his words so warmly and flowing eloquent.[10]

Perhaps this passage, more than any other in the juvenilia, sums up how powerful the drover/aristo coupling can be. One moment the hero's a dusty figure on the road, the next he's a glamorous, drawing room charismatic. Just how much this effect could be carried intact from 'the world below' of the Angrian saga into 'the world above' of a plausible, realistic novel set in contemporary England was the next aesthetic problem Branwell and Charlotte faced.

If *And the Weary Are at Rest* is a fragment from a novel Branwell was working on in 1845 and not an Angrian story, then he seems to have been able to do without the drover effect as a means of anchoring Northangerland; the only hint of it appears in S'death being called a 'groom'. Charlotte, however, in her uncompleted *Mr Ashworth and Son*, 1840, allows Percy Northangerland his droverhood, and I rather wonder if it would not appear in the early chapters she evidently excised from the final version of *The Professor*, the professor being, after all, a son of Percy in a secret, Angrian past. 'Ashworth' is an alias for Percy both she and Branwell had used five years earlier, and, in this unfinished attempt to turn her Angrian material into some sort of Richardsonian romance, not only does Percy Northangerland as drover appear, but this time Liverpool is mentioned is a destination for has trading vetures: 'many mercantile men, too, are yet living in Leeds and Manchester and Liverpool who can remember the market dinners given by Ashworth'. Ashworth-Percy works with four helpers who are said to have been chosen 'for his associates in his great triple character of demagogue, cow-jobber, and horse-jockey. Their names are: Gordon 'a penniless scoundrel', Daniels 'who knew well how to disguise a traitor's heart under the features of a jovial Irish gentleman', McShane, an Irishman with 'the advantage of a Gallic education' and Robert King, 'his hair very red'.[11] If the question 'why drover?' can be answered, then I think that 'Liverpool' and 'Irish gentleman' may also fall into place.

The above question can be answered by the earlier mentioned hypothesis that the drover motif belongs to stories their father told them about his own Irish past and that of some of his ancestors in County Down and elsewhere. This sounds like quite a leap to take, but hypotheses, which is all this at present can be, must take wide enough leaps to let in enough material for the inevitable sorting, rejecting, and possible accepting to come when, long overdue, Branwell's youthful writings have, at last, all been edited and published.* Having taken the leap, the next question is from whom did Patrick Brontë (originally Brunty until he made an inspired upward mobility change) hear them from his father, Hugh Brunty, and this now leads us to a much reviled book published in 1893, *The Brontës in Ireland* by the Rev. W. D. Wright, D.D.

Untidy as Dr. Wright's chronology may be, and really wild as some of his conclusions are, nevertheless, he did hear and record some remarkable oral traditions with regard to the Brunty family in Ireland, and it may very well be that it is exactly the wildness of such stories that may have attracted the attention of young genii not particularly interested in getting the facts straight about Wellington and Napoleon either, but eager for any material that would keep a story going. And one such Irish story about their family was that one of their uncles named Walsh or Welsh was named after a demonic foundling who was brought into the family by their great grandfather who was himself a drover down near Drogheda. The foundling grew up to take over his benefactor's business by devious means.

The great grandfather 'used to live on a farm on the banks of the Boyne, somewhere above Drogheda. Besides being a farmer he was a cattle-dealer, and he often crossed from Drogheda to Liverpool to dispose of his cattle'. On the way back, the story goes, a foundling discovered in the hold of the ship was rescued by the cattle drover and his wife and taken home with them where it was not beloved by its foster sisters and brothers. Called 'Welsh', he was favorite of the cattle driving Brunty who:

> . . . took him to fairs and markets, instead of his own sons, as soon as he was able to go, and he found him of the greatest service. His very insignificance added to his usefulness. He would mingle with the people from whom Brontë wished to purchase cattle, find out from their conversation among themselves the lowest price they would be willing to take, and report to his master. Brontë would then go to the dealers, and without the usual weary process of bargaining offer them straight off a little less than he knew they wanted, and secure the cattle.

In no time at all, Welsh takes over the old cattle drover's business;

> They were returning from Liverpool after selling the largest drove of cattle that had ever crossed the Channel, when suddenly Brontë died on board. Welsh, who was with him at the time of his death, professed to know nothing of the master's money, and as all books and accounts had been made away with, no one could tell what had become of the cash received for the cattle.[12]

Not long after this, Welsh had taken over the Brunty farm and married one of his late master's daughters. Childless, the couple adopt a nephew, Hugh Brunty, so much mistreated that he runs away at the age of fifteen. Yet survives to prosper in County Down, marry, father a large family, the first born of which is known to us as Patrick Brontë with, among other brothers and sisters, a brother known as Welsh or Walsh, presumably named after the demonic foundling.

Here, then, is a possible answer to why a drover, keeps reappearing in the Glasstown and Angrian tales. There may be other explanations, and they are welcome, but at least this one also explains something that has always puzzled me. Using the persona of Lord Charles Albert Florian Wellesley, Charlotte writes *My Angria and the Angrians* (1834) and meets on his/her travels in Angria her brother Branwell whom she calls Patrick Benjamin Wiggins. She asks him what relations he has and he replies:

> Why, in a way I may be said to have no relations. I can't tell who my father and mother were no more than that stone. I've some people who call themselves akin to me in the shape of three girls not that they are honoured by possessing me as a brother, but I deny that they be my sisters. Robert Patrick S'DEATH Esqre is partly my uncle, but he's the only relative I'll acknowledge.[13]

For 'partly my uncle' then, read 'my uncle named after a foster great-uncle' who did some rather inspiring things so far as literary children in search of material were to be concerned: for example, stow away on a boat sailing out of Liverpool to Ireland where he behaved in peasant terms to his benefactors the way Percy Northangerland behaves in aristocratic Gothic terms. Some years later, like S'Death, he even writes old Mr Brunty out of the script. There is no reason why Gothic romance material should always be gentlemanly and upper class; just as Branwell and Charlotte showed the way in other Angrian stories where factory life is involved, they also showed how invigorating a drover could be when cross-hybridized with the more usual titled neurotic.

NOTES

*Since this article was first written, the prose works of Branwell have been published as *The Works of Patrick Branwell Brontë: an Edition.* Edited by Victor A. Neofeldt, 3 vols. Garland Publishing, N. Y. and London, 1997-2000.

1. Charlotte Brontë, *The Foundling* in *The Miscellaneous and Unpublished Writings of Charlotte and Patrick Branwell Brontë* (The Shakespeare Head Brontë) henceforth cited as *SHCBM.* ed. by T. J. Wise and J. A. Synsington (Oxford: Basil Blackwell, 1936), p. 288.

2. Branwell Brontë, *SHCBM,* i. pp. 104–107.

3. Branwell Brontë, No. 41, ti, TS, p. 33. This and all other typescripts cited are in the Hatfield transcripts of Juvenilia, Brontë Parsonage Museum.

4. As above, p. 181.

5. Branwell Brontë, *SHCBM,* i. pp. 148.

6. As above, p. 181.

7. Branwell Brontë, No. 42, iii, TS, p. 121–123.

8. As above, No. 41, ii, TS, p. 38–40.

9. As above, No. 65, iii, TS, p. 382.

10. As above, p. 370.

11. Charlotte Brontë, No. 65, TS, pp. 32–35.

12. William Wright, *The Brontës in Ireland, or Facts Stranger Than Fiction* (New York: D. Appleton, 1893), p. 190.

13. Charlotte Brontë, *SHCBM,* ii, pp. 9–10.

MEGHAN BULLOCK

Abuse, Silence, and Solitude in Anne Brontë's The Tenant of Wildfell Hall

Anne Brontë's The Tenant of Wildfell Hall *is a much overlooked and impor-tant text in terms of early feminist writing. Its themes of marital abuse and women's silence, separation from society, and solitude are all explored in depth. This article considers the themes of silence in the face of abuse and the solitude it causes. It focuses on the relationship between Helen and Milicent, examin-ing the lack of communication between them and the connection between their silence and the cycle of abuse within families and within society.*

If there were less of this delicate concealment of facts—this whispering 'Peace, peace,' when there is no peace, there would be less of sin and misery to the young of both sexes who are left to writing their bitter knowledge from experience.[1]

T*he Tenant of Wildfell Hall* is an unusual text, both shockingly modern and graphic for its time, and still relevant today in Anne Brontë's treatment of the questions of women's silence and how the 'delicate concealment of facts' only leads to more trouble, both for the women concealing their plight from each other, and for the other women who see and follow their example.

Anne says in her preface to the second edition that the reason for her writing this novel is to 'tell the truth'.[2] She has decided to speak for those women who can't, who, like Helen, Milicent, and Aunt Maxwell, suffer at the

Bronte Studies, Volume 29, Number 2 (July 2004): pp. 135–141. © The Brontë Society 2001.

hands of others and are unable for one reason or another to make themselves heard. In exploring the story of Helen Huntingdon, Anne is able to give her readers a look into the lives of different women and their relationships, their motivations, and the abuses they suffer. As readers, we can surmise that there is much going on in the lives of these women that is not explicitly stated. Even though we have access to Helen's diary, we are not privy to everything that is going on in her marriage, especially with the added insulation of reading her diary through Gilbert's eyes, and Anne does not give any hints about whether or not the diary was edited because of its being used as the text of a letter. This insulation is one way in which Anne herself silences Helen in the text, and is also only one example of Helen being silenced. Whether the silencing is her own doing or that of others is a question that pervades the text.

Those who have grown up surrounded by abused women and who have been victims of abuse themselves generally learn from mothers and grandmothers how to deal with it; they either learn to he silent, or, because their mothers have made that mistake, they learn the necessity of seeking support from other women, and this breaks their silence. Helen's diary begins with her aunt, the mother figure in the novel, giving her warnings about marriage. She is full of advice but strangely reticent on the subject of her own treatment by her husband. The subject of marriage is introduced because Aunt Maxwell noticed Helen's attraction to Arthur and was uneasy about it. She says

> 'Now I want to warn you, Helen, of these things, and to exhort you to be watchful and circumspect from the very commencement of your career, and not to suffer your heart to be stolen from you by the first foolish or unprincipled person who covets the possession of it [. . .] I may as well tell you likewise — for if I don't others will — that you have a fair share of beauty, besides — and I hope you may never have cause to regret it!' (p. 148)

Helen, of course, trusts in her own strength and clear perception of people to guide her in her choice of husband. Anne never shows that she has experience of her own or others to warn her otherwise. Helen admits to being 'vexed at her incredulity; but I am not sure her doubts were entirely without sagacity; I fear I have found it much easier to remember her advice than to profit by it — indeed, I have sometimes been led to question the soundness of her doctrines on those subjects' (p. 151). She does not take her aunt's advice, or even take her warnings to heart, but she does ask her aunt if this is the voice of experience. When Helen asks if she has 'been troubled in that way' (p. 149) Aunt Maxwell replies 'No, Helen [. . .] but I know many that have; and some, through carelessness, have been the wretched victims of deceit; and some, through weakness, have fallen into snares and temptations terrible to relate' (p. 149). Anne has made Helen's uncle a selfish reprobate, and this is what prompts Helen's curiosity about her aunt's experience. Her uncle keeps friends similar to Arthur's, and shows the signs of having lived like him at one time in his life. Helen's aunt serves as Helen's model for how to deal with marital troubles: silence.

When Helen is first introduced as the widow Graham, the reader is struck by her solitude. In her diary, no friends are mentioned prior to her first season in London, which is where she meets Milicent. There is no friendship in the text with the ladies she is shown to be on good terms with at Wildfell Hall, and the relations with most ladies in the neighborhood seem barely cordial. Milicent Hargrave is the only woman in the novel that Helen is shown to have any kind of close or open relationship with. This could be a reason why she is silent — she has no one to talk to except for Milicent, and Milicent is so innocent at first that she would have no way to sympathize with Helen in her troubles, and thus arguably be of no help to her whatsoever.

When she first meets Milicent, Helen describes her as 'gentle' and says that 'she had taken a violent fancy to me, mistaking me for something vastly better than I was' (p. 160). She refers to her as 'poor Milicent'. Milicent appears in the subsequent chapter as Helen's intimate friend as well as a houseguest, invited by Helen's aunt to benefit Helen by her example of 'gentle deportment, and lowly and tractable spirit' (p. 169). Milicent is praised by many of the characters in the book for what they deem her humble spirit, hut that same gentleness is what causes her to be a victim of her husband for so long. In this novel, Milicent is shown to he a 'sweet, good girl' (p. 169), but ironically, the things that would make her seem so to a Victorian audience are the very things that Anne, Helen, and later Milicent's husband Hattersley see as faults in her character.

Anne devotes the remainder of chapter 18, as well as chapter 19, to Helen's descriptions of what has passed between her and Arthur, who is beginning to show himself as he really is. Even though Helen has her 'intimate friend' (p. 170) Milicent in her house, she does not speak to Milicent about her uneasiness over Arthur but chooses to write about it instead, saying,

> This paper will serve instead of a confidential friend into whose ear I might pour forth the overflowing of my heart. It will not sympathize with my distresses, but then it will not laugh at them, and, if I keep it close, it cannot tell again; so it is, perhaps, the best friend I could have for the purpose. (pp. 169–170)

It seems strange that Helen would not talk to Milicent instead. If she really is such a gentle, good, kind person, she would not laugh at what Helen had to say, she would sympathize with her, and keep her own counsel. It seems as though Milicent has all the qualities Helen attributes to a piece of paper.

Of course, a pragmatic reason for Helen's silence is that if Helen had spoken these things to her friend, there would be no diary to use as a device for the novel. Nevertheless, even had Anne not told the story through Helen's diary (through Gilbert and then Halford), it is arguable that she still would not have had Helen tell Milicent her troubles.

Anne introduces shame into Helen's life: she begins to feel ashamed of Arthur and her attraction to him, and does not want to reveal either his conduct or the depth of her attachment to him. After all, he does have 'the audacity to put his arm around my neck and kiss me' (p 173), he flirts with Annabella, and he violates Helen's privacy. Arthur's general conduct is not calculated to gain approval, and it would be especially offensive to someone like Milicent, who is pure and gentle. To open herself up to Milicent would be to risk being looked down upon for her taste in men, or to be lectured at, or some other unpleasant consequence. However, as the story progresses and the characters unfold, the reader learns that Milicent would indeed be a good confidant, but Helen does not realize this soon enough, and does not take advantage of it when she can.

Milicent is as guilty of not speaking out about her husband's treatment of her as Helen is, but she is at least honest in her reaction to Helen when the letter tells her of impending marriage to Arthur. Milicent is no more support than Helen's aunt, much to Helen's displeasure; she say that 'she rather provoked me by her manner of taking it' (p. 195). Milicent's reaction to Helen's announcement of her engagement was, 'Well, Helen, I suppose I ought to congratulate you [. . .] but I did not think you would take him, and I can't help feeling surprised that you should like him so much' (p. 195). She continues to try and bring things about to Arthur to Helen's attention that may prove to be problematic later on, perhaps to make her think of these things while there is still a way out. It is ironic, however, that she didn't volunteer any of this before matters reached this point. Helen silences her friend, though, by simply ignoring her. Though not done on purpose, it takes the power from Milicent's speech all the same, and she never levels with Helen like this again. Helen silences her Aunt in the same way and is herself a victim of silencing through being ignored — her protestations being ignored by Hargrave and Gilbert, her ideas being ignored by the society surrounding Wildfell Hall, and so on. Anne's women, even those who do speak, are consistently ignored. By having Helen ignore Milicent's observations and intended advice, Anne makes her forfeit some valuable insights as well as the opportunity to develop a deeper friendship with Milicent. This is not uncommon in either women's literature or real life.

By ignoring everybody's advice and observations concerning Arthur, Helen gets herself into a brutal, unhappy marriage. It is ironic that Anne uses Helen, a woman, and one who is strongly in favor of independent womanhood, as a silencer of *other women* who have chosen to say things that are on their minds; things that could be dangerous. The question is, though, would Helen have listened to advice more intently, and not silenced her aunt, if she had shared more of her *personal* experiences with Helen? For example, if Helen had known that her aunt was speaking about marriage to a man like Arthur from an intensely personal experience, would she have given her more credit and heeded her hard-earned wisdom? Perhaps, if she had shared her own experience rather than just good advice, Helen's aunt could have helped to break the cycle of abuse and silence sooner. However, because Anne was writing this piece as a representation of real life, this would have been impossible as, arguably, it happened so rarely in Victorian society.

After the first few weeks of marriage, Helen makes the observation that 'Arthur is not what I thought him at first' (p. 215) and realizes, 'I might have known him, for everyone was willing enough to tell me about him [. . .] but I was willfully blind' (p. 215). This would seem to be a turning point, Anne giving her a realization about not ignoring the things others have to say, and perhaps it is, but from this point on in the novel, Helen (like many women in Anne's audience) internalizes her pain and struggles even more than before, to the point of not writing it all out in her diary. There are points where she is obviously leaving out details, or perhaps entire (important) exchanges between Arthur and herself. Helen, like Anne's contemporaries, is either lying to herself, or does not want there to be any chance that her darkest secrets be discovered. Women lacking the support and benefit of the past experience of other women are more liable to fall into this trap of either excusing their husbands' bad treatment or else hiding it out of shame. If the women in Helen's family, and those surrounding her, had been more open about their own sufferings, Helen probably would not have settled for justifying Arthur's actions; but that is not the story that Anne wanted to tell.

Discovering Arthur's past intrigues so angers Helen that she locks herself into her bedroom and admits to her diary, 'for the first time in my life, and I hope the last, I wished I had not married him' (p. 222). This is their first real argument, at the end of which she tries to convince him that she never would have married him if she had known these things that the other characters would have told her. He responds:

> Do you know that if I believed you now, I should be very angry? — but thank Heaven I don't. Though you stand there with your white face and flashing eyes, looking at me like a very tigress, I know the heart within you, perhaps a trifle better than you know it yourself. (pp. 222–223)

In spite of Helen's words and actions, Arthur does not listen to or believe her, so she writes a letter to her aunt; 'of course telling her nothing of all this'

(p. 223); the legacy of silence continues. This letter is not the only example Anne gives of Helen's desire to reach out to her family. During Arthur's first absence, she would 'beg my uncle and aunt, or my brother, to come and see me, but I do not like to complain of my loneliness to them' (p. 233). Anne continues relating her and her family in this fashion: even though Helen realizes that her aunt knows that something is amiss, she keeps it a secret until she finally leaves Arthur. She writes letters to all of those close to her telling them what she has done, but her aunt is the only one she gives a reason to. She says of writing this last letter, '[it was] a much more difficult and painful undertaking [. . .] but I must give her some explanation of that extraordinary step I had taken [. . .] At last, however, I told her I was sensible of my error' (p. 391). This is as close as she comes in the text to opening up to her aunt. She apparently does not tell her much more than she has to, and yet says that 'if they knew all, I was sure they would not blame me' (p. 391). If she told them everything she thought they needed to know in order to pardon her fully, she would not need to have worries about their reception of her and the step she had taken. Anne uses this to reinforce the legacy of silences that Aunt Maxwell left Helen.

Helen's aunt passed silence on to Helen, and so it is natural that Anne would have Helen pass it on to Milicent. Since Helen is the only other woman Milicent knows in an obviously less-than-happy marriage, and since Helen is possibly Milicent's only real friend, Milicent takes all her cues on how to deal with things from her. The letter that Milicent writes to Helen to tell her of her engagement to Hattersley is the most open communication the two women ever have about their troubles with their men. Of her impending marriage, Milicent says,

> To tell you the truth, Helen, I don't like the thought of it at all. If I am to be Mr. Hattersley's wife, I must try to love him; and I do try with all my might: but I have made very little progress yet [. . .] he frightens me with his abrupt manners and strange hectoring ways, and I dread the thought of marrying him. 'Then why have you accepted him?' you will ask; and I didn't know I had accepted him; but mamma tells me I have, and he seems to think so too. I certainly didn't mean to do so; but I did not like to give him a flat refusal for fear mamma should be grieved and angry [. . .] mama is so delighted with the idea of the match; she thinks she has managed so well for me [. . .] I do object sometimes and tell her what I feel, but you don't know *how* she talks [. . .] Do *you* think it nonsense, Helen? [. . .] Do write to me, and say all you can to encourage me. Do not attempt to dissuade me, for my fate is fixed [. . .] and don't say a word against Mr. Hattersley, for I want to

think well of him [. . .] After all, I think he is quite as good as Mr. Huntingdon, if not better; and yet you love him, and seem to be happy and contented. (pp. 234–235)

Helen responds in her *journal* saying, 'Alas! Poor Milicent, what encouragement can I give you? — or what advice — except that it is better to make a bold stand now, though at the expense of disappointing and angering both mother and brother, and lover, than to devote your whole life, hereafter, to misery and vain regret?' (pp. 235–236). Anne does not say how Helen responded to Milicent, and one can only assume based on the rest of the text that this advice was not given. Milicent's letter is a plea to Helen, to somehow help her out of the mess she is in. Helen is in no position to help her friend as, in the text, she ignored all the advice given her, and that is part of the reason for her resigned tone upon reading the epistle. She has already given Milicent a model to follow, that of seeming 'to be happy and contented' even when she suffers tremendously. Whether implicitly or explicitly, Milicent picks up on this, and never opens herself up again the way she does in this section of the novel. Her later letters provoke Helen's distrust based on her own self-deception and deception of others. Chapter 25 ends with this description of Milicent's letters:

> She either is or pretends to be quite reconciled to her lot. She professes to have discovered numberless virtues and perfections in her husband, some of which, I fear, less partial eyes would fail to distinguish, though they sought them carefully with tears; and now that she is accustomed to his loud voice and abrupt, uncourteous manners, she affirms she finds no difficulty in loving him as a wife should do, and begs I will burn that letter wherein she spoke so unadvisedly against him. So I trust that she may yet be happy; but if she is, it will be entirely the reward of her own goodness of heart; for had she chosen to consider herself the victim of fate, or of her mother's worldly wisdom, she might have been thoroughly miserable [. . .]. (pp. 239–240)

Helen is unable to believe that Milicent is truly happy because she knows too well the methods that women use to deal with terrible situations. Like Helen, Milicent is silent, but she is better at self-deception than Helen is. Anne gives her a gentler temperament, so Milicent is able to make herself feel that she is happy and content, unlike Helen, who feels her sorrows keenly though she hides them. Helen is perceptive enough to see that Hattersley makes 'life a curse' (p, 269) to her friend, and 'as for her own misery, I rather *feel* it than *see* it expressed in her letters' (p. 270).

The women in the novel do the best they can to avoid admitting the truth to themselves or others. When Arthur accuses Helen and Milicent of abusing their husbands in correspondence, Helen offers a possible, though partial, explanation for their silence: 'We are both of us far too deeply ashamed of the errors and vices of our other halves, to make them the common subject of our correspondence. Friends as we are, we would willingly keep your failings to ourselves — even *from* ourselves if we could' (pp. 270–271). Later, Anne offers further explanation for Helen's silence when Helen recounts a visit with her aunt, who she fears is more perceptive than she would have liked. She muses

> Was it pride that made me extremely anxious to appear satis-
> fied with my lot, — or merely a just determination to bear my
> self-imposed burden alone, and preserve my best friend from the
> slightest participation in those sorrows from which she had striven
> to save me? It might have been something of each, but I am sure
> the latter motive was more predominant. (p. 276)

Shame or wounded pride, and the reluctance to draw her closest friends into her pain are the recurring excuses that are given for Helen's silence. She seems to feel guilty when she thinks of sharing her burdens with others; Anne was faulted for these unpleasant portrayals of Helen's burdens, because they were far too 'coarse and brutal' (according to the *Spectator*, 8 July 1848). With such reception to the fictionalized stories of women's suffering, one can only wonder if there would be any difference in the reception of the fully authentic, fully detailed stories of what women really went through in their own homes. False guilt for marrying Arthur may have been the main motive Anne gave Helen for silence, but surely she knew that women are silent also because their stories were usually not received.

It is gratifying that Helen does not end the novel in silence. As previously mentioned, the story of her life with Arthur was told through her diary, which was couched in the narrative of Gilbert Markham.[3] In order for him to have been able to share what she has written of her story with the readers of the novel (or his friend Halford, as the novel is presented as a letter to him), Gilbert would first have had to have read her diary. In order for this to happen, she would have had to have given him her diary to read. When she does this, it is an act of resistance against the people starting rumors against her, as well as resistance against Gilbert and his weakness in believing them. This is the point where Anne finally allows Helen to break her silence — after finding herself so strongly drawn to Gilbert, and realizing that only the truth, her *own story*, would clear her of whatever shame the countryside was attempting to bring down on her. She makes the first move to confront

Gilbert about his sudden change in demeanor toward her, and when he is reluctant to listen to her reasoning, confronts him again, protesting, 'I would have told you all!' (p. 141) when he suggests that he has, from eavesdropping on her conversation with Lawrence, learned more than she would ever have let him know. Later on, when Gilbert comes to hear the explanation, which she has decided him unworthy of, he explains to her why he feels that the gossip of the countryside is believable. Her response to this, which is the vocalized tuning point in her struggle against silence, is: 'You should have come to me after all [. . .] and heard what I had to say in my own justification. It was wrong to withdraw so secretly and suddenly, immediately after such ardent protestations of attachment, without ever assigning a reason for the change. You should have told me all — no matter how bitterly — *it would have been better than this silence*' (p. 145, italics mine).

Anne allows Helen to physically liberate herself when she runs away from Arthur; she is able to resist him physically all along, but it is not until she can bring herself to share her experiences with Gilbert that she is able to begin transformation. The cultural transformation that her experiences make her responsible for can only be brought about through her sharing with other women, building solidarity, and encouraging others to do the same. This stage of her development is not shown in the text; rather, Anne takes it upon herself to provide the avenue for abused women to speak through.

References

1. Anne Brontë, Preface to the Second Edition of *The Tenant of Wildfell Hall*, 1848.

2. Anne Brontë, *The Tenant of Wildfell Hall* (Viking Penguin, 1980), p. 29.

3. In 'The Voicing of Feminine Desire in *The Tenant of Wildfell Hall*', Elizabeth Langland points out that this female narrative nested inside an ostensibly male's story was considered a 'correct' form of presentation of women's stories in Victorian times; ironically, in order to get her heroine heard, Brontë had to silence her in the context of the writing of the novel, by not giving her anything to say firsthand.

PAUL EDMONDSON

Shakespeare and the Brontës

When Virginia Woolf was invited to lecture at Cambridge in 1928, she famously remarked that 'a woman must have money and a room of her own, if she is to write fiction'. Her papers were later published as a short book, *A Room of One's Own*, in which she frames her thoughts like this:

> But, you may say, we asked you to speak about women and fiction—what has that got to do with a room of one's own? I will try to explain. When you asked me to speak about women and fiction I sat down on the banks of the river and began to wonder what the words meant. They might mean simply a few remarks about Fanny Burney; a few more about Jane Austen; a tribute to the Brontës and a sketch of Haworth Parsonage under snow, some witticisms about Miss Mitford, a respectful allusion to George Eliot; a reference to Mrs. Gaskell and one would have done.[1]

A tribute to the Brontës and a sketch of Haworth Parsonage covered in snow. Already we have an image of quaintness, an image of isolation, an image of an entire family, which included both male and female writers, deserving of our tribute. But, you may think, this is an article about Shakespeare and the Brontës, what has that got to do with a room of one's

Brontë Studies, Volume 29 (November 2004): pp. 185–198. © The Brontë Society 2001.

own, or Virginia Woolf? I will try to explain. *A Room of One's Own* proposes more than the necessity of financial independence for women who write; it proposes the necessity of an imaginative space, and the Brontë sisters certainly had that in abundance, if not the complete privacy of their own rooms. In her work, Woolf also proposes an evolutionary community of women writers, a creative sisterhood whose transcendental influence makes it possible for women to write, for ordinary women to write and struggle for independence. For most of their lives, a varied experience of the world and extensive travel was denied the Brontë sisters, Woolf reminds us, and their novels:

> were written by women without more experience of life than could enter the house of a respectable clergyman; written too in the common sitting-room of that respectable house and by women so poor that they could not afford to buy more than a few quires of paper at a time upon which to write *Wuthering Heights* and *Jane Eyre*.[2]

Now you and I know, as did Virginia Woolf, that the Brontës did travel from Haworth, but her exaggeration here serves her over-arching hypothesis. Imagining their struggle against social restrictions, Woolf muses how much more impossible it would have been 'for any woman to have written the plays of Shakespeare in the age of Shakespeare'. And so Woolf imagines that Shakespeare:

> had a wonderfully gifted sister, called Judith [. . .]. She was as adventurous, as imaginative, as agog to see the world as he was. But she was not sent to school. She had no chance of learning grammar and logic, let alone reading Horace and Virgil. She picked up a book now and then, one of her brother's perhaps, and read a few pages. [. . .] Perhaps she scribbled some pages up in an apple loft on the sly, but was careful to hide them or set fire to them. [Then, one day, escaping the prospect of an awful marriage she . . .] made up a small parcel of belongings, let herself down by a rope one summer's night and took the road to London. She was not seventeen. The birds that sang in the hedge were not more musical than she was. She had the quickest fancy, a gift like her brother's for the tune of words. Like him she had a taste for the theatre. She stood at the stage door; she wanted to act, she said [. . .] at last Nick Greene, the actor-manager took pity on her; she found herself with child by that gentleman and so—who shall measure the heat and violence of the poet's heart when caught and tangled

in a woman's body?—killed herself one winter's night and lies buried at some cross-roads where the omnibuses now stop outside the Elephant and Castle.[3]

Shakespeare's imaginary sister 'never wrote a word', Woolf reminds us towards the end of her essay, but 'she lives; for great poets do not die; they are continuing presences; they need only the opportunity to walk among us in the flesh'.[4] And so we arrive at Haworth Parsonage buried in snow to pay tribute to the Brontës: Charlotte, Emily, and Anne; who, in Virginia Woolf's view, are sisters of Shakespeare who *could* and *did* write, and whose words *were* published and started to become famous during their tragically short lives. Importantly for us, Woolf refers to the Brontës several times during the course of *A Room of One's Own*, and speculates that:

> when one reads of a witch being ducked [. . .] a wise woman selling herbs [. . .] then [. . .] we are on the track of a lost novelist, a suppressed poet, of some mute and inglorious Jane Austen, some Emily Brontë who dashed her brains out on to the moor or mopped and mowed about the highways crazed with the torture that her gift put her to.[5]

It is significant, I think, that here, Emily Brontë is directly associated with Shakespeare's Lady Macbeth who says that she would have 'dashed the brains out' of her innocent child, rather than be in any way uncertain about her vow to kill King Duncan, as Macbeth is (*Macbeth*, I. 7. 58).[6] 'Mopped and mowed' is also an allusion to *King Lear*, and Edgar as Poor Tom's 'Flibbertigibbet, of mopping and mowing, who since possesses chambermaids and waiting-women' (*King Lear*, IV. I. 64). In his Arden edition, Reg Foakes suggests this may mean: 'making faces and grimacing (as chambermaids do behind the back of their mistress?)'.[7] Although only a passing reference, Woolf's remarks about Emily Brontë are deeply revealing in their characterization of her as darkly neurotic—conjuring up immediately a woman, like Lady Macbeth, given to fits of madness and sleepwalking—and possessing a deeply disturbing, violent imagination. One only has to recall Virginia Woolf's own unhappiness, madness, and her suicide to realize that here she is also writing about herself. Interestingly, too, she associates Emily explicitly with tragedy: *Macbeth*, a Scottish play set in a not dissimilar landscape to that of Emily's own beloved Haworth. The reference to *King Lear* perhaps evokes something of the immense frustration that Woolf perceives in Emily's character, as viewed through her work. For Woolf, the Brontës are the most Shakespearian of all of Shakespeare's imaginary sisters, and Emily the most Shakespearian of all.

The size of the Brontë sisters' output is too large for me to consider very much of it in the course of a single article. So, after sketching an impression of the Shakespeare that the Brontës might have known, I am going to turn to Charlotte Brontë's *Shirley* and Emily Brontë's *Wuthering Heights* to draw out some of their Shakespearian parallels, and to discuss the kind of importance they attach to Shakespeare.

Although it includes the *Life of Sir Walter Scott.*, the Lord Wharton Bible, and Milton's *Paradise Lost,* no edition of Shakespeare is listed in the inventory of 'Books belonging to or inscribed by members of the Brontë family and held in the Brontë Parsonage Museum'. This should not be too surprising. The inventory is small and the most commonly read books tend not to survive, being so well-thumbed that they fall to pieces. Remarkably, though, Anne's copy of Shakespeare *does* survive in the Folger Shakespeare Library, Washington, D.C., and is signed by its owner (*The Dramatic Works*, London: I. J. Chidley, 1843, 4 vols). Jane Austen conducts a discussion between Henry Crawford and Edmund Bertram in that Titanic-on-still-waters of a novel, *Mansfield Park* (chapter thirty-four). The heroine Fanny Price overhears Henry Crawford reading Shakespeare's *Henry VIII* to Lady Bertram and taking all the parts himself with an excellent variety of voices. Edmund remarks that the play must be a favourite of Henry's, who replies:

'It will be my favourite I believe from this hour [. . .] but I do not think that I have had a volume of Shakespeare in my hand, since I was fifteen.—I once saw Henry the eighth acted.—or I have heard of it from somebody who did—I am not certain which. But Shakespeare one gets acquainted with without knowing how. It is part of an Englishman's constitution. His thoughts and beauties are so spread abroad that one touches them everywhere, one is intimate with him by instinct—No man of any brain can open at a good part of one of his plays, without falling into the flow of his meaning immediately.'

'No doubt one is familiar with Shakespeare in a degree,' said Edmund, 'from one's earliest years. His celebrated passages are quoted by every body; they are in half the books we open, and we all talk Shakespeare, use his similes, and describe with his descriptions.[8]

It is probably safe to assume that the all-pervasive influence of Shakespeare as outlined in this extract was the same for the Brontës as it was for Henry Crawford, Edmund Bertram and, one supposes, Jane Austen herself. In her biographical novel, *Dark Quartet: The Story of the Brontës,* Lynne Reid

Banks sketches what the reading climate of the young Brontës might have been like:

> When he [the Reverend Patrick] saw Branwell in a reverie over some book, written in a more permissive age, Patrick wondered if he was wise in allowing his children access to any volume in his library or that at Ponden Hall, which they frequently visited to borrow books. At first he had felt that they were safe from the grosser allusions in Shakespeare, for instance, by virtue of an inability of their essentially innocent minds to understand. Now he was no longer sure.[9]

Perhaps the Reverend Patrick might have made sure that his children were kept safe from Shakespeare's sexier passages by acquiring the relatively recent four-volume edition of twenty plays in *The Family Shakespeare*, edited by Henrietta Bowdler (1754–1830), which cut all the so-called 'grosser allusions'? Or he may have steered his children towards the ten-volume, completely Bowdlerized edition of 1818 (the same year in which Emily was born, and still less than 200 years after the publication of the First Folio), by Henrietta's twin brother, Thomas? A translation of August Wilhelm Schlegel's *Lectures on Dramatic Art and Literature* was published in 1815; William Hazlitt's *Characters of Shakespeare's Plays* appeared in 1817 and his theatrical criticism, *A View of the English Stage*, appeared in 1818. It is likely that these classics among Shakespearian criticism were relished by the Brontë family. Their favourite novelist, Sir Walter Scott, was himself profoundly influenced by Shakespeare, and the Brontës probably enjoyed noticing the imaginative and prolific connections with Shakespeare that stream through Scott's fiction.

The Brontës might have read with interest, too, Anna Jameson's *Characterisations of Women, Moral, Poetical and Historical* of 1832. Later this became known as *Shakespeare's Women* and is a character study of the leading roles. The Brontës might have been aware of the great Shakespearian actor Edmund Kean's (1787–1833) flashes of lightning across the London stage. Charlotte herself saw William Charles Macready's (1793–1873) Shakespearian performances as Macbeth and Othello at the Theatre Royal, Covent Garden. To her friend Margaret Wooler she confessed to finding his style of acting 'false and artificial'. John Forster (who Charlotte met in December 1849) vibrantly reviewed Macready's productions of *King Lear* and *Coriolanus* in February and March 1838 for *The Examiner*. Macready helped to restore *King Lear* to something closer to Shakespeare's version, post-Nahum Tate, by re-instating the role of the Fool. Helena Faucit was a similar age to the Brontë sisters, just twenty, when she appeared as Hermione opposite

Macready's Leontes in *The Winter's Tale* in 1837; the year the Age of Victoria began, when the Queen herself was only a young woman of eighteen. Writing to her dear friend, Ellen Nussey, at around this time, Charlotte Brontë very usefully provides an inventory of her own, a recommended reading list:

> You ask me to recommend some books for your perusal; I will do so in as few words as I can [she writes on 4 July 1834]. If you like poetry let it be first rate, Milton, Shakespeare, [James] Thomson, Goldsmith, Pope (if you will, though I don't admire him) Scott, Byron, [Thomas] Camp[b]ell, Wordsworth and Southey. Now Ellen don't be startled at the names of Shakespeare, and Byron. Both these were great Men and their works are like themselves. You will know how to chuse the good and avoid the evil, the finest passages are always the purest, the bad are invariably revolting you will never wish to read them over twice, Omit the Comedies of Shakespeare and the Don Juan, perhaps the Cain of Byron though the latter is a magnificent Poem and read the rest fearlessly, that must indeed be a depraved mind which can gather evil from Henry the 8th from Richard 3 from Macbeth and Hamlet and Julius Caesar.[10]

What is so interesting about this extract from Charlotte's letter is that although Shakespeare is recommended at the same time as several other writers, it is *Shakespeare* whom Charlotte seems most keen to impress upon Ellen. After mentioning Shakespeare once, then Byron, Charlotte comes back to Shakespeare, perhaps implying that the 'bad invariably revolting' passages are to be found mainly in Shakespeare's *comedies*. One wonders, too, if there is a criticism of the Bowdlerized editions lurking at the back of 'you will know how to chuse the good and avoid the evil [. . .] that must be a depraved mind indeed which can gather evil from Henry the 8th from Richard 3 from Macbeth and Hamlet and Julius Caesar'. Notice, too, how Ellen is to omit Shakespeare's comedies altogether. This does not mean that Charlotte herself did not like them, only that they are not part of her selective reading list. Perhaps she thought that in themselves the comedies would not lead to the intellectual improvement that Ellen was apparently seeking. Charlotte also makes explicit mention of *Henry VIII*, the play so admired by Henry Crawford in *Mansfield Park*, with all his associations of Shakespeare being part of an English constitution.

In Charlotte Brontë's novel *Shirley*, it is *Coriolanus*, the role so well portrayed by Macready, that becomes the all-important play. The critic Marianne Novy, who is primarily interested in the way women novelists engage with Shakespeare's plays in order to express their own political and emotional concerns, believes that 'three images of Shakespeare have particular resonance for women's history: the outsider, the artist of wide-ranging identification and the actor'.[11] The Brontës were natural outsiders in the margins of their social sphere, not least precociously and geographically. The Shakespeare that the Brontës inherited from the Romantic writers—Keats, Hazlitt, and Coleridge—was understood to be predominantly a poet of Nature and one who engaged with the whole of creation on equal terms. For the Romantics, Shakespeare did not judge others on moral or political grounds and seemed to avoid expressing an opinion about any one of the characters, or moral standpoints, in his plays. Shakespeare seemed to be the ultimately sympathetic artist, and it is this that Charlotte is exploring in *Shirley*.

On the whole, the Brontës never seem to think *through* Shakespeare in any of their writing, in the way that Walter Scott and, later, Charles Dickens did; rather, Shakespeare is made present as an implied influence throughout their work, and at odd intervals. Chapter six of *Shirley* is called '*Coriolanus*'and provides the most overt example of what Shakespeare meant to the Brontës as far as their fiction was concerned. In *Shakespeare and the Victorians*, Adrian Poole notices that *Coriolanus* was an important play for Victorian novelists: Dickens names a character Lady Volumnia Dedlock in *Bleak House* (1852–1853) and George Eliot's *Felix Holt* (1866) includes several references to the play.[12] Here Charlotte presents a heroine who *does* think through Shakespeare. During 1811–1812, at the time of the Luddite rebellions, Caroline Helstone tries to persuade her distant cousin the mill owner, Robert Moore, to be kinder to his workers. Robert is described as being not even half-English and the fact that he comes from Belgium and speaks French to his sister, Hortense, makes him an outsider from the community in which he is the chief industrialist. For their evening entertainment, Caroline suggests to Robert that they read:

'[. . .] an old English book, one that you like; and I will choose a part of it that is toned quite in harmony with something in you. It shall waken your nature, fill your mind with music: it shall pass like a skilful hand over your heart, and make its strings sound. Your heart is a lyre, Robert; but the lot of your life has not been a minstrel to sweep it, and it is often silent. Let glorious William come near and touch it; you will see he will draw the English power and melody out of its chords.'

'I must read Shakespeare?'

'You must have his spirit before you; you must hear his voice with your mind's ear; you must take some of his soul into yours.'

'With a view to making me better; is it to operate like a sermon?'

'It is to stir you; to give you new sensations. It is to make you feel your life strongly; not only your virtues, but your vicious, perverse points.'[13]

One wonders how much of Charlotte Brontë there is in the voice of Caroline at this point. Shakespeare makes one feel life more strongly and draws a distinctly English power out of a person's heart. And so Robert and Caroline settle down to read *Coriolanus*. There is a strain of Paulina and Leontes in this extract. Towards the end of *The Winter's Tale*, Paulina tells the King of Sicilia, 'It is required | You do awake your faith' (V. 3. 94), here Caroline says that Shakespeare 'shall waken [Robert's] nature'. Similarly, just as Julius Caesar mistrusts the rational Cassius because 'he hears no music' (*Julius Caesar* I. 2. 203), so too Caroline suggests that Robert needs more music in his intellectual and emotional outlook. Shakespeare, she hopes, will 'fill [Robert's], mind with music: it shall pass like a skilful hand over [his] heart, and make its strings sound'.

> The very first scene in 'Coriolanus' came with smart relish to his intellectual palate, and still as he read he warmed. He delivered the haughty speech of Caius Marcius to the starving citizens with unction; he did not say he thought his irrational pride right, but he seemed to feel it so. Caroline looked up at him with a singular smile.
>
> 'There's a vicious point hit already,' she said; 'you sympathise with that proud patrician who does not sympathise with his famished fellow-men, and insults them.'[14]

As they continue to read, Charlotte Brontë tells us that Robert 'did not read the comic scenes well, and Caroline, taking the book out of his hand, read these parts for him'.[15] Perhaps there is here an answer to Charlotte telling Ellen Nussey to omit the comedies of Shakespeare from her course of reading. Ellen, like Robert, might not have read the comedy well enough on her own and might have lost her taste for Shakespeare. How many school children, one wonders, have suffered a similar fate when, looking at a so-called Shakespearian comedy, they have not found anything in it to make them laugh? At the end of their reading, Caroline asks Robert:

> 'Now, have you felt Shakespeare?'[. . .]
> 'I think so.'
> 'And have you felt anything in Coriolanus like you?'
> 'Perhaps I have.'
> 'Was he not faulty as well as great?'[16]

Caroline goes on:

> '[. . .] you must not be proud to your work-people; you must not neglect chances of soothing them, and you must not be of

an inflexible nature, uttering a request as austerely as if it were a command.'

'That is the moral you tack to the play. What puts such notions into your head?'

'A wish for your good, a care for your safety, dear Robert, and a fear caused by many things which I have heard lately, that you will come to harm.'[17]

Perhaps Charlotte Brontë chose *Coriolanus* because of its military aspects. Her novel is set at the time of Napoleon, and she herself had great admiration for the Duke of Wellington, whom she called '*le moderne* Coriolan'.[18] One thinks of the Reverend Patrick Brontë's account to Elizabeth Gaskell for her biography of Charlotte:

> When mere children, as soon as they could read and write, Charlotte and her brother and sisters used to invent and act little plays of their own, in which the Duke of Wellington, my daughter Charlotte's hero, was sure to come off conqueror; when a dispute would not infrequently arise amongst them regarding the comparative merits of him, Buonaparte, Hannibal and Caesar. When the argument was warm, and rose to its height, as their mother was then dead, I had sometimes to come in as arbitrator, and settle the dispute according to the best of my judgment.[19]

Of all of Shakespeare's plays, *Coriolanus*, like *Julius Caesar*, shows the power of a crowd most effectively. In Caroline Helstone's reading, this becomes synonymous with the disenfranchised working class in Robert Moore's mill: 'I cannot help thinking it unjust to include all poor working people under the general and insulting name of "the mob" and continually to think of them and treat them haughtily.'[20] The word 'mob' does not occur anywhere in Shakespeare, but is used here in relation to the dramatic crowd in *Coriolanus*. John Forster's review of the 1838 production, which has already been mentioned, explains how Macready's *Coriolanus* was the first to use a sizeable on-stage crowd. Forster, too, uses the word 'mob':

> The mob in *Coriolanus* were now for the first time shown upon the stage, on a level with the witches in *Macbeth*, as agents of the tragic catastrophe. [. . . Here] was not the one, or two, or half-dozen inefficient *sawnies* [simpletons, fools] of former times, when John [Philip] Kemble stalked and *thinvoiced* it among them, like the ghost of the Roman State; but a proper massy crowd of dangerous violent fellows, fit to hustle Macready's flesh and blood.[21]

In this context, the 'mob' which Caroline Helstone perceives in *Coriolanus* might in fact be influenced by Charlotte's own knowledge of the play in performance from twenty-seven years later than the period in which *Shirley* is set. Margaret J. Arnold, in an essay about Shakespeare's play in relation to *Shirley*, notices how Robert Moore, through the influence of both Caroline Helstone and Shirley Keeldar, 'achieves a more comprehensive manhood'.[22] In short, he is a Coriolanus who is tamed, unlike St. John Rivers in *Jane Eyre*, another Coriolanus figure, who remains 'true to his lonely integrity but [is] difficult to domesticate'. Marianne Novy observes simply that Charlotte uses *Coriolanus* in *Shirley* 'to give women more power'.[23]

I now want to consider how Emily Brontë interweaves and adapts Shakespeare through *Wuthering Heights*, and how this adds to the power and impact of her novel. There is a long tradition of comparing Emily Brontë to Shakespeare. Two contemporary reviewers of *Wuthering Heights* seem to have been the first to do so publicly. G. W. Peck, reviewing the novel for the *American Review* in 1848, mentions that 'in conversation we have heard it spoken of by some as next in merit to Shakespeare for depth of insight and dramatic power'.[24] Sydney Dobell, assuming that Currer, Ellis, and Acton Bell were one and the same, praises *Wuthering Heights* for its psychological insights: 'it has been said of Shakespeare, that he drew cases which the physician might study; Currer Bell has done no less [he means Ellis Bell, Emily not Charlotte, since he's writing about *Wuthering Heights*]'.[25] Dobell's comparison was endorsed by Algernon Charles Swinburne in 1877. He goes on to notice the landscape:

> which serves as overture to the last fierce rapturous passage of raging love and mad recrimination between Heathcliff and the dying Catherine; the mention of the church-bell that in winter could just be heard ringing across the naked little glen, but in summer the sound was lost, muffled by the murmur of blowing foliage and branches full of birds.[26]

Swinburne compares this passage to Banquo noticing the 'temple-haunting martlet and its loved mansionry which serves as prelude to the entrance of Lady Macbeth'.[27] This time a moment in Emily's *work* is being compared to Lady Macbeth, rather than a comparison being made between Lady Macbeth and Emily herself, as Virginia Woolf does. Swinburne's comparison relates very much to the tradition of comparing *Wuthering Heights* to Shakespearian tragedy. Angus Mackay, writing about Emily for the *Westminster Review* in 1898, again anticipates to a later comparison by Virginia Woolf:

> It is scarcely too much to say of Emily that she might have been Shakespeare's youngest sister. [. . .] what is there comparable to

this romance except the greater tragedies of Shakespeare? The single peasant in the story, Joseph, is of the kin of Shakespeare's clowns, and yet is quite distinct from them [. . . Heathcliff] reminds us of Shylock and Iago—not, indeed, by any likeness to their characters, but by the sense of wonder he awakens in us at the power that could create such a being. Catherine Earnshaw, again, and Catherine Linton—are not these by their piquancy and winsomeness almost worthy of a place in Shakespeare's gallery of fair women? The whole story has something of the pathos of *King Lear* and much of the tragic force of *Macbeth*.[28]

In *A Room of One's Own*, Virginia Woolf says that 'Emily Brontë should have written poetic plays'.[29] In 1949, an article by Melvin R. Watson suggested that Heathcliff was neither like Macbeth nor like Iago, 'but rather a Hamlet without Hamlet's fatal irresolution'.[30] Watson goes on to impose an unlikely five-act structure over the novel to complete his comparison with Elizabethan drama. At the end of the 1970s, Sandra Gilbert and Susan Gubar's influential study, *The Madwoman in the Attic: The Woman Writer and the Nineteenth-Century Literary Imagination*, drew further comparisons between *Wuthering Heights* and *King Lear*. In Gilbert and Gubar's reading Heathcliff is the bastard son of Nature (like *Edmund*), set against *Edgar* Linton of Thrushcross Grange. Catherine Earnshaw plays the parts of Goneril, Regan, and Cordelia 'to the Lear of her father and her husband'.[31] When speaking at a service of remembrance for the one hundred and fiftieth anniversary of Emily Brontë's death, Inga-Stina Ewbank quoted the lines of Catherine Earnshaw about Heathcliff:

> He's more myself than I am. Whatever our souls are made of, his and mine are the same, and Linton's is as different as moonbeam from lightning, or frost from fire [. . .] My love for Heathcliff resembles the eternal rocks beneath: a source of little visible delight, but necessary. Nelly, I *am* Heathcliff—he's always, always in my mind—not as a pleasure, any more than I am always a pleasure to myself—but as my own being.

Inga-Stina Ewbank comments that:

> This double movement within the text—inwards as well as outwards, defining as well as suggesting—is typical of *Wuthering Heights*. It corresponds to the quality this novel has—much like that of a Shakespeare play—of existing on several levels at once: being at one and the same time an exciting tale of Yorkshire life,

set with great precision in place (the moors, the beck, the two houses) and time and weather, and a metaphysical exploration of identity and—indeed—of immortality.[32]

Embracing *all* these comments and comparisons, I would like to offer some more of my own, the better to appreciate how closely Emily Brontë relates *Wuthering Heights* to the plays of Shakespeare.

There is, first and foremost, the distinctive structure of *Wuthering Heights*. Like several of Shakespeare's plays, it seems essential that there are two main imaginative spaces: Wuthering Heights and Thrushcross Grange. These two homes are separated by the moors. The warm domesticity of the Grange is contrasted to the wild austerity of the Heights. This contrast is as crucial to the depiction of the novel's characters as the Forest is in relation to the Court in *As You Like It* or *A Midsummer Night's Dream;* as crucial a contrast for the genres at work within the novel as the cold and wintry Sicilia is to the warm and pastoral Bohemia in *The Winter's Tale.* Moreover, the generational change which makes *Wuthering Heights* seem like two novels in one also bears strong comparison to *The Winter's Tale.* This would make Heathcliff the Leontes figure, nursing his hurt and despondency over the years, until 'a wide gap of Time' (*The Winter's Tale*, V. 3. 155) itself brings in its revenges (in the words of Feste in *Twelfth Night*, V. I. 373), and these events to their conclusion. This effect is heightened by the narrator, Mr. Lockwood, going away from the village of Gimmerton for almost a year, missing the final events leading up to Heathcliff's death, and having to have them reported by Nelly Dean. This takes, by my reckoning, the number of narratives in the novel up to sixteen; the number of years that Time moves forward at the beginning of act four in *The Winter's Tale.*

Shakespearian allusions are indeed plentiful in *Wuthering Heights* and what follows now are just a few of them. Some of the contexts for love in the novel, perhaps surprisingly, refer to Shakespearian comedy, rather than tragedy. Emily seems to do this in order to show the failure of the comic situation. So when Mr. Lockwood explains in chapter one how he made himself unworthy of a 'comfortable home, and only last summer', he explains how he met 'a real goddess' of a woman somewhere on the coast. 'I "never told my love" vocally; still, if looks have language, the merest idiot might have guessed I was over head and ears [. . .] and what did I do? I confess it with shame—shrunk icily into myself, like a snail, at every glance retired colder and farther'.[33] Here Lockwood quotes directly from Viola in *Twelfth Night*, who tells Orsino of an imaginary half-sister who:

> never told her love
> But let concealment, like a worm i'th'bud,
> Feed on her damask cheek. She pined in thought,

And with a green and yellow melancholy,
Sat like patience on a monument,
Smiling at grief. (*Twelfth Night* II. 4. 110)

There is, too, an allusion to *Love's Labour's Lost*, with Lockwood shrinking into himself 'like a snail'. The simile is common enough, but following on immediately from the self-conscious reference to *Twelfth Night*, I think Emily is reminded of the Lord Berowne in act four, scene three:

Love's feeling is more soft and sensible
Than are the tender horns of cockled snails.
(*Love's Labour's Lost*, IV. 3. 314)

It is as if Lockwood, punished by denying the potential comedy in his life, is displaced to the 'misanthropist's heaven' of Wuthering Heights and has to sit 'like patience on a monument' while Nelly Dean tells him stories of those whom love has tortured and who have committed extreme acts of violence because of it. Similarly, a twisted parallel is made to *Much Ado About Nothing* In the great episode of chapter nine, Heathcliff, unlike Benedick, *does not* overhear how much Catherine loves him, but how much she loves Edgar Linton instead, and how it would degrade her to marry himself. And, unlike Beatrice in *Much Ado*, Catherine explains that 'If I were in heaven, Nelly, I should be extremely miserable.' In *Much Ado*, Beatrice explains to Leonato how she imagines herself leading apes into Hell, as an unmarried woman, but:

[. . .] there will the devil meet me, like an old cuckold, with horns on his head, and say, 'Get you to heaven, Beatrice, get you to heaven; here's no place for you maids:' So deliver up I my apes, and away to Saint Peter fore the heavens; he shows me where the bachelors sit, and there live we as merry as the day is long. (*Much Ado About Nothing*, II. 1. 38)

For Catherine Earnshaw, quite the reverse seems true. She has dreamt that she was in heaven but it

did not seem to be my home; and I broke my heart with weeping to come back to earth; and the angels were so angry that they flung me out, into the middle of the heath on top of Wuthering Heights, where I woke sobbing for joy.[34]

There is even an inversion of *The Taming of the Shrew* towards the end of the novel when Catherine Linton is being held prisoner by Heathcliff. She wants freedom and she is hungry, but unlike her namesake, Kate, she is resolved not to eat: 'I wouldn't eat or drink here, if I were starving'.[35] So allusions to Shakespearian comedies in *Wuthering Heights* serve to invert any comic possibility and contribute instead toward the novel's overriding tragic outcome.

Adrian Poole notices *King Lear* and *Macbeth* in *Wuthering Heights* and interestingly shows how Emily's God-forsaken universe paves the way for Thomas Hardy's.[36] But Poole does not mention *Hamlet* and *Antony and Cleopatra*, which are also present. *King Lear* is mentioned explicitly in chapter two. When Mr. Lockwood is attacked by two large dogs, Gnasher and Wolf, on first arriving at Wuthering Heights, he curses them as he struggles: 'I ordered the miscreants to let me out—on their peril to keep me one minute longer—with several incoherent threats of retaliation that, in their indefinite depth of virulence, smacked of *King Lear*.'[37] 'Miscreant' is the word that Lear uses against Kent in the opening scene, and 'incoherent threats' seems to refer to act two, scene two when he says to Goneril and Regan:

> I will have such revenges on you both,
> That all the world shall—I will do such things—
> What they are, yet I know not, but they shall be
> The terrors of the earth. (*King Lear*, II. 2. 453)

Mr. Lockwood's allusion to *King Lear* provides an initial context for Heathcliff's terrible revenges which emerge during the course of the novel. Here Heathcliff laughs at the 'copious bleeding at the nose' that his dogs have inflicted upon Lockwood. Later, Hindley, drunk and cursing, 'vocifering oaths dreadful to hear', calls his son Hareton an 'unnatural cub',[38] a curse Lear-like in its tone and comparable to 'detested kite' and 'unnatural hags', which Lear uses against Goneril and Regan. More generally, it is the location of the moorland, the blasted heath, that evokes *King Lear*. The open space which isolates Wuthering Heights also serves as refuge and escape; it is the place of lovers and fugitives, ghosts and madmen, and like Lear's heath, provides a way in which identities are shaped in the novel and where universal questions can be asked. Heathcliff's very name brings together both a sense Lear's blasted *heath* and of Dover *Cliff* from which the blinded Gloucester tries to throw himself. Here, in *Heath-cliff's* name and person the extremes of human suffering become intertwined: the heath of Lear's pain unites with the cliff of Gloucester's to give 'Heathcliff.' *Hamlet* is evoked with the appearance of the ghost of Catherine Earnshaw to Mr. Lockwood, which, like the Ghost of Hamlet's father, returns to a private chamber, as though looking for the love it left behind. Later, Heathcliff, like Hamlet, will have a conversation with the sexton in the graveyard and hold

Catherine's, rather than Yorick's, dead face. Like Hamlet, Heathcliff too is reminded of bodily decay:

> I got the sexton, who was digging Linton's grave, to remove the earth off her coffin lid, and I opened it. I thought, once, I would have stayed there, when I saw her face again—it is hers yet—he had hard work to stir me; but he said it would change, if the air blew on it.[39]

Macbeth is evoked first of all to make *Wuthering Heights* into a house of witches, who control fate. On going downstairs 'to the lower regions' after seeing the ghost of Cathy, Mr. Lockwood says 'nothing was stirring except a brindled, grey cat, which crept from the ashes, and saluted me with a querulous mew'.[40] 'Thrice the brinded cat hath mewed' says the First Witch at the beginning of act four, scene one before they conjure up the spirits for Macbeth. A sentence later, Mr. Lockwood names the cat 'Grimalkin', the name of the witches' cat as mentioned in the first scene of the play: 'I come, Grimalkin'. On the evening that Heathcliff disappears, there is a violent storm which knocks down 'a portion of the east chimney stack'.[41] A similar storm takes place on the night of King Duncan's murder:

> LENNOX   The night has been unruly: where we lay,
>   Our chimneys were blown down;
>
> and, as they say,
>
>   Lamentings heard i'th'air; strange
>
> screams of death.
>
> (Macbeth, II. 3. 53)

Catherine Earnshaw, like Macbeth and Lady Macbeth, is tormented by nightmares: 'I dread sleeping, my dreams appal me'.[42] Over her dead body, Heathcliff echoes the occasion, and the words, of Macbeth on seeing the ghost of Banquo:

> The murdered *do* haunt their murderers. I believe—I know that ghosts *have* wandered on earth. Be with me always—take any form—drive me mad![43]

In contrast, Macbeth does not want to see the ghost of Banquo: 'Take any shape but that, and my firm nerves | Shall never tremble' (*Macbeth*, III. 4. 100).

Antony and Cleopatra is suggested when Catherine Earnshaw says 'Every Linton on the face of the earth might melt into nothing, before I could consent to forsake Heathcliff!'.[44] 'Melt Egypt into Nile!' says Cleopatra when she hears of Antony's marriage to Octavia (*Antony and Cleopatra*, II. 5. 78); 'Let Rome in Tiber melt, and the wide arch | Of the ranged Empire fall', says Antony in describing his love to Cleopatra (*Antony and Cleopatra*, I. 1. 35). Finally, in sharing the same grave Heathcliff and Cathy evoke something of the transcendental love of Antony and Cleopatra themselves, of whom it is said:

> No grave upon the earth shall clip in it
> A pair so famous.
>
> (*Antony and Cleopatra*, V. 2. 353)

Of all Shakespeare's plays, it is *The Tempest* that features most strongly in *Wuthering Heights*. *The Tempest* is the play with which the Brontës might have felt the deepest affinity. As children, they presided over their imaginary Glass Town, Prospero-like, as four genii: Tallii (Charlotte), Brannii (Branwell), Emmii (Emily), and Annii (Anne). In a letter of 20 August 1840, Charlotte Brontë signs herself 'Caliban', due to the quality of her handwriting for which she apologizes at the end of the letter:

> Preserve this writing as a curiosity in calligraphy—I think it is exquisite—all brilliant black blots, and utterly illegible letters.[45]

In *Wuthering Heights* there are many Calibans. They begin to appear when Heathcliff, like Prospero, is in full control of the Heights. Nelly Dean goes to visit Hindley and meets Hareton at the gate, 'an elf-locked, brown-eyed boy setting his ruddy countenance against the bars'.[46] He throws a flint at her which strikes her bonnet,

> and then ensued, from the stammering lips of the little fellow, a string of curses which, whether he comprehended them or not, were delivered with a practised emphasis, and distorted his baby features into a shocking expression of malignity. [. . .] 'Who has taught you these fine words, my barn?' [asks Nelly, to which Hareton eventually replies] 'Devil daddy [. . .] Daddy cannot bide me, because I swear at him.'[47]

We also learn that Heathcliff tells Hareton to swear at his own father, Hindley. Shortly after this exchange, Heathcliff, rather than Hindley, appears at the door and Nelly runs away 'as scared as if [she] had raised a goblin'.[48] Nelly does not run away in disgust or out of pride, but in terror. Her account does not explain exactly why she runs away, and with the reference to 'goblin'—with possible echoes of Hamlet's 'goblin damned'—the reader is left to surmise that something darkly magic might have induced her sudden fear. With its Shakespearian suggestions of *The Tempest*, this episode makes Hareton seem the Caliban to Heathcliff's wicked Prospero:

> You taught me language, and my profit on't
> Is I know how to curse. The red plague rid you
> For learning me your language!
>
> (*The Tempest*, I. 2. 365)

Heathcliff is later described as an 'evil genius'.[49] However, he too is capable of being like Caliban. Hindley locks him out of the Heights in the snow and Nelly notices Heathcliff's 'sharp cannibal teeth'.[50] It is as if Heathcliff and Hindley are during this episode competing for the role of Prospero and subsequent rule over Wuthering Heights. Hareton's position again sounds like Caliban's at the end of the same chapter. Heathcliff is victorious and Hindley's inheritance is lost. Hareton, unlike Caliban, remains ignorant of his father's (or, in Caliban's case, mother's) misfortunes. Caliban's tragedy is that he remembers that he has a claim on the island through Sycorax his mother, and that Prospero has taken it from him; Hareton's tragedy is detailed at the end of chapter seventeen by Nelly:

> In that manner, Hareton, who should now be the first gentleman in the neighbourhood, was reduced to a state of complete depen-dence on his father's inveterate enemy; and lives in his own house as a servant deprived of the advantages of wages, and quite unable to right himself, because of his friendlessness, and his ignorance that he has been wronged.[51]

There is a final Shakespearian sting in Emily's wild tale. Lockwood discovers 'the three head-stones' on the slope next to the moor: Edgar's, Cathy's and Heathcliff's. And then come the final, beautiful and justly famous concluding lines:

> I lingered round them, under that benign sky watched the moths fluttering among the heath and hare-bells; listened to the soft wind breathing through the grass; and wondered how any one could ever imagine unquiet slumbers, for the sleepers in that quiet earth.

As well as the clear allusion to the musical ending of Samuel Taylor Coleridge's great conversational poem 'Frost at Midnight', in which the frost continues to perform its 'secret ministry [. . .] unhelped by any wind', 'Quietly shining to the quiet moon', there is a direct allusion to Shakespeare's *Richard III* In act three, scene two, an anonymous messenger from Lord Stanley sounds out the loyalty of Lord Hastings to Richard. Lord Stanley, we learn, has been unable to sleep, racked by dreadful dreams of the boar. Hastings replies:

> Tell him his fears are shallow, without instance.
> And for his dreams, I wonder he's so simple,
> To trust the mock'ry of unquiet slumbers.
> (*Richard III*, III. 2. 22–24)

Hastings's speech is painfully and brutally ironic, since just a few moments later than this in stage time, Richard will order his head to be cut off. Lockwood, too, is being ironic. He wants to believe that the dead will not walk again, but everything he has experienced and heard about thus far proves otherwise. By evoking *Richard III*, Emily is very definitely locating the final impressions of her novel in a world of angry ghosts, violence, and revenge. After hearing all the accounts from Nelly Dean, Lockwood will no doubt be unquiet for some time to come, and so indeed might we by the time we've reached the haunting end of Emily's masterpiece.

These Shakespearian allusions that contribute so powerfully to the mood and drama of Emily Brontë's novel are by no means exhaustive. Likewise, it has been impossible to cover other connections to Shakespeare that can be found in Emily and Charlotte's poetry. More articles need to be produced on this subject. And that is before one turns to Anne and Branwell. I want to go back to where I started from, though, and to Virginia Woolf's account of Shakespeare's forgotten but imaginary sister, Judith. From a consideration of Charlotte Brontë's *Shirley* and Emily Brontë's *Wuthering Heights*, it is clear that, although for the purposes of Virginia Woolf's necessarily feminist argument, Shakespeare's sister's grave is long-forgotten—'buried at some cross-roads where the omnibuses now stop outside the Elephant and Castle'—she is also to be found in the Brontë family vault in Haworth Church and, in the case of Anne, high on a cliff, in a churchyard overlooking Scarborough.

NOTES

1. Virginia Woolf, *A Room of One's Own* and *Three Guineas*, ed. by Hermione Lee (London: Chatto and Windus, 1984), p. 3.
2. Woolf, p. 65.
3. Woolf, pp. 44–45.
4. Woolf, pp. 104–105.
5. Woolf, p. 46.

6. All quotations from Shakespeare's work, unless otherwise stated, are from: William Shakespeare, *The Complete Works*, Compact Edition, ed. by Stanley Wells, Gary Taylor, John Jowett, and William Montgomery (Oxford: Clarendon Press, 1988).

7. William Shakespeare, *King Lear*, ed. by R. A. Foakes (Walton-on-Thames: Thomas Nelson and Sons Ltd., 1997), p. 308.

8. Jane Austen, *Mansfield Park*, ed. by Tony Tanner (Harmondsworth: Penguin, 1966; repr. 1985), p. 335.

9. Lynne Reid Banks, *Dark Quartet: The Story of the Brontës* (London: Weidenfelg and Nicolson, 1976; repr. Penguin, 1986), p. 66.

10. See Chorlotte's letters of: 5 December 1849, 14 February 1850, 19 December 1849 for references to Macready, Wooler and Forster respectively, in *The Letters of Charlotte Brontë*, ed. by Margaret Smith, vol. 2. (Oxford: Clarendon Press, 2000). Her letter to Ellen Nussey is in Smith, vol. 1 (1998).

11. *Women's Revisions of Shakespeare*, ed. by Marianne Novy (Chicago and Urbana: University of Illinois Press, 1991), p. 2.

12. Adrian Poole, *Shakespeare and the Victorians* (London: Thomson Learning, 2004), p. 106.

13. Charlotte Brontë, *Shirley*, ed. by Andrew and Judith Hook (Harmondsworth: Penguin, 1974), pp. 114–115.

14. *Shirley*, p. 116.

15. *Shirley*, p. 116.

16. *Shirley*, p. 117.

17. *Shirley*, p. 117.

18. Poole, p. 106.

19. Elizabeth Gaskell, *The Life of Charlotte Brontë*, ed. by Alan Shelton (Harmondsworth: Penguin, 1975; repr. 1985), p. 94.

20. *Shirley*, p. 118.

21. John Forster on W. C. Macready as Coriolanus at the Theatre Royal, Covent Garden, London, from *The Examiner*, reprinted in *Dramatic Essays by John Forster, George Henry Lewes*, ed. by William Archer and Robert W. Lowe (1896), pp. 54–65, quoted in *Shakespeare in the Theatre: An Anthology of Criticism*, ed. by Stanley Wells (Oxford: Clarendon Press, 1997), p. 81.

22. Margaret J. Arnold, '*Coriolanus* Transformed: Charlotte Brontë's Use of Shakespeare in *Shirley*', in *Women's Revisions of Shakespeare*, ed. by Marianne Novy (Chicago and Urbana: University of Illinois Press, 1991), pp. 76–88 (p. 83).

23. Novy, p. 9.

24. *The Brontë's: The Critical Heritage*, ed. by Miriam Allott (London: Routledge and Kegan Paul, 1995), p. 141.

25. Allott, p. 181.

26. Allott, p. 411.

27. Allott, p. 411.

28. Allott, pp. 446–447.

29. Woolf, p. 62.

30. Melvin R. Watson, 'Tempest in the Soul: The Theme and Structure of *Wuthering Heights*', in *Nineteenth-Century Fiction* (1949–1950), pp. 87–100 (p. 90).

31. Sandra M. Gilbert and Susan Gubar, *The Madwoman in the Attic: The Woman Writer and the Nineteenth-Century Literary Imagination* (London: Yale University Press, 1979), pp. 259, 285.

32. Inga-Stina Ewbank, 'Emily Brontë and Immortality'; a talk given at the end of the service of remembrance for Emily Jane Brontë, 19 December 1998.

33. Emily Brontë, *Wuthering Heights*, ed. by David Daiches (Harmondsworth: Penguin, 1965; repr. 1985), p. 48.

34. *Wuthering Heights*, pp. 120–121.

35. *Wuthering Heights*, p. 302.

36. Poole, p. 144.

37. *Wuthering Heights*, p. 59.

38. *Wuthering Heights*, p. 114.

39. *Wuthering Heights*, p. 319.

40. *Wuthering Heights*, p. 71.

41. *Wuthering Heights*, p. 125.

42. *Wuthering Heights*, p. 162.

43. *Wuthering Heights*, p. 204.

44. *Wuthering Heights*, p. 121.

45. Gaskell, p. 205.

46. *Wuthering Heights*, p. 148.

47. *Wuthering Heights*, p. 148.

48. *Wuthering Heights*, pp. 148–149.

49. *Wuthering Heights*, p. 215.

50. *Wuthering Heights*, p. 212.

51. *Wuthering Heights*, p. 223.

BIRGITTA BERGLUND

In Defence of Madame Beck

Introduction

*V*illette is Charlotte Brontë's last novel and arguably her most accomplished work. It has never been the most popular one, though. That has always been *Jane Eyre* with its passionate heroine, Byronic hero, dramatic plot, and happy ending. Part of the reason why *Villette* has never been a popular novel is obviously that it has none of these things: the heroine, Lucy Snowe, is quiet, secretive, self-righteous, and singularly unhappy for most of the novel; the hero, Paul Emanuel, is a little choleric school-master who has none of the powerful masculinity of Mr Rochester; the plot, although seething with repressed feelings and containing some memorable scenes, can hardly be called dramatic; and, finally, the ending is not a happy one — Lucy Snowe never gets her 'angry little man'.

However, part of the problem also seems to be connected to the point of view. The choice of a first-person narrator, together with the fact that the text is undeniably to some extent autobiographical, dealing with Charlotte Brontë's unhappy experiences in Brussels some years prior to the writing of the book, has led to an unfortunate habit of reading *Villette* as merely thinly veiled autobiography. This way of reading is obvious in the very first reviews and comments on the publication of the novel[1] and was confirmed after Elizabeth Gaskell's *Life of Charlotte Brontë*, which presented

Brontë Studies, Volume 30, Number 3 (November 2005): pp. 185–211. © The Brontë Society 2005.

Charlotte as a pious and suffering tragic heroine, an Angel in the House surrounded by the wild Yorkshire moors, rather than as an experienced artist and early-Victorian intellectual. Readers from Thackeray onwards have thus unhesitatingly equated Lucy Snowe with Charlotte Brontë and assumed that Lucy's experiences, opinions, and prejudices are identical with Charlotte's. For instance, Juliet Barker, in her excellent 1994 book on the Brontës, warns against 'literalists [who] argue the facts of the Brontës' lives from their fiction, which they persist in regarding as autobiographical'[2] — and then goes on to do precisely that when she comes to *Villette*.[3]

Thus it is generally taken for granted not only that Paul Emanuel and Madame Beck are portraits of Monsieur and Madame Heger, but also that what Lucy Snowe tells us of these fictional characters should be taken as the author's own words about their originals, the only question being to what extent Charlotte Brontë is 'right' — i.e. to what extent Monsieur and Madame Heger were really like this. Such an attitude is doubly surprising. Firstly, because Lucy Snowe is far from a reliable narrator; as many readers have noted, she frequently equivocates and suppresses facts both to the reader and to the people around her. Secondly, because *the author* herself, on several separate occasions, clearly distanced herself from her narrator. In one letter she refers to Lucy as 'morbid and weak';[4] in another she states: '[. . .] I am not leniently disposed towards Miss Frost — from the beginning I never intended to appoint her lines in pleasant places'.[5]

Lucy Snowe's feelings for Paul Emanuel have indeed been questioned by readers who have failed to see his charm. When it comes to Madame Beck, however, readers and critics alike seem to have accepted the narrator–protagonist's judgement of her; and since Lucy strongly dislikes Madame Beck, she has been regarded as an unlikeable woman. Although there are a fair number of critics who have come to the defence of Madame Heger, claiming that this is an unfair portrait of her, nobody so far seems to have defended Madame Beck.

However, it is my intention to show that the portrait given of Madame Beck is actually that of a woman who is both admirable and likeable, and that the overwhelmingly negative attitude towards this character is due partly to an unwillingness to appreciate strong and successful women characters and partly to the persistent habit of reading *Villette* as autobiography. Regarding Lucy Snowe as a self-portrait of the author is a habit which — maintaining the image of Charlotte Brontë as a tragic heroine writing true life romances — ultimately denies her powers as a creative writer able to handle her materials with the mature author's distance and control.

The Narrator

That the portrait of Madame Beck is a negative one seems, as stated above, to be taken for granted by virtually all critics of the novel: 'The fair, compact, neat, able and false Madame Beck with her system of *surveillance,* her spying in list slippers, her reading of other people's letters, her coldly practical world views, was so like Madame Heger as to make Charlotte anxious to prevent a French edition of *Villette*, wrote Phyllis Bentley in 1947,[6] while Valerie Grosvenor Myer in 1987 claimed that '[i]t is possible to feel considerable sympathy for Madame Heger, watching the plain, clever, intense young *Anglaise* falling in love with Monsieur, and behaving correctly to protect her marriage, only to find herself recognizably vilified in print'.[7] More recently Sue Lonoff also sympathizes with the Hegers in this regard: 'Apparently the Hegers never read *The Professor*, whose Zoraïde Reuter they might have found even more offensive than *Villette*'s Modeste Beck. But to anyone aware of Charlotte's originals, *Villette* (which they did read) was sufficiently vengeful, a vilification of the woman whose sole fault had been to see what Charlotte hid from herself'.[8] In *The Oxford Companion to the Brontës*, Madame Beck is likewise said to be 'in essence an acid portrayal of Mme Zoë Heger'.[9] She has been described as 'calculating',[10] 'dissembling',[11] 'dangerous',[12] 'ruthless',[13] and 'evil';[14] there are references to 'Madame Beck's "hollow system", where all is stealth, uncertainty, and latent hostility',[15] to 'Madame Beck's shrewdness, her cold rationality, her open commitment to self-interest',[16] and simply to her 'villainy'.[17] The character and extent of this villainy may be defined in slightly different ways by different critics depending on their theoretical positions, but whether Freudian, Marxist, or feminist, they all seem to agree about its existence. Thus according to one 'Madame Beck [...] functions simultaneously as a suppressive figure of espionage and hidden control and as a sexually aggressive opportunist';[18] to another she is 'a spying, scheming little bourgeoise who [...] is finally exposed as a thorough villain',[19] while a third claims that 'Madame Beck is Charlotte Brontë's last and best variant of the Bitch-Rival [...]'.[20] In the introduction to the Everyman edition of the novel from 1992, we are told not only that 'Madame Beck, with her shoes of silence, her face of stone and her dead heart, is clearly a witch',[21] but also that she is 'gradually revealed as a death-dealing monster of selfishness and deceit'.[22]

To what extent are these allegations supported by the text? That depends, of course, on how we read that text. Above all, it depends on how we read Lucy Snowe. It is certainly not difficult to find examples of Lucy accusing Madame Beck of being, variously, cold, hard, hostile, worldly, false, jealous, deceitful, sensual, unloving, untrustworthy, and dangerous. But Lucy is, as was pointed out above, a notoriously unreliable narrator as well as a somewhat dishonest character. Apart from the fact that she sometimes jumps to faulty conclusions, she also lies, equivocates, and, above all, withholds and suppresses facts. She does this both in her relations to the other characters in the book and in her function as narrator.[23]

Thus, although it is not surprising that a fourteen-year-old girl does not let on to the people around her that she has a crush on the sixteen-year-old son of the family she is staying with, it *is* somewhat surprising to the reader that Lucy-the-narrator only indicates this after ten years and some two hundred pages of the story have passed. Even then it is done in an oblique way, when Lucy-the-character encounters the portrait of John Graham as a boy in Mrs Bretton's home in Villette and reflects:

> Ah! That portrait used to hang in the breakfast-room, over the mantel-piece: somewhat too high, as I thought. I well remember how I used to mount a music-stool for the purpose of unhooking it, holding it in my hand, and searching into those bonny wells of eyes, whose glance under their hazel lashes seemed like a pencilled laugh; and well I liked to note the colouring of the cheek, and the expression of the mouth. I hardly believed fancy could improve on the curve of that mouth, or of the chin; even *my* ignorance knew that both were beautiful, and pondered perplexed over this doubt: How was it that what charmed so much, could at the same time so keenly pain?[24]

It is even more surprising that when meeting John Graham in Villette and actually recognizing him in 'Dr John' of the *pensionnat*, Lucy never mentions this either to the reader or to John Graham himself. Even though she is so struck by the realization that she involuntarily gives away her surprise, and John Graham asks her what the matter is — thus giving her an easy opportunity — she refuses to tell him. It is only when, some hundred pages further on, Lucy has fainted in the street and been taken to the Brettons' home, that she reveals the situation to the reader and refers back to the moment of recognition, adding: 'To *say* anything on the subject, to *hint* at my discovery, had not suited my habits of thought, or assimilated with my system of feeling. On the contrary, I had preferred to keep the matter to myself' (p. 248). The idea that her way of behaving could be seen as both deceitful and rude does not seem to enter her mind, and the only explanation she gives for her conduct is: 'I liked entering his presence covered with a cloud he had not seen through, while he stood before me under a ray of special illumination, which shone all partial over his head, trembled about his feet, and cast light no further' (p. 248). Neither does Lucy make herself known to Mrs Bretton, a kind and caring woman who is Lucy's godmother, until that lady herself recognizes Lucy. 'I saw how it must end', Lucy-the-narrator then comments, 'so I thought it best to anticipate' (p. 249). If that had not been the case, would she then never have made herself known to the Brettons? Apart from being disturbingly dishonest, Lucy's behaviour on these occasions is highly irrational. She has absolutely nothing to gain by it — on the contrary, she almost misses her only chance of regaining two true friends in a situation where she is sick with loneliness. Taken together with several other, less significant, occasions when Lucy likewise withholds information from either the reader or the people around her, this way of acting can only be seen as evidence of a habitually secretive and unreliable personality, one who gathers knowledge about other people and hoards it for the feeling of power it gives her.

Lucy also frequently equivocates: she avoids answering straightforward questions from the people around her and is generally evasive or misleading when giving her opinions. Because hers is the central intelligence of the narrative, the mind through which the story is filtered and which chooses what facts to reveal and what to withhold, it is necessarily more difficult to prove that she actually lies to the reader, though. However, there are some instances where this seems to be the case.

One is the case of the pink dress. Being neither rich nor beautiful, Lucy makes a virtue out of necessity by keeping her mode of dressing plain to the point of Quakerish. Then Mrs Bretton gives her a pretty, pink dress to wear for a concert. Lucy is flustered and at first states that she will not wear it: 'I thought no human force should avail to put me into it. A pink dress! I knew it not. It knew not me. I had not proved it' (p. 283). When she does put it on, it is, she claims, not of her own free will: 'I found myself led and influenced by another's will, unconsulted, unpersuaded, quietly over-ruled. In short, the pink dress went on, softened by some drapery of black lace. I was pronounced to be en grand ténue, and requested to look in the glass. I did so with some fear and trembling; with more fear and trembling, I turned away' (pp. 283–284). This is ambiguous. Why does Lucy turn away in fear from her reflection? Is it because she is struck by her own plainness? Or is it because she actually notices herself looking attractive? Graham's 'kind smile and satisfied nod' (p. 284) when he sees her would seem to bear out this interpretation. Lucy claims that she is afraid of being regarded as overdressed, and that she would much rather have worn something dark and sober. However, '[s]ince Graham found in it nothing absurd, my own eye consented soon to become reconciled' (p. 284). Lucy's choice of words here is consistently negative: 'unpersuaded', she is only 'reconciled' to the wearing of the dress when the effect of it is 'softened' and she is assured that there is 'nothing absurd' in it. At no point either then or later, when she is complimented on her dress by Ginevra Fanshawe, does she admit that she likes the dress, or that she enjoys looking good, and she never expresses any gratitude for Mrs Bretton's gift. However, six months later Lucy herself actually acquires a new pink dress for the May Day picnic with Paul Emanuel, the man she is now more than half in love with. She even recreates the exact effect of Mrs Bretton's 'drapery of black lace' by wearing a black silk scarf with it (p. 470). Again, Lucy denies all intention of looking pretty, though. Her dress is *not* pretty, she claims, although M. Paul compliments her on it, and the only reason for the pink colour is that it happens to be cheaper and to wash better than any other colour (p. 471). This explanation is so patently untrue that it is half comic, half touching.[25] However, the whole episode is typical of Lucy's lack of candour, of how the reader can never take her word for granted but has to scrutinize her behaviour in order to get an indication of what her true feelings and opinions are.

Above all, Lucy denies her feelings on almost every occasion. Most importantly, Lucy-the-narrator denies ever being in love with John Graham Bretton. 'I disclaim, with the utmost scorn, every sneaking suspicion of what are called "warmer feelings": women do not entertain these "warmer feelings" where, from the commencement, through the whole progress of an acquaintance, they have never once been cheated of the conviction that to do so would be to commit a mortal absurdity', she says (p. 335.) Again, the statement is so obviously untrue in all its aspects that one cannot be sure that Lucy expects to be taken seriously. It could, and perhaps would be, ironic if, again, it were not so pathetic.

A similar, although minor, instance of Lucy denying her feelings, and even her behaviour towards another person, is on the occasion when she and Paulina de Bassompierre decide to learn German and therefore employ a German mistress. Lucy gives a venomous description of this woman's clumsiness and vulgarity and how 'her direct and downright Deutsch nature seemed to suffer a sensation of cruel restraint from what she called our English reserve; though we thought we were very cordial with her: but we did not slap her on the shoulder, and if we consented to kiss her cheek, it was done quietly, and without any explosive smack' (p. 388). After a further contemptuous comment on how Fraülein (*sic*) Braun, who is used only to the laziness and stupidity of 'foreign girls', is awed by the intellectual ability and rapid progress of her English pupils, as well as by their cold and proud manners, Lucy placidly continues: 'The young Countess *was* a little proud, a little fastidious: and perhaps, with her native delicacy and beauty, she had a right to these feelings; but I think it was a total mistake to ascribe them to me' (p. 388). Since everything that has been said in the previous paragraph contradicts this statement, the reader again has to ask whether Lucy really expects us to believe her.

Irrespective of what intentions we as readers ascribe to the fictional character/narrator Lucy Snowe, the question of whether the author expects us to believe this narrator is another one altogether. If we could disregard the fact that Lucy Snowe 'is' Charlotte Brontë in Brussels (and that Madame Beck 'is' therefore Madame Heger), it would seem to be an obvious example of an author who consciously uses the narrative strategy of an unreliable narrator

— one whose statements we are meant to see through, and one whose actions we are meant to judge for ourselves.

Certainly, if we cannot trust Lucy Snowe's comments about Fraülein Braun, who is a very minor character, then how can we trust her when it comes to Madame Beck — a person of great importance in Lucy's life, a person of whom Lucy has every reason to be jealous or envious? For one thing, it should be remembered that Lucy Snowe describes Madame Beck from the perspective of an employee. The relationship between employer and employee is seldom an easy one even at the best of times; there is always an element of inequality and dependence, and this must particularly be the case when, as here, the employee does not have a separate home but is also part of her employer's household. It is clear from the text that Lucy is expected to ask Madame Beck's permission whenever she wants to leave the house, even when it is to go and visit her friends in her hours off. There are many people who would find this annoying; and Lucy is a fiercely independent soul. Thus she declines the offer of becoming Paulina de Bassompierre's companion (at three times her present salary), partly because of the further sacrifice of liberty and independence that such a post would involve and partly, it seems, because of the very fact that she likes Paulina and wants to stay her friend, which would not be possible if Paulina were to become her employer (pp. 382–383).

There are, in other words, strong reasons why we should adopt a very cautious stance when considering Lucy Snowe's words about Madame Beck, and at the very least try to compare what Madame Beck actually seems to say and do in the book with Lucy's claims about her character and personality.

Lucy's Accusations

So what are Lucy's allegations exactly? First and foremost, the accusation which Lucy comes back to on numerous occasions in the narrative, and which is most often referred to by critics, is Madame Beck's habit of spying. This is certainly borne out by acts contained in the text. On the very first meeting between the two, there is a hint of something of the kind as Lucy does not immediately notice Madame's coming into the room: '[S]he had entered by a little door behind me, and being shod with the shoes of silence, I had heard neither her entrance nor her approach' (p. 127). How long had she been standing there watching Lucy, unseen? is the unspoken question. Later that night Madame Beck goes through Lucy's things, and on other occasions she reads Lucy's letters and tries to eavesdrop on her when Lucy is in the garden with either John Graham Bretton or Paul Emanuel. She also freely admits to Lucy that her school is built upon a system of surveillance.

To Lucy, all this is proof of Madame Beck's fundamental dishonesty, of her deceitful character and general Jesuitism. But how justified is such an opinion in view of the situation and setting depicted in the text?

Surveillance in various forms was the rule in most schools at the time, and boarding schools in particular, in England as well as on the continent. It was customary, for instance, for letters to be opened and read by the management of the school to check that there was nothing improper in them.[26] Nor is this particularly surprising, since schools for girls were seen as institutions where the acquisition of proper manners and morals was at least as important as general knowledge. What makes Madame Beck different from other headmistresses is not the fact that she keeps a watch on the girls and their behaviour at all times, but that she does this so discreetly and tactfully, never openly interfering unless it is absolutely necessary and always avoiding confrontations and accusations.

Lucy is not surprisingly hurt when Madame Beck goes through *her* things and reads *her* letters; but again, this is understandable. In running a fashionable girls' school Madame Beck is a businesswoman whose marketable product is an approved model of upper-class femininity, which includes general knowledge, elegant accomplishments, and, above all, impeccable conduct. Any suspicion that one of the teachers at such an institution is lacking in this respect would be damaging for the school, and thus for Madame Beck's livelihood. It should be remembered that Lucy Snowe turns up at the school in circumstances which would probably make most proprietors turn her away on the spot: unannounced, unexpected, in the middle of the night, and with no references (not to mention the fact that she is a foreigner unable to speak the language of the country). Still, we are told that Madame Beck is daring enough, unconventional enough, and intelligent enough to decide to employ Lucy on the strength of her personality alone. Seen in this light, the fact that she searches Lucy's things that night after she thinks Lucy is asleep is less surprising than the fact that she employs her at all.[27]

The other occasions when Madame Beck 'spies' on Lucy are likewise accounted for by circumstances. The first time is when she sees Lucy doing something surreptitious with the English doctor in the garden after dark. She then, naturally enough, walks down into the garden to see what is going on. Characteristically, she avoids confrontations and accusations, gracefully pretending that she just felt like an evening walk and treating Lucy in the kindest manner possible. Later on she listens in on a meeting between Lucy Snowe and Dr John, obviously to determine the degree of familiarity between the two and whether anything untoward is going on. Finally, she reads Dr John's letters to Lucy. This may seem like an unforgivable violation of privacy; but again, it is important to remember the context. A correspondence between a man and woman not married or engaged to be married was considered highly improper at the time. In fact, such a correspondence would be seen as proof of either a secret engagement or an illicit liaison.[28] For Madame Beck to be worried by these letters and to want to make sure that there is nothing improper in them is thus perfectly understandable. In fact, Lucy herself implicitly admits this — she is pained by having her privacy violated, but not surprised or shocked at Madame's action. It is only when she has reason to believe that other people have read her letters that she reacts by deciding to get rid of them.

This also points to the other objection to condemning Madame Beck on the grounds of spying, namely that she is far from the only person in the book to engage in such pursuits. As many readers and critics have noticed, there is a general atmosphere of mistrust, deceit, and voyeurism in *Villette*. Most notably, perhaps, there is Paul Emanuel, the man who gradually rises to the position of the hero of the novel. He is the other person whom Lucy suspects of having read her letters, the one whose right to do so she does not accept. He is the one who silently watches Lucy from an adjoining room when, believing herself to be alone, she has for once broken down crying, thus triggering her outburst: 'This was a strange house, where no corner was sacred from intrusion, where no tear could be shed, nor a thought pondered but a spy was at hand to note and to divine' (p. 310). He regularly ransacks the contents of Lucy's desk, he has a key that makes it possible for him to enter the garden of the school unseen, and, as he freely admits to Lucy, he has taken a room overlooking the school garden, with the express purpose of 'observation' — sometimes using binoculars. In contrast to Madame Beck, Paul Emanuel has no rational reason for his behaviour, and there is something decidedly disturbing about the notion of this middle-aged bachelor watching the girls and the women teachers of the school for hours on end, simply because, as he says, 'it is my way — my taste' (p. 453).

At this point of the story Lucy is indignant at M. Paul's behaviour, which she regards as immoral; but she too, although in a less methodical fashion, is a persistent voyeur. On a number of occasions, Lucy watches other people without making herself known to them — sometimes from a corner of a public room, like the museum or the concert hall; sometimes in a public space outdoors, like the school garden or the park where she follows first Count de Bassompierre's party, then Madame Beck's on the night of the feast, listening to their conversations; often, like M. Paul, from an adjoining room; and several times from her bed, pretending to be asleep. It is after all only because she pretends to be asleep, while really watching through half-closed eyelids when her new employer comes into her room that first night at the school, that Lucy knows of Madame Beck's going through her things.

Several of these occasions could perhaps be explained — and have been explained — with reference to Lucy's vulnerable situation as an outsider and a foreigner, and in general a person whom nobody takes notice of and who is therefore left almost inevitably to play the part of an observer rather than a participant. However, this is not the case when Lucy is a girl at Bretton; and even then watching seems to have been her habit. When little Paulina Home first arrives at Bretton and is trying to fight her tears at leaving her father, Mrs Bretton tactfully tells Lucy to take no notice of the child who has gone to sit in a corner of the room. 'But I did take notice: I watched [. . .]' says Lucy. 'I observed [. . .] I heard [. . .]' (p. 65) The next morning she pretends to be asleep and again watches little Polly as she is washing, dressing, and saying her prayers. Like Paul Emanuel, Lucy often really has no rational reason for her watching: it simply seems to be her way — her taste.

In fact, the only person who has rational and understandable motives for her watching is Madame Beck. She, too, is the only person who does not really seem to relish the idea of spying in the way Paul Emanuel and Lucy Snowe do. Even Lucy admits that 'madame knew what honesty was, and liked it' (p. 135), and that she uses her methods of surveillance only because it is the only way she knows to keep control of the girls under her care. There is something convincing and almost moving about Lucy's description of how '[o]ften in the evening, after she had been plotting and counterplotting, spying and receiving the reports of spies all day, she would come into my room — a trace of real weariness on her brow — and she would sit down and listen while the children said their little prayers to me in English' (p. 135). This is a single parent with three children to support, who works hard to do so using the means available to her. Her methods may be wrong, but considering the circumstances it does not seem quite so evident that she should be blamed for using them.[29]

Still, blamed she has certainly been, and the main reason for this seems to be a lack of discernment on the part of readers — even skilled and experienced academic critics — when it comes to handling the point of view. Lucy's perspective is so all-encompassing, and as a narrator she is such a powerful personality, that it is very difficult for a reader to slip out of her moral universe and see things from another perspective than hers. Thus, since it is not painful to Lucy to watch others but it is painful for her to be watched, we accept Madame Beck's watching as implicitly worse than Lucy's.

Madame Beck's system of surveillance is closely connected to her kindness, her tactfulness, and her consistent habit of avoiding confrontation, qualities which Lucy seems to have genuine difficulties in understanding and which she therefore regards as deceitfulness. Lucy, for instance, implicitly accuses Madame Beck of a lack of sincerity because of her habit of never openly criticizing her staff. Instead she treats them all kindly, and when displeased with somebody she simply keeps an eye on this person's behaviour while at the same time looking out for a substitute. The moment she has found a better option, the offending person is dismissed and a new employee takes his or her place. It can certainly be claimed that this way of dealing with the staff is less honest than open criticism and rebuke would have been. Still, the question is to what extent it would have been possible for a woman in Madame Beck's position to act differently, to be openly critical or confrontational, and what would have been gained by such a course of action. Many people — and women in particular — find confrontations difficult to handle and try to avoid them. Apart from the internalized suppression of aggression which is still typical of many women, and which was certainly even more so at a time when the approved model of femininity was the mild, soothing, supporting mother/daughter/ sister, there is also the added problem that even today women who openly criticize others or are openly angry or aggressive will run the risk of being seen as not very feminine or ladylike. This would of course be particularly devastating to a woman in Madame Beck's situation, one who makes her living by selling the acquisition of feminine and ladylike qualities. By not criticizing her staff she also avoids resentment and bad feelings in what is not just her workplace and her business but also her home. Again, while it is possible to claim that Madame Beck's methods are wrong (that you should not behave as if you are pleased with an employee when in fact you are not) it seems very harsh indeed to condemn her for using them.

Lucy is likewise critical of Madame Beck's way of handling her children, in particular Désirée, the eldest, who is a difficult child ('vicious', according to Lucy, p. 157), given to fits of anger and destructivity as well as general mischief. It is somehow implied by Lucy, and seems to be accepted by readers, that the wickedness of this child is proof of her mother's bad qualities and the general evil of the house.[30] Whatever the reason for the child's behaviour, Lucy is certain that Madame Beck's way of treating Désirée is wrong. She ought, according to Lucy, to 'confront the child with her vices' (p. 158), and her failure to do so Lucy regards as a moral weakness. However, bringing up children is a difficult task even at the best of times, and particularly so when one is dealing with a highly strung child who has lost her father not so long ago. Perhaps in the circumstances Madame Beck's way — unfailing kindness and patience, pretending that she does not notice bad behaviour instead of rewarding it with her attention, avoiding violent scenes and punishments, keeping the child close to her as much as possible — is just as efficient, and certainly kinder.

It should also be borne in mind that Lucy consistently maintains that all parents treat their children too leniently. Not only does she claim, when speaking about the Labassecouriens, that 'the indulgence of offspring is carried by them to excessive lengths; the law of most households being the children's will' (p. 166); she also sees Mrs Bretton as far too partial to her son, and obviously too passive or lenient in allowing little Paulina Home some privacy when grieving for her father's absence. About the heartbreaking spectacle of little Polly blissfully waiting on Mr Home when he unexpectedly visits them, Lucy says: 'Candidly speaking, I thought her a little busy-body; but her father, blind like other parents, seemed perfectly content to let her wait on him, and even wonderfully soothed by her offices' (p. 72). The impression gained is of a person (Lucy) who really does not like children — or who perhaps grudges other children the happy childhood she herself never had.

It is all the more surprising, then, that Lucy also accuses Madame Beck of not being affectionate and loving enough as a mother. The impression given is that she is an efficient and caring mother to her children, doing all she can for them and often worrying about what will become of them, although she is obviously not a sentimental one. She does not, for instance, lose her composure when Fifine, the middle child, has had a fall and broken her arm. Instead she quickly summons a doctor and then assists him with a steady hand, receiving praise for her calm, which is, he says, a thousand times better than a misplaced sensibility (p. 160). Still, Lucy holds Madame Beck's calm and efficiency against her — because she is jealous of the compliment?

Lucy's words about Madame Beck's attitude towards her children are worth citing in full because they are so untypical of Lucy. She claims that '[Madame] never seemed to know the wish to take her little children upon her lap, to press their rosy lips with her own, to gather them in a genial embrace, to shower on them softly the benignant caress, the loving word' (p. 157). Can the person speaking here really be the same one who coldly referred to Polly Home as 'a little busy-body', to Mr Home as 'blind like other parents' and to Madame Beck's eldest child as 'that tadpole, Désirée Beck' (p. 556)? Lucy's language on this occasion seems to break down into a clichéd sentimentality which signals her lack of sincerity. She also claims to love little Georgette, Madame Beck's youngest daughter, presumably better than Madame herself, since 'to hold her on my lap, or carry her in my arms was to me a treat' (p. 188). It stretches the imagination to believe that Lucy Snowe as we know her would consider it a treat to carry around any child, let alone a child of Madame Beck's. (And Georgette is not a tiny baby; she seems to be about two or three years old.) In fact, this does not seem plausible, unless it is, consciously or unconsciously, a way for Lucy of showing her moral superiority to the child's mother, who — or so she has told us — will not generally carry or caress her children.[31]

It seems that Lucy is playing a double game: on the one hand she claims for herself the right not to be judged by conventional standards, not to be pressed into the mould of sentimental, Victorian femininity; on the other hand she implicitly criticizes Madame Beck for not fitting into this mould. Lucy repeatedly hints at Madame Beck's lack of femininity, often by damning with faint praise, as when she describes her employer's administrative qualities:

> I say again, madame was a very great and a very capable woman.
> That school offered for her powers too limited a sphere: she ought

to have swayed a nation: she should have been the leader of a turbulent legislative assembly. Nobody could have brow-beaten her, none irritated her nerves, exhausted her patience, or over-reached her astuteness. In her own single person, she could have comprised the duties of a first minister and a superintendent of police. Wise, firm, faithless; secret, crafty, passionless; watchful, and inscrutable; acute and insensate — withal perfectly decorous — what more could be desired? (p. 137)

To Victorian readers such a description of a woman might be seen as damaging. To the modern reader, however, who is neither surprised nor shocked at the idea of a woman lawyer, a woman Member of Parliament, a woman police inspector or even a woman Prime Minister, and who accepts that there must have been a number of more or less frustrated nineteenth-century women with such qualities, this passage ought not to be automatic proof of Madame Beck's lack of either femininity or morality. Likewise, the fact that this busy working woman sometimes has an 'absorbed air and brow of hard thought' which Lucy smugly comments on as making her 'look so little genial' (p. 138) can hardly in itself condemn her.[32]

Even so, Lucy assumes a very condemning attitude towards Madame Beck because of her general briskness and lack of sentimentality; and this is the more surprising since not only Lucy herself (with the exceptions mentioned above), but also the people she respects, are very far from sentimental, and this is a quality that Lucy approves of: 'Indisputably Mr Home owned manly self-control, however he might secretly feel on some matters' (p. 71), she says about little Polly's fond father, and there is no doubt that this is meant as praise from Lucy. Even more important is the fact that she describes her godmother in a very similar way: 'Mrs Bretton was not generally a caressing woman: even with her deeply-cherished son, her manner was rarely sentimental, often the reverse […]' (p. 64). Particularly when it comes to Mrs Bretton, this is a quality that Lucy returns to several times, and always approvingly.[33] Again it is necessary to ask why qualities that are seen as praiseworthy in other characters are represented as faults in Madame Beck, and the answer can only be: because Lucy says so.

Thus Lucy actually manages to condemn her employer's most attractive quality, namely her generosity. She tells us that Madame is always ready to open her purse to the poor, that she participates freely in all sorts of philanthropic schemes, and that she does so cheerfully. However — and here is the rub for Lucy — she does so without any show of feeling, and although she 'would give in the readiest manner to people she had never seen' (p. 137) she will not be moved by the individual case. Madame Beck is, in other words, benevolent for rational rather than sentimental reasons. Which is the more admirable attitude must be a matter of opinion. It does seem, however, that regarded from the point of view of results achieved, 'the poor' are just as well served by a person who gives generously to organizations meant to alleviate their conditions as they are by somebody who sheds tears over an individual case. This was also the opinion of a number of writers from the eighteenth century onwards who warned, in particular female readers, about the dangers of an overwrought sensibility. One of them was Hannah More; and it is interesting to note that the following passage is underlined in the Haworth copy of More's *Moral Sketches*: 'Judgement is so far from a cooler of zeal, as some suppose, that it increases its effects by directing its movements; and a warm heart will always produce more extensive, because more lasting good, when conducted by a cool head'.[34] It is difficult not to side with Hannah More as well as with 'Dr John' here and conclude that Madame Beck's children are better served by a cool-headed, efficient, and hard-working parent than by a doting or a sentimental one.

Madame Beck's Kindness and Generosity

Madame Beck's generosity is worth stressing, as this a quality that is in marked contrast to Lucy Snowe's characteristics.[35] Thus Madame not only gives freely to the poor; Lucy is also compelled to praise the plentiful allowances of food and drink in the school. The girls are well fed and taken care of, and they all look healthy and blooming as a result. That this is not just good policy by a shrewd proprietor of a school but a natural — and attractive — quality in Madame Beck is further borne out by a number of instances when she provides Lucy with nourishment. In fact, the very first thing Madame does after she has decided to employ Lucy is to see to it that she is placed by a warm fire and given a hot meal, having perceived that the girl is cold and hungry. All the meals in the school are also well prepared and tasty.[36]

Lucy has great difficulties in accepting this quality in Madame Beck, however, and she is very ambivalent in her references to it. Thus, whereas on the one hand she praises the fact that the food is good and abundant at the *pensionnat*, she is consistently scornful of those who enjoy it. Ginevra Fanshawe's hunger at breakfast, for instance, which makes her exchange her morning cup of coffee for one of Lucy's rolls, is clearly held against her. Likewise, when at the charity-concert Lucy notices some former pupils of the school sitting above her in the royal compartment, she seems to console herself for this fact — as well as for the fact that the girls are young, happy, and beautiful — by gleefully thinking not only of their stupidity in class but also of the fact that at least one of them had a hearty appetite, eating large quantities of bread, butter, and fruit for lunch every day. Her smug comment, 'Here be truths — wholesome truths, too', shows how damaging she obviously feels this is to the girl's character (p. 292). Lucy's jealousy at M. Paul's protégée Justine Marie, who is also young, beautiful, and protected, is likewise expressed in her scornful comment that 'she looks well-nourished, fair, and fat of flesh' (p. 563).[37]

Lucy obviously feels that her smaller appetite makes her superior to these young girls, not taking into account the fact that they are just that — young, healthy, growing girls. But there is more to it than that. She seems actually to grudge the girls their food, or their pleasure in it, just as she seems in some ways really to dislike the generosity that supplies it. This attitude is visible on the May Day picnic when Paul Emanuel treats the boarders and teachers to a farmhouse breakfast, described by Lucy in the following way:

> Clean knives and plates, and fresh butter being provided, half a dozen of us, chosen by our professor, set to work under his directions, to prepare for breakfast a huge basket of rolls, with which the baker had been ordered to provision the farm, in anticipation of our coming. Coffee and chocolate were already made hot; cream and new-laid eggs were added to the treat, and M. Emanuel, *always generous*, would have given a large order for 'jambon' and 'confitures' in addition, but that some of us, who presumed perhaps upon our influence, insisted that it would be a most reckless waste of victual. He railed at us for our pains, terming us 'des ménagères avares;' but we let him talk, and managed the economy of the repast our own way (p. 473, emphasis added).

The passage is typical of Lucy's narrative style in many ways: there is a simple sensual pleasure in the description of the clean plates, fresh butter, hot chocolate, and new-laid eggs, while at the same time there is a fear lest there should be too much pleasure; she praises M. Paul for his generosity, while at the same time disapproving of it; and she is evasive when it comes to actual facts. Who are the 'some of us' referred to who, in spite of M. Paul's railings, manage to prevent him from being too generous? It seems unlikely that they would include Madame Beck, who never openly opposes anybody if she can help it, and who is herself consistently generous in matters of food and drink; and it seems even more unlikely that any of the other teachers (not to mention the pupils) would have the courage to go against M. Paul. It can only be Lucy herself. Only she would actually enjoy a confrontation with the hot-blooded little professor, and only she would be really pained by the idea of too many delicacies.

The same troubled attitude to food and drink, bordering on the neurotic or anorexic, is evident in Lucy's description of her last meal with Paul Emanuel. Here, however, the ambivalence seems to be resolved: there is pleasure but not too much of it, there is generosity but it is tempered: 'Our meal was simple: the chocolate, the rolls, the plate of fresh summer fruit, cherries and strawberries bedded in green leaves, formed the whole; *but it was what we both loved better than a feast*, and I took a delight inexpressible in tending M. Paul', she says (p. 588, emphasis added). It is tempting here to question Lucy's statement that they both preferred this moderate enjoyment, asking whether it should be taken at face value or perceived as an attempt on Lucy's part to persuade herself that she has finally succeeded in curbing M. Paul's 'reckless' generosity, thus removing him at last from any kinship with Madame Beck.[38]

It is certainly possible to see Lucy's ambivalent attitude towards food as part of a generally ambivalent attitude towards sensual pleasures in general and sexuality in particular. The anorexic girl's fear or hatred of the rounded female body is often connected to a fear of sexual maturity and maternity — sometimes also to a hatred of or rivalry with her own mother. Madame Beck, who is referred to as 'the little buxom widow' by John Graham (p. 259), and whom Lucy gradually comes to regard as her rival, is a sexually mature, sexually experienced, and sexually attractive woman, whose motherliness is consistently stressed in the text — usually in connection with her roundness of figure. Lucy's vehement attack on her employer at the end of the book — 'Madame [...] you are a sensualist. Under all your serenity, your peace, and your decorum, you are an undenied sensualist [...] Leave me [...] *Leave me*, I say!' (p. 543) — seems to indicate that what is by now a hatred and fear of Madame Beck, is indeed connected with a general fear of the sensuality that the mature woman represents. Lucy also has the typical anorexic's contempt of or distaste for food and for people who enjoy eating at the same time as she is obsessed with the idea of food and food metaphors. Her description of Dr John's eagerly awaited letter as 'natural and earth-grown food [...] the wild, savoury mess of the hunter, nourishing and salubrious meat, forest-fed or desert-reared, fresh, healthful and life-sustaining' (p. 318) is certainly rather striking for a person who claims not to care very much for food. Later on she also says about M. Paul's letters that they 'were real food that nourished, living water that refreshed' (p. 594).

Madame Beck's generosity is not just limited to meat, drink, and money, though. There is a generosity of spirit in her which makes her see the good as well as the bad in any person and which makes it easy for her to give praise. For instance, when Lucy asks her employer's leave to go and visit the Brettons, Madame instantly and graciously answers:

'Oui, oui, ma bonne amie: je vous donne la permission de coeur et de gré. Votre travail dans ma maison a toujours été admirable, rempli de zèle et de discrétion. Vous avez bien le droit de vous amuser. Sortez donc tant que vous voudrez. Quant à votre choix de connaissances, j'en suis contente; c'est sage, digne, louable' (p. 376).[39]

This kind comment is much more than the occasion demands and in no way accounted for by any ulterior motives on Madame's part. It seems simply to be a spontaneous emanation of good will and appreciation. Lucy also admits and refers to this deeper generosity when she says that although she is not happy about the fact (discussed above) that Madame has read her letters, it does not trouble her very much, because she knows that Madame will 'see things in a true light, and understand them in an unperverted sense' (p. 378). The reason she is deeply troubled by the idea of M. Paul having read them, though, is that '*He*, I believed, was not apt to regard what concerned me from a fair point of view, nor to judge me with tolerance and candour' (p. 379).

Obviously, fairness, tolerance, and 'candour' are qualities that Lucy as a matter of course ascribes to Madame Beck.[40] Unfortunately, these qualities do not characterize Lucy. Her caustic comments on such things as the paintings in the museum or the performances at the charity concert may be funny, but they are also sad in that they speak of a personality who lacks the ability to see the positive side of things or to enjoy uncritically. She consistently sees the faults rather than the merits of people as well as performances, be they the 'usually large' ears of the Labassecourien schoolgirls (p. 147), the 'tawdry' and 'grossly material' ceremonies of the Catholic Church (p. 516), a translation of Shakespeare, which, 'being French, was very inefficient' (p. 416), or the countless deficiencies of foreigners in general.[41] When this judgemental attitude is applied to religious matters it comes close to simple bigotry;[42] when applied to other people it speaks of a lack of charity — all the more notable since according to Lucy's Protestant faith this is the greatest of all human virtues. This lack of charity is perhaps particularly offensive when Lucy's disgust is directed towards defects which can only be regarded as the calamities of nature, such as the mental deformity of the retarded pupil, consistently referred to merely as 'the cretin', whom Lucy is in charge of during the long vacation, or the physical deformity of Madame Walravens, who is said to be 'hideous as a Hindoo idol' (p. 559).

In fact, even when Lucy is for once full of admiration for something or someone, it is extremely difficult for her to express it. Thus, although she finds it easy to contradict or quarrel with the man she is in love with, and sometimes almost seems to enjoy hurting him, on the one occasion when she would like to praise M. Paul (after his rousing speech at the Athénée) she finds she cannot: 'I would have praised him: I had plenty of praise in my heart; but, alas! no words on my lips' (p. 397).

This lack of charity or inability to show kindness to other people also seems to be what makes Lucy mistrust Madame Beck's kindness, which she can only view as insincerity. Madame's kindness in general and towards Lucy in particular is stressed throughout the text: 'There never was a mistress whose rule was milder', Lucy says (p. 134); 'That worthy directress had never from the first treated me otherwise than with respect' (p. 376). It is noteworthy that on the one occasion when Madame Beck could actually be seen as unkind or inconsiderate, the author has taken care that we will not make this interpretation. This is when the headmistress leaves Lucy alone and in sole charge of a retarded pupil during the long vacation, and when Lucy consequently has what we would now term a nervous breakdown. Lucy then actually (and uncharacteristically) is made to defend Madame Beck. It was not Madame's fault, Lucy says; she could not know that Lucy would fall ill, and as for the care of the girl it was meant to fall on the lot of a servant who had left and in the rush of the holidays starting not been replaced. Her breakdown Lucy attributes to a combination of her own personality and unfortunate circumstances.

Nevertheless, almost every act of kindness by Madame Beck is either viewed with suspicion or made fun of by Lucy. On the occasion when Madame Beck has come down late in the evening to find out what is going on in the school garden (where Lucy is handing over the billet-doux intended for Ginevra Fanshawe to Dr John), Lucy expects to be reprimanded for being out so late. This is not the case, however; instead Madame Beck's behaviour to her is kind and friendly. This may be seen as proof of her generosity of mind in that she allows a person to be regarded and treated as innocent until guilt is proved. After all, she has no right to suppose that Lucy is guilty and thus to treat her unkindly, although her position does give her the right to investigate in order to make sure whether this is the case. Lucy, however, interprets Madame's behaviour as proof of her duplicity and seems to feel that this gives her the upper hand over her employer: 'I caught myself smiling as I lay awake and thoughtful on my couch — smiling at madame. The unction, the suavity of her behaviour offered, for one who knew her, a sure token that suspicion of some kind was busy in her brain' (p. 182). This seems a case of projection — the person whose brain is busy with suspicion is Lucy, who, herself unable to show tactfulness and kindness, cannot accept these as positive qualities without ulterior motives in other people.

Therefore, when Madame Beck comes to pay Lucy a visit during her convalescence at La Terrasse (which is furthermore prolonged a couple of weeks beyond the end of the vacation, thus leaving Madame without an English teacher for this period), this attention is merely regarded as a nuisance by Lucy, and explained away with the words 'I suppose she had resolved within herself to see what manner of place Dr John inhabited' (p. 270). After she has left, Lucy and John Graham together make fun of Madame Beck in a manner which seems remarkably unkind, but which Lucy obviously relishes: 'How he laughed! What fun shone in his eyes as he recalled some of her fine speeches, and repeated them, imitating her voluble delivery! He had an acute sense of humour, and was the finest company in the world [. . .]' (p. 271).[43]

Madame Beck's habit of kindness and Lucy's habit of belittling her attentions are perhaps nowhere more obvious than on the occasion when Lucy has fallen asleep one hot Sunday afternoon in one of the classrooms and does not wake up until after sunset:

> On waking, I felt much at ease — not chill, as I ought to have been after sitting so still for at least two hours; my cheek and arms were not benumbed by pressure against the hard desk. No wonder. Instead of the bare wood on which I had laid them, I found a thick shawl, carefully folded, substituted for support, and another shawl (both taken from the corridor where such things hung) wrapped warmly around me.
>
> Who had done this? Who was my friend? Which of the teachers? None, except St Pierre, was inimical to me; but which of them had the art, the thought, the habit, of benefiting thus tenderly? Which of them had a step so quiet, a hand so gentle, but I should have heard or felt her, if she had approached or touched me in a day-sleep?
>
> As to Ginevra Fanshawe, that bright young creature was not gentle at all, and would certainly have pulled me out of my chair, if she had meddled in the matter. I said at last: 'It is Madame Beck's doing; she has come in, seen me asleep, and thought I might take cold. She considers me a useful machine, answering well the purpose for which it was hired; so would not have me needlessly injured [. . .]' (p. 449).

As it turns out, it is actually M. Paul who is Lucy's 'friend' on this occasion, the one who had seen her asleep and covered her up. However, this is not the relevant issue here. The interesting point is the way in which the questions are posed in the text. Lucy asks herself not only who in the school has 'a step so quiet, a hand so gentle' — we already know that the proprietress has these qualities — but also who has 'the art, the thought, the habit, of benefiting thus tenderly', and her own answer to these questions is unequivocal: Madame Beck does. Then Lucy cannot feel content until she has resolved this problem by once again denigrating Madame's kindness and ascribing it to ulterior motives: her action cannot in Lucy's eyes be due simply to human warmth or motherly care; it must therefore be the outcome of cold economic calculation.[44]

Madame Beck's kindliness and warmth are also manifested in the fact that she possesses the ability to make friends. In her free time she is consistently — and in marked contrast to the solitary and lonely Lucy, who has no such ability — mentioned as being in the company of friends. Admittedly, the word 'friends' in the nineteenth century still retained some of its older meaning of 'family' or 'relations'. Still, the expressions used in connection with Madame Beck seem to point to a wider circle of acquaintance than mere family. She spends the summer holidays 'at a cheerful watering place with her children, her mother, and a whole troop of friends who had sought the same scene of relaxation' (p. 230); she sits in the evening 'in the salle à manger with her mother and some friends' (p. 323); and she spends a spring Sunday in the garden with 'a gay party of friends, whom she had entertained that day at dinner' (p. 448).

What is especially noteworthy is the fact that Madame Beck seems to be willing to be Lucy's friend — had Lucy allowed her to be so. From the very beginning, when Lucy is just the nursery governess and Madame likes to come and sit with her and the children in the evening, she shows her appreciation of Lucy's worth and her pleasure in Lucy's company. Later, as Lucy advances to the position of teacher, Madame Beck treats her with a kindness and consideration which are quite remarkable. It is also clear that she increasingly regards Lucy as an equal rather than as an employee. This is shown for instance on the occasion when the directress has been called away for a fortnight on account of a relative's illness and returns home anxious about her school. She then gives each of the teachers a present as a token of her gratitude for their loyalty and efficiency in running the school in her absence. Only Lucy receives nothing:

> To my bedside she came at twelve o'clock at night, and told me she had no present for me. 'I must make fidelity advantageous to the St Pierre', said she; 'if I attempt to make it advantageous to you, there will arise misunderstanding between us — perhaps separation. One thing, however, I *can* do to please you — leave you alone with your liberty: c'est ce que je ferai.'
>
> She kept her word. Every slight shackle she had ever laid on me, she, from that time, with quiet hand removed. Thus I had pleasure in voluntarily respecting her rules; gratification in devoting double time, in taking double pains with the pupils she committed to my charge (p. 383).

This is not only a gesture of appreciation and recognition which stands out in itself. Of all the characters in the book, I would claim that it is Madame Beck rather than Paulina de Bassompierre who alone *sees* Lucy and respects her for what she is. It is also a mark of tact and sensitivity and an offer of friendship on equal terms which Lucy at least to some extent recognizes and is grateful for. At this point it seems as if the two women might actually become friends; and the relationship that Lucy could have enjoyed with Madame Beck would have been of a quite different quality from the one she has with seventeen-year-old Paulina. Paulina is Lucy's only friend and companion, but not only is Lucy aware that this is a very temporary companionship which will in effect end with Paulina's marriage, there are also great gaps between the two which preclude any real intimacy between them — gaps of age, of social class, and of experience. A friendship between Lucy and Madame Beck, on the other hand, would have been one of maturity and equality.

Lucy's Jealousy

Why, then, does such a friendship never materialize? Why is Lucy for such a large part of the book so bitterly, and seemingly unfairly, opposed to this warm, friendly, intelligent, and generous woman, who is a good teacher, a good mother, and a good housekeeper, and whose many qualities Lucy cannot but acknowledge? The most obvious answer is simply sexual jealousy. Almost from the very beginning Lucy sees Madame Beck as her rival, first for the attentions of Dr John, later for M. Paul. For a great part of the book, Lucy is, in spite of her protestations to the contrary, strongly attracted to the masculinely handsome Dr John. He, on the other hand, while keeping up a lighthearted flirtation with Madame Beck, barely notices Lucy. At this stage Madame Beck is hardly a serious rival, though, as Lucy knows of Dr John's infatuation with Ginevra Fanshawe and obviously finds it unlikely that he would fall for the older woman. Still, Madame Beck's competent handling of the situation makes Lucy's awkward position stand out more clearly. Like a Cinderella in her corner by the fire, Lucy — herself plain, poor, shy, and reserved, but passionate — watches her employer's youthful looks, feminine fullness of figure, simple but elegant dress, easy manners, and general ability to charm. There is genuine admiration in Lucy's description of Madame Beck at this stage:

> I scarcely think [. . .] that her intention in this went further than just to show a very handsome man that she was not quite a plain woman: and plain she was not. Without beauty of feature or elegance of form, she pleased. Without youth and its gay graces, she cheered. One never tired of seeing her: she was never monotonous, or insipid, or colourless, or flat. Her unfaded hair, her eye with its temperate blue light, her cheek with its wholesome fruit-like bloom – these things pleased in moderation, but with constancy. (p. 167)

In other words, Madame Beck has all the qualities that Lucy lacks. Still, at this stage Lucy is more fascinated than envious, and when Madame Beck, watching her own reflection in the mirror, finally realizes the truth that Lucy has seen all along, that she is too old to attract Dr. John, Lucy warms to her: 'Never had I pitied madame before, but my heart softened towards her, when she turned darkly from the glass. A calamity had come upon her. That hag disappointment was greeting her with a grisly 'all-hail!' and her soul rejected the intimacy' (p. 170). In spite of the obvious differences between Madame Beck and Lucy, there is a strong element of identification in this passage; and as Lucy sees Madame show real strength of character in overcoming her disappointment, the identification as well as the admiration grows even stronger:

> I believe madame sermonized herself. She did not behave weakly, or make herself in any shape ridiculous. It is true she had neither strong feelings to overcome, nor tender feelings by which to be miserably pained. It is true likewise that she had an important avocation, a real business to fill her time, divert her thoughts, and divide her interest. It is especially true that she possessed a genuine good sense which is not given to all women nor to all men; and by dint of these combined advantages she behaved wisely, she behaved well. Brava! once more, Madame Beck. I saw you matched against an Apollyon of a predilection; you fought a good fight, and you overcame! (p. 171)

There are in fact many points of similarity between Lucy and Madame Beck.[45] They have both, to begin with, fallen from the position of a protected middle-class wife or daughter to a state of things where they have to provide for themselves.[46] The options were few for such women at that time, and between the two of them they fairly cover them: Lucy first works as a nurse/companion, then as a nursery governess, and finally as a teacher, while Madame Beck opens a school. Both of them are intelligent, hardworking, and good at their work; and they both recognize these qualities in each other. At the beginning of their acquaintance Lucy admires Madame Beck's administrative ability and her generally pleasant and sensible way of running the school. She also praises Madame Beck's qualities as a teacher: '[S]he taught well', Lucy says in the early part of the book (p. 225), and even towards the end, when matters between them are more fraught, Lucy likes to listen to Madame's 'orderly and useful lessons' (p. 491) and admits to being 'pleased and edified with her clear exposition of the subject (for she taught well)' (p. 492). Madame Beck, on her side, instantly recognizes Lucy's ability when she overhears her teaching the little Beck children. As time passes, Lucy comes to feel more and more strongly that what Madame can do, she can do too, and she dreams of having the same success as her employer:

When I shall have saved one thousand francs, I will take a tenement with one large room, and two or three smaller ones, furnish the first with a few benches and desks, a black tableau, an estrade for myself; upon it a chair and table, with a sponge and some white chalks; begin with taking day-pupils, and so work my way upwards. Madame Beck's commencement was — as I have often heard her say — from no higher starting-point, and where is she now? All these premises and this garden are hers, bought with her money; she has a competency already secured for old age, and a flourishing establishment under her direction, which will furnish a career for her children (p. 450).

There is a moment of mutual identification as well as appreciation between the two on the morning of the great fête, when they happen to meet on the stairs, the only women in the house to be dressed and ready so early, and the only two to have chosen extreme simplicity and sobriety in their dress. However, a note of difference and discord is present, too: Madame Beck compliments Lucy on her dress, while Lucy is inwardly sarcastic both about Madame's taste and her compliment, and also implicitly envious of her jewels and the blooming complexion which has been pointed out several times as Madame's particular claim to beauty:

> I had no flowers, no jewel to relieve [the simplicity of the dress]; and what was more, I had no natural rose of complexion. — However, in this same gown of shadow I felt at home and at ease; an advantage I should not have enjoyed in anything more brilliant or striking. Madame Beck, too, kept me in countenance; her dress was almost as quiet as mine, except that she wore a bracelet, and a large brooch bright with gold and fine stones. We chanced to meet on the stairs, and she gave me a nod and a smile of approbation. Not that she thought I was looking well — a point unlikely to engage her interest — but she considered me dressed 'convenablement,' 'décomment,' and la Convenance et la Décence were the two calm deities of madame's worship. She even paused, laid on my shoulder her gloved hand, holding an embroidered and perfumed handkerchief, and confided to my ear a sarcasm on the other teachers (whom she had just been complimenting to their faces). (p. 200)

Earlier in this article I emphasized the differences rather than the similarities between Lucy and Madame Beck; however, in order to fully understand Lucy's growing hatred of Madame and her consequently warped presentation of her, I believe that it is necessary to take the similarities into consideration as well. It is Lucy's partial understanding of Madame Beck, her admiration for her and her initial identification with her that constitute the key to her bitterness, as she comes to realize the truth: that she can never be Madame Beck. Apart from the fact that Madame's situation differs from Lucy's in that she has been born with good looks and is surrounded by a family group consisting of her mother, her children, and several other close relatives, she also has personal qualities of kindness, tactfulness, generosity, and what would today be called social skills, which — together with the qualities that she shares with Lucy (such as intelligence and diligence) — make for professional as well as social success.

Lucy's jealousy of Madame is therefore not just sexual rivalry; it goes much deeper than that. With her unwillingness to confess the truth about herself and her own feelings, though, Lucy refuses to see this, and instead gradually focuses her jealousy on one person: M. Paul. As it becomes more and more obvious that she is in love with him and that he is falling in love with her, and as it is likewise obvious that his relatives are not happy about Paul's marrying Lucy, her jealousy and hatred of Madame Beck, who now comes to represent all the obstacles to her happiness, take on hysterical proportions. Since in this case there is also a religious element involved, and since Lucy is vehemently anti-Catholic, she now sees plots and conspiracies all around her.

However, if one looks at Madame Beck's actions rather than at what Lucy says about her presumed motives — and particularly if one keeps in mind Lucy's habit of ascribing evil intentions to quite innocent actions — it is possible to interpret things in a much less sinister light. Thus, to begin with, Madame, who is obviously much more worldly-wise than Lucy, notices the lonely young English teacher falling in love with her kinsman. Knowing of his confirmed bachelorhood (and having seen other teachers trying to lure him into marriage but failing) but not wishing to offend Lucy by bringing this up openly, she arranges for somebody else — Père Silas — to tell Lucy about Paul Emanuel's love story. Lucy of course sees through this stratagem and, as could be expected, sees it as devious rather than tactful. Madame then openly refers to Paul Emanuel's other obligations and his determination not to marry, finishing her conversation with the kindly suggestion: 'But I hinder you from taking refreshment, ma bonne meess, which you must need; eat your supper, drink your wine, oubliez les anges, les bossues, et surtout, les Professeurs — et bon soir!' (p. 489).

Instead of accepting Madame Beck's words at face value — as advice kindly meant — Lucy immediately begins to perceive a conspiracy, and from now on everything that happens is the work of 'them' trying to hinder her. It is certainly true that when M. Paul's friends realize that he is in love, they are worried. However, this is not surprising, considering the context. Quite apart from her personal qualities, which both Madame Beck and Père Silas do full justice to, Lucy is a foreigner and a Protestant and such 'mixed marriages' were far from common or even accepted. In *The Brontës and Religion* Marianne Thormählen says: 'Both in works of fiction and in real life, close and loving proximity between Protestants and Roman Catholics was generally seen as problematic, if not impossible. An untroubled marriage along these lines was barely conceivable.'[47] One need only imagine Lucy's reaction were Paulina de Bassompierre to fall in love with a foreigner and a Catholic, to see how problematic such a union would be.[48]

It is also true, however, that when 'they' realize that M. Paul's love for Lucy is serious, 'they', i.e. Père Silas and Madame Beck, arrange for Lucy to have religious instruction, a fact which seems to point to some kind of acceptance of the situation. Even when Madame is still opposed to the idea of Lucy marrying her cousin (after it is clear that Lucy will not convert to Catholicism) her opposition has none of the vehemence of Lucy's hysterical jealousy, as she suddenly accuses Madame Beck of wanting to marry M. Paul herself: 'I knew she secretly wanted him, and had always wanted him', Lucy says, adding, 'she did not love, but she wanted to marry, that she might bind him to her own interest' (p. 544). That Madame Beck should want to marry her cousin in order to keep him as a teacher at the school hardly seems believable, and there is no other foundation for this in the text than Lucy's sudden 'intuition' or 'inspiration' (p. 544). Lucy's allegation that Madame has 'secretly wanted' M. Paul for a long time seems again more like a projection of Lucy's own feelings, as does her further statement: 'In the course of living with her, too, I had slowly learned, that [. . .] she must ever be a rival. She was *my* rival, heart and soul, though secretly, under the smoothest bearing, and utterly unknown to all save her and myself' (p. 544). In this scene Lucy lashes out vehemently against Madame Beck, who takes her behaviour surprisingly quietly and kindly, asking her to calm down, suggesting that she go to bed, and offering her a sedative, which Lucy refuses. The next night Madame Beck sees to it that Lucy is actually given an opiate — a circumstance which Lucy presents as a poisoning. However, it should be remembered that opium was really the only tranquilliser available at the time, as well as the only painkiller, and considering Lucy's hysterical state of mind, the excruciating headache that she complains of, and the fact that she has had no sleep the preceding night, Madame Beck's having it administered it to her does not seem entirely out of order.

As for Lucy's accusations that 'they' keep M. Paul from her and lie to her about his departure, they turn out to be not true: M. Paul has changed the date of his departure of his own accord, and he has consciously kept out of Lucy's way simply because he has been afraid of unintentionally revealing the surprise of the school he is preparing for her. Likewise, Lucy's jealousy of M. Paul's young ward, whom she is sure 'they' mean for him to marry, turns out to completely unfounded.

In a key passage towards the end Lucy does in fact admit that her interpretation of facts is far from reliable:

> I might have paused longer upon what I saw; I might have deliberated ere I drew inferences. Some perhaps would have held the premises doubtful, the proofs insufficient; some slow scep- tics would have incredulously examined, ere they conclusively accepted the project of a marriage between a poor and unselfish man of forty, and his wealthy ward of eighteen; but far from me such shifts and palliatives, far from me such temporary evasion of the actual, such coward fleeing from the dread, the swift-footed, the all-overtaking Fact, such feeble suspense of submission to her the sole sovereign, such paltering and faltering resistance to the Power whose errand is to march conquering and to conquer, such traitor defection from the TRUTH. (p. 566)

What is ironically celebrated as truth here is in fact the opposite. Admittedly Lucy is referring to a single incident, and one that took place when she was under the influence of opium. Nevertheless this passage is significant in that it illustrates Lucy's general tendency to jump to conclusions, and in particular her tendency to see things as generally worse than they are — and it contains the author's as well as the narrator's admission that this is so. It is this tendency in a deeply troubled personality which, together with her initial identification, her growing jealousy, and her final hatred of her employer, makes Lucy misinterpret Madame Beck's actions and motives.

Lucy Snowe — 'both morbid and weak'

In Lucy Snowe, Charlotte Brontë has painted a portrait of a repressed, unhappy, even neurotic woman.[49] One of Lucy's 'morbid' characteristics is her tendency to see other people in a very negative light. This tendency is, for reasons discussed above, particularly pronounced in her attitude to Madame Beck. The conscious artist Charlotte Brontë gives us a picture of Madame Beck as a competent, successful, generous, and attractive woman. At the same time she shows us how the character/narrator Lucy,[50] project- ing her own fears and insecurities on the woman she comes to see as her rival, gradually constructs a picture of this woman first as an insincere and cold-hearted businesswoman and then — as Lucy's paranoia develops — as a life-threatening monster.

We cannot blame Lucy for her weaknesses, since Charlotte Brontë so clearly shows us how they are a result of her circumstances. As a young woman with a great deal of sharp intelligence but with neither wealth nor beauty, Lucy's chances on the marriage market are slender to begin with, and as a poor and plain spinster with no family connections she is a person whom her society has no place for and would rather forget about, a person many of the people in the book hardly notice. (Kate Millett has compared her to a piece of furniture.[51]) In such circumstances how would it be possible for her to develop into an easy-going, generous, and charitable woman? In the words of Pauline Nestor, 'Lucy Snowe is the true daughter of a society in which repression and disguise are necessary strategies for women striving to behave appropriately and all the less attractive features of her personality [. . .] can be seen as direct reflections of social pressures'.[52] Or as Charlotte Brontë put it herself: 'You say that she may be thought both morbid and weak unless the history of her life be more fully given. I consider that she *is* both morbid and weak at times — the character sets up no pretensions to unmixed strength — and anybody living her life would necessarily become morbid'.[53]

Lucy is a product of her society, as are the other women in the book, and one thing Charlotte Brontë shows us in *Villette* is how the oppressed turn against one another instead of against their oppressors: Lucy, in fact, has more reason to bear a grudge against Graham Bretton than against Madame Beck. John Graham Bretton is a man who, although intelligent and perceptive enough to see and appreciate the sterling qualities of Madame Beck and Lucy, and to respond to them with a kind of careless flirtation, nevertheless ultimately approves of, and rewards, the childish prettiness of Ginevra Fanshawe and Paulina Home. Both of these are naturally clever girls who could have developed into intelligent, independent, and mature women, had such qualities been appreciated in their society. As it is they seem to remain in a kind of perpetual girlishness, because that is what men like John Graham Bretton appreciate and reward.[54] Even worse than Graham Bretton is M. Paul, a man who simply cannot cope with independent women: he spies on the teachers as well as the schoolgirls in order to feel in control, and he can really only behave decently to women if they are in a dependent position. Thus he is kind to small children but as soon as the girls grow up he starts to bully them, taking a sadistic pleasure in making them cry; he hounds the only teacher who is not afraid of him from her post and can only be kind to her when she is (because of him) destitute; he teaches Lucy but does not like it when she succeeds in learning, and he is the one who, appalled by her independence of mind, puts her in a corner of the art gallery, telling her to study the dreary series of pictures of a conventional woman's life.

Men like these are the real enemies of both Madame Beck and Lucy Snowe, who are both, although in different ways and to different extents, victims of patriarchal structures.[55] Lucy, however, is so jealous of Madame Beck's relative success that she cannot see this, and instead of appreciating another intelligent and independent woman who could have become her friend, she turns against her.

Reading Charlotte Brontë

Lucy's hostile picture of Madame Beck is not borne out by the text. Why, then, when Lucy's narrative unreliability is an established fact, has the overwhelmingly negative picture of Madame Beck remained unchallenged?

One answer, paradoxically, has to do with Charlotte Brontë's skill as an author. We may not like Lucy, and we may not want to accept her view of the world, but we are still drawn into that world by the emotional power she exerts on the reader and the pain we feel in reading about her situation. This emotional power affected readers from the very beginning and is probably at the root of some of the more hostile reactions to *Villette* as a novel.[56]

There is also the reason of narrative patterns. In a story which presents a young, poor and vulnerable protagonist pitched against an older, richer, and stronger character, our sympathies seem automatically to go to the young protagonist against his or her older adversary. In other words, if Lucy Snowe is Cinderella (or Snow White, as her name seems to indicate), Madame Beck has to be the wicked stepmother. This pattern is particularly prevalent when we are dealing with female characters. According to Victorian notions of femininity, which saw mental and physical weakness as an accepted, almost laudable, part of the female character, a strong woman was by definition unfeminine. Therefore, the more Madame Beck's intelligence, strength, and professional success are stressed, the more unfeminine she seems, and the more she risks losing the readers' sympathies. Within the text Paul Emanuel mockingly refers to Madame Beck as 'cette maîtresse-femme, my cousin Beck' (p. 453), and John Graham Bretton, who initially praises Madame Beck for her strength, ends up making fun of her. Readers, then as well as now, seem to have taken the same attitude.

Another reason why readers have accepted Lucy Snowe's rather than Charlotte Brontë's picture of Madame Beck is one that I have already touched upon at the beginning of this article: the persistent habit of reading Charlotte Brontë's books in general, and *Villette* in particular, as only slightly veiled autobiography. In other words, we still see Lucy Snowe as Charlotte Brontë in the end, and if we do not accept Madame Beck as a true portrait of Madame Heger, we still accept Lucy's picture of her as Charlotte's. This image of the Brontë sisters as unconsciously pouring out their hearts in their books, not really aware of what they were creating, is part of 'The Brontë Myth' recently explored by Lucasta Miller.[57] Miller shows that Charlotte herself was to some extent responsible for the origin of the myth in her

'Biographical Notice of Ellis and Acton Bell', in which she tried to mitigate criticism against her sisters' works as being 'coarse': 'Charlotte presented her sisters as naïve artists responding only to the dictates of nature, rather than as knowing and ambitious writers who had produced consciously constructed novels. This defence combined her Romantic ideal of the natural genius with the conventional idea of female modesty and simplicity which, she hoped, would counterbalance public perceptions of the Bells as women unsexed.'[58] She thus prepared the ground for Gaskell's *Life of Charlotte Brontë*, which would firmly establish this romantic view of all three sisters, but perhaps above all of Charlotte herself. Finally, the publication in *The Times* in 1913 of Charlotte's passionate letters to M. Heger created a sensation after which it has been virtually impossible to separate the life from the work.

For any reader familiar with Charlotte's story who has also read *The Professor* there is also the added temptation of seeing Zoraïde Reuter as a kind of blueprint for Madame Beck, or both as only slightly different versions of Zoë Heger. Zoraïde Reuter is definitely a dishonest and unpleasant character, who, although engaged to be married to another man, tries to seduce the hero of the book and behaves cruelly and deceitfully towards the young, half-English teacher–pupil who is the heroine. Mlle Reuter's actions and character will then imperceptibly influence our impression of Madame Beck, who to the 'knowledgeable' reader comes to be seen as just a more sophisticated version of basically the same character. Indeed, this is the claim of many critics who read Charlotte Brontë's works in connection with her life.[59]

All artists use personal experiences as material for their work to a greater or lesser extent, and Charlotte Brontë did so to a great extent. However, the operative word is *use*, as the conscious artist uses the personal experience as the raw material from which art is created. Thus, Charlotte Brontë used her experiences — the general setting as well as individual characters and incidents — of the Cowan Bridge school in *Jane Eyre*, but that does not mean that Jane's story is Charlotte's. In the same way she used her experiences — again the general setting as well as individual characters and incidents — of the girls' school in Brussels for *Villette*, but that does not mean that Lucy's story is Charlotte's.

Lucy Snowe obviously has some similarities to Charlotte Brontë herself, just as Jane Eyre has. In the character of Jane Eyre, the author perhaps exaggerated the positive aspects of her own personality — the passion, the independence, the belief in her own vision — in short, the vitality and strength that make Jane's story a success story. In Lucy Snowe, on the other hand, I think she exaggerated the negative aspects of the same personality — the inability to assert herself in company with others, the tendency to depression, the morbidity — while showing these traits to be both the result of the life Lucy leads and, to some extent, the reason for her difficulties and unhappiness.[60]

If we still think of *Villette* as to some extent autobiographical, or at least as the artist's way of dealing with traumatic experiences by sublimating them into art, it is worth remembering that Charlotte Brontë was a woman who could be extremely severe on herself and who believed in facing the truth, however unpleasant.[61] In *Jane Eyre* the author makes her heroine face what Jane herself believes to be unrequited love by painting two portraits: one of a rich, cherished, adored beauty, the other of a poor, plain, obscure governess — making sure that she stresses rather than tones down the differences between the two. It could be argued that this is what Brontë is doing in *Villette*, as she shows the readers on the one hand the poor, plain, and embittered young girl who rages at life's unfairness, and on the other hand the mature, generous, and attractive woman who seems to have it all.

But I do not think that it is necessary to bring in the autobiographical aspect at all. Charlotte Brontë was a professional writer who took her own writing seriously. She was hurt and distressed at the way in which readers and reviewers tended to speculate about the person behind the work. More than one hundred and fifty years have gone since the publication of *Villette*. Is it not time to admit that Charlotte Brontë was indeed a creative writer who, in this novel, plays a sophisticated narrative game with the reader? Is it not time to accept that a strong, intelligent, and successful woman can be a warm, generous, and likeable person? In short, is it not time to give Madame Beck a chance?

NOTES

1. See *The Edinburgh Review*, April 1853: 'It is clear at a glance that the groundwork and many of the details of the story are autobiographic; and we never read a literary production which so betrays at every line the individual character of the writer' (p. 387); the *Spectator*, 12 February 1853: 'Villette is Brussels, and Currer Bell might have called her new novel "Passages from the Life of a Teacher in a Girls' School at Brussels, written by herself"' (p. 155); and the *Guardian*, 23 February 1853: 'Lucy Snowe is *Jane Eyre* over again; both are reflections of Currer Bell [. . .]' (p. 128).

2. Juliet Barker, *The Brontës* (London: Weidenfeld & Nicolson, 1994), p. xix.

3. See the description of Charlotte Brontë returning alone to Brussels in 1843 where Barker starts off by describing the known facts of the journey, then goes on to conjecture: '*If, as seems likely*, Charlotte used this adventure in her novel *Villette*, she had a frightening experience which would have fully justified her aunt's concerns about the impropriety of a young woman travelling alone.' This is followed by the passage from the novel where Lucy is frightened by the boatmen fighting for her fare. Barker then describes the rest of Charlotte's voyage, her arrival in Brussels, and her letter to Ellen Nussey '*omitting to tell her about the incident on London Bridge Wharf*, which would undoubtedly have outraged her friend's sensibilities' (Barker, p. 410, emphasis added). In other words, Barker here goes from guessing that Charlotte

might have had the same experience as Lucy, to regarding this as a fact, the question being not *if* this really happened but why Charlotte did not tell her friend about it.

4. Letter to William Smith Williams, 6 November 1852, in *The Letters of Charlotte Brontë*, ed. by Margaret Smith, vol. III (Oxford: Clarendon Press, 2004), p. 80.

5. Letter to George Smith, 3 November 1852, in *Letters*, vol. III, p. 78.

6. Phyllis Bentley, *The Brontës* (London: Home & Van Thal Ltd, 1947), p. 77.

7. Valerie Grosvenor Myer, *Charlotte Brontë: Truculent Spirit* (London & Ottawa, NJ: Vision & Barnes & Noble, 1987), p. 193.

8. Sue Lonoff, 'Introduction' in Charlotte Brontë and Emily Brontë, *The Belgian Essays*, ed. and trans. by Sue Lonoff (New Haven & London: Yale University Press, 1996), p. xix.

9. *The Oxford Companion to the Brontës*, ed. by Christine Alexander and Margaret Smith (Oxford: Oxford University Press, 2003), p. 30.

10. Lyndall Gordon, *Charlotte Brontë: A Passionate Life* (London: Vintage, 1995), p. 256.

11. Margaret Smith, 'Introduction', in *Villette* (Oxford & New York: Oxford University Press, The World's Classics, 1990), p. xi.

12. W. A. Craik, *The Brontë Novels* (London: Methuen, 1968), p. 171.

13. Robert Bernard Martin, *The Accents of Persuasion: Charlotte Brontë's Novels* (London: Faber & Faber, 1966), p. 180.

14. Lucasta Miller, *The Brontë Myth* (London: Vintage, 2002), p. 47.

15. Tony Tanner, 'Introduction', in *Villette* (Harmondsworth: Penguin, 1979), p. 49.

16. Helene Moglen, *Charlotte Brontë: The Self Conceived* (New York: Norton, 1976), p. 206.

17. Tom Winnifrith, *The Brontës and Their Background: Romance and Reality* (New York: Barnes & Noble, 1973), p. 55.

18. John Maynard, *Charlotte Brontë and Sexuality* (Cambridge: Cambridge University Press, 1984), p. 178.

19. Terry Eagleton, *Myths of Power: A Marxist Study of the Brontës* (London: Macmillan, 1988), p. 5.

20. Susan Ostrov Weisser, *A Craving Vacancy: Women and Sexual Love in the British Novel, 1740–1880* (New York: New York University Press, 1997), p. 78.

21. Lucy Hughes-Hallett, 'Introduction', in *Villette* (London: Everyman's Library, 1992), p. xiii.

22. Ibid.

23. Virtually all critics who have commented on *Villette* mention Lucy's unreliability as a narrator, mostly just in passing as an established fact. However, a further study of this aspect of the novel shows that there are different opinions about exactly how Lucy is unreliable and to what extent. Thus, for instance, Lucasta Miller refers to her as a narrator 'who frequently conceals vital information from the reader and offers misleading interpretations of her own character and behaviour' (Miller, p. 48), while Robert Bernard Martin claims that 'she is premature, unfair and illogical in her assessment of others' (Miller, p. 147). Harriet Björk feels that Lucy is unreliable because she is 'evasive, contradictory, hysterical as a person' (Harriet Björk, *The Language of Truth: Charlotte Brontë, the Woman Question and the Novel* [Lund: Gleerup, 1974], p. 111). Rachel M. Brownstein simply comments on 'the perverse-

ness of Lucy the narrator' (Rachel M. Brownstein, *Becoming a Heroine: Reading about Women in Novels* [Harmondsworth: Penguin, 1984], p. 170) while Pauline Nestor refers to Lucy's narration as 'frequently vague, distorted and unreliable' (Pauline Nestor, *Women Writers: Charlotte Brontë* [London: Macmillan, 1987], p. 85). Lucy Hughes-Hallett, although claiming that '[t]here has seldom been a first-person narrative which withheld so much from its readers', nevertheless feels that Lucy is 'not so much unreliable as evasive' (Hughes-Hallett, pp. v, vi). Similarly, Suzanne Keen regards Lucy as a 'shifty and not-entirely-divulging narrator' (Suzanne Keen, *Victorian Renovations of the Novel* [Cambridge: Cambridge University Press, 1998], p. 109). John Maynard argues, somewhat surprisingly, that Lucy Snowe is actually a more reliable narrator than Jane Eyre, as she eventually comes to a more complete understanding of herself than Jane Eyre does: 'What makes Lucy different from an unreliable narrator from whom we turn to establish a separate implied author's position is that it is to Lucy herself that we turn for eventual clarification of her own distortions. [. . .] Hence, we look at her finally as a reliable guide to the central subject of her work, herself' (Maynard, pp. 166–167). This is also the line pursued by Helene Moglen, who claims that Lucy's apparent contradictions are unconscious, since '[. . .] it is not until she learns to trust her imagination as she must trust her feelings and intuitions that she can become "reliable" as a narrator, "whole" as a woman' (Moglen, p. 200). Finally, Brenda R. Silver is most radical in her interpretation of Lucy as a narrator when she ventures that '[. . .] it can also be argued that Lucy is less evasive and even less unreliable than most critics have assumed — that she is, in fact, a self-consciously reliable narrator of unusual circumstances whose narrative choices ask her "readers" to perceive her on her own terms' (Brenda R. Silver, 'The Reflecting Reader in *Villette*', in *The Voyage In: Fictions of Female Development*, ed. by Elizabeth Abel, Marianne Hirsch, and Elizabeth Langland [Hanover & London: University Press of New England, 1983], p. 91).

24. Charlotte Brontë, *Villette* (Harmondsworth: Penguin, 1979), p. 243. All subsequent references will be to this edition and will be given parenthetically within the text.

25. So, in fact, is Lucy's claim that on both occasions she wears black with her pink dress in order to soften or modify the effect. But black decorations would not do that. On the contrary, they would set off and highlight the pink colour.

26. This was certainly the case at the Cowan Bridge school. Gaskell quotes the school rule stating that 'All letters and parcels are inspected by the superintendent'; and adds that 'this is a very prevalent regulation in all young ladies' schools, where I think it is generally understood that the school mistress may exercise this privilege, although it is certainly unwise in her to insist too frequently upon it'. Elizabeth Gaskell, *The Life of Charlotte Brontë* (Penguin: Harmondsworth, 1975), p. 98. It is interesting to note that Gaskell, a woman known for her tact and charm, does not object to the idea as such, only to antagonizing the pupils by insisting too frequently on it. She seems to favour a non-confrontational attitude very like that of Madame Beck.

27. It was also not unusual for headmistresses at the time to treat young female teachers almost like pupils. Lucasta Miller gives the example of how as late as 1889 'some young teachers at a girls' boarding school wanted to read *Jane Eyre* but were forbidden to do so by the headmistress until they reached the age of twenty-five' (Miller, p. 89). Jane Eyre herself goes out of her way to hide the fact that she is writing and mailing a letter of application for another post while still at Lowood, thus

indicating that there might be some kind of checking of the young teachers' letters there too (*Jane Eyre*, chapter X).

28. The reviewer of *Villette* in the *Guardian* evidently felt that Paulina de Bassompierre's correspondence with John Graham Bretton was problematic from this point of view: 'In these very volumes Paulina, the perfect character, represented as a miracle of innocence and delicate perception, corresponds with a young man clandestinely for months; and Currer Bell narrates it evidently without feeling that it interferes with the refinement of her heroine', he complains indignantly (p. 128).

29. They are certainly not worse than Lucy's methods of ruling, when she is promoted to be a teacher at the school, which include physical violence and ridiculing the pupils' efforts.

30. See, for instance, Tony Tanner on how Madame Beck is 'confronted by the vicious violence of her daughter Désirée instinctively rebelling in an hysterical way against the frigid coercions and deprivations of her home'; Tanner, p. 32.

31. This seems to be in accordance with a prevalent motif in many governess novels of the time, in which the poor, plain, and neglected governess is often depicted as superior in motherly qualities to her wealthy and worldly employer. See Cecilia Wadsö Lecaros, *The Victorian Governess Novel* (Lund: Lund University Press, 2001), pp. 193–237.

32. It is interesting to compare Lucy's assessment of Madame Beck's capacities with that of Emily Brontë given by Monsieur Heger: 'She should have been a man — a great navigator. Her powerful reason would have deduced new spheres of discovery from the knowledge of the old; and her strong, imperious will would never have been daunted by opposition or difficulty; never have given way but with life.' Quoted from Barker, p. 392.

33. Madame Beck and Mrs Bretton, in fact, have many qualities in common: both are widows who care on their own for their children, and do so well; and both are intelligent and generous but unsentimental women. Kate Millett calls them 'two of the most efficient women one can meet anywhere in fiction'; Kate Millett, *Sexual Politics* (London: Sphere Books, 1971), p. 141. Margot Peters also comments on their similarity: 'Mrs. Bretton and Madame Beck are two facets of the middle-aged Victorian matron. Both are blooming, efficient, and full of sexual vitality that can find no market'; Margot Peters, *Charlotte Brontë: Style in the Novel* (London & Madison, Wisconsin: University of Wisconsin Press, 1973), p. 93.

34. Hannah More, *Moral Sketches of Prevailing Opinions and Manners, Foreign and Domestic: with Reflections on Prayer*, 3rd edn (London, 1819), pp. 124–125. I am indebted to Professor Marianne Thormählen for this observation.

35. In strong contrast to Madame Beck's cheerful generosity, Lucy finds giving very difficult. On the one occasion when she plans to give a present to another person (the watch-chain for M. Paul's birthday which she works so lovingly), she can hardly make herself actually hand it over.

36. There is one instance when Madame Beck might be suspected of parsimoniousness. This is in her payment of Lucy, as the English girl is promoted from nursery governess to the status of teacher of English. 'Madame raised my salary', says Lucy, adding cattily: 'but she got thrice the work out of me she had extracted from Mr Wilson, at half the expense' (p. 144). However, in this Madame Beck is simply following the custom of the time, since female teachers were habitually paid much less than male — and expected to do more work. When Branwell Brontë was employed as tutor in the Robinson family in 1845, for instance, he was paid exactly

twice as much as his sister Anne who was governess in the same family, in spite of the fact that she taught the three daughters of the family and he just the one boy (Barker, p. 466). Unfair as this may seem to us, Charlotte's salary at this time was still only half of Anne's (Barker, p. 351). It would thus seem that Madame Beck pays Lucy the same salary as her other female teachers, which, considering the fact that Lucy has no formal qualifications and no teaching experience, is in fact quite generous.

37. Lucy's scorn for the painting of the supposedly seductive Cleopatra figure in the picture gallery is also phrased in terms very similar to those used of Justine Marie and the girls in the *pensionnat*: 'She was, indeed, extremely well fed: very much butcher's meat — to say nothing of bread, vegetables and liquids — must she have consumed to attain that breadth and height, that wealth of muscle, that affluence of flesh' (p. 275).

38. See also Lucy's comment on this occasion on M. Paul's attitude to money a page later: 'I more than suspected in him a lamentable absence of the saving faculty; he could get, but not keep; *he needed a treasurer*' (p. 589, emphasis added).

39. 'Yes, yes, my good friend; I give you permission from the heart willingly. Your work in my house has always been admirable, full of zeal and discretion: you certainly have the right to amuse yourself. Go out as much as you like. As to your choice of acquaintances, I am happy with it; it is sensible, dignified and praiseworthy' (translation from the Penguin edition of *Villette*).

40. The word 'candour' is presumably used here in the sense of 'fairness, impartiality, justice' rather than 'frankness' (which is not one of Madame Beck's qualities). The word also seems to me to carry some of its older meaning of 'freedom from malice, favourable disposition, kindliness'. See *Oxford English Dictionary*, which also gives Dr Johnson's definition of the word as 'sweetness of temper, kindness'.

41. With all her critical acumen Lucy is obviously quite unaware of her own deficiencies, since she often censures other people for faults that are also her own. Not only does she thus criticize M. Paul for his habit of spying and for his 'severe and suspicious' (p. 379) attitude, she also complains about Ginevra Fanshawe being prejudiced against foreigners (pp. 148–149).

42. On anti-Catholicism in *Villette*, see Marianne Thormählen, *The Brontës and Religion* (Cambridge: Cambridge University Press, 1999), pp. 29–36.

43. One shudders at the thought of a turning around of this situation and how this would be described by Lucy, i.e. a scene in which Madame Beck and M. Paul (or, indeed, Madame Beck and Dr John) were overheard making fun of Lucy herself.

44. She jumps to exactly the same conclusion about Madame Beck's allegedly mercenary feelings and motives when Ginevra Fanshawe elopes without a note of explanation in the middle of the night. Since the girl is a minor left in Madame Beck's care, it is not surprising that the headmistress is upset and worried. However, Lucy is certain that this is only because of the possible damage done to the reputation of the school, 'Never had I seen Madame Beck so pale or so appalled', she says, continuing venomously: 'Here was a blow struck at her tender part, her weak side; here was damage done to her interest' (p. 572).

45. This has been noted by some critics. See for example Margot Peters: 'Lucy [. . .] and Madame are alike rather than the opposites they seem. Both are hardworking, independent, proud, strong-willed personalities. Both hide a passionate nature under a surface [. . .]' (p. 91). Brenda R. Silver comments on Lucy's 'confused

reaction of admiration and shock at discovering a woman so powerful, so independent, so successful, and, in many ways, so like her!' (p. 106). 'In almost all the other characters Lucy Snowe can see facets of her own nature [. . .] most subtly in Madame Beck, who is Lucy's most formidable enemy, and yet has qualities of feeling and self-control which Lucy understands and applauds', says Margaret Smith, in her 'Introduction' in Charlotte Brontë, *Villette* (Oxford & New York: The World's Classics, 1990), p. xvi.

46. We learn very little of the former life of either woman. However, since Madame Beck obviously belongs to the upper middle classes, and since she is a widow, it seems reasonable to assume that the death of her husband has made it necessary for her to support herself, even though she must have started her teaching career before that. As for Lucy, we see nothing of her home life as a child, but her relationship to Mrs Bretton as well as the reference to 'an old servant of our family — once my nurse' (p. 103) points to an earlier state of some affluence. Her comment, 'I know not that I was of a self-reliant or active nature; but self-reliance and exertion were forced upon me by circumstances' (p. 95) likewise points to this interpretation of her situation.

47. Thormählen, p. 35.

48. In fact, this is an argument that Lucy uses in order to make Paulina's father accept her engagement to John Graham Bretton: If his daughter does not marry John Graham, she might marry into the aristocracy of Villette — a possibility which Count de Bassompierre obviously does not want to contemplate.

49. The question of Lucy Snowe's, and often, by implication, Charlotte Brontë's, sanity has been discussed by a number of readers and critics. To mention but a few, as early as 1920 Lucile Dooley published an article in *The American Journal of Psychology* claiming that Charlotte Brontë herself was a neurotic. See 'Psychoanalysis of Charlotte Brontë as a Type of the Woman of Genius', *American Journal of Psychology*, 31.3 (July 1920). This view has been challenged most forcefully by John Maynard in *Charlotte Brontë and Sexuality* (1984), in which he not only argues convincingly that Lucy's author was perfectly sane and that her texts are the products of a conscious artist, but also, less convincingly in my view, claims that the portrait of Lucy Snowe is that of a woman who, having suffered from repression and depression, finally reaches full sexual and emotional maturity. In the chapter on *Villette* in *Charlotte Brontë and Victorian Psychology* (Cambridge: Cambridge University Press, 1996), Sally Shuttleworth shows how the portrait of Lucy illustrates Charlotte Brontë's interest in and knowledge of Victorian psychological theory, and how she partly adheres to and partly questions established (male) assumptions of the female psyche.

50. In narratological terminology Lucy is a homodiegetic narrator, i.e. one who is also a character in the situations and events she recounts.

51. Millett, p. 140.

52. Pauline Nestor, *Women Writers: Charlotte Brontë* (London: Macmillan, 1987), p. 86.

53. Letter to W. S. Williams, 6 November 1852, in *Letters*, vol. III, p. 80.

54. Admittedly Ginevra and Paulina are not exactly similar as characters; Ginevra is much more shallow and flirtatious, Paulina more serious and also more submissive. But neither seems to develop her full potential because they are both too anxious to win the approval of the men around them — Ginevra because she wants economic security, Paulina more for emotional reasons. Paulina's numerous rewrit-

ings of her letter to John Graham shows that she is just as eager as Ginevra to 'secure' her man, only more sophisticated in her means.

55. Kate Millett, while regarding Lucy as a victim of 'a male-supremacist society', nevertheless sees Madame Beck as the villain, since she is a collaborator, 'a perpetual policewoman, a virtual forewoman of patriarchal society' (p. 140). This seems to me an unfair judgement of a woman who makes the best of her situation and who is just as much a product of her society as Lucy is.

56. See Christina Crosby on this aspect of *Villette*: 'In fact, as her publishers had feared, the novel was read as a record of "subjective misery" that is "almost intolerably painful", from which the author "allows us no respite", an obsessive representation which is too singular to be "a true presentment of any large portion of life and experience". Harriet Martineau forfeited Charlotte Bronte's friendship by that review, but her opinion is hardly unique. She is seconded by the *Guardian*, which declares that the novel "is too uniformly painful, and too little genial, to be accepted by the generality as the unmingled truth". Thackeray, in a private letter, is more blunt: "That's a plaguey book that *Villette*. How clever it is — and how I don't like the heroine".' Christina Crosby, *The Ends of History: Victorians and 'The Woman Question* (New York & London: Routledge, 1991), pp. 111–112.

57. Lucasta Miller, *The Brontë Myth* (London: Vintage, 2002).

58. Miller, p. 24.

59. It is significant that the entry on Mme Beck in *The Oxford Companion to the Brontës* ends with the words 'See also Reuter, Mlle Zoraïde'. See *The Oxford Companion to the Brontës*, ed. by Christine Alexander and Margaret Smith (Oxford: Oxford University Press, 2003).

60. In a letter to Ellen Nussey Charlotte wrote: 'As to the character of "Lucy Snowe" my intention from the first was that she should not occupy the pedestal to which "Jane Eyre" was raised by some injudicious admirers. She is where I meant her to be, and where no charge of self-laudation can touch her.' Letter to Ellen Nussey, 22 March 1853, in *Letters*, vol. III, p. 137. Elizabeth Gaskell, herself a novelist and aware of the complex psychological mechanisms involved in creative writing, commented shrewdly on Charlotte's work: 'I am sure she works off a great deal that is morbid into her writing, and out of her life'. Letter from Elizabeth Gaskell to Lady Kay-Shuttleworth, 7 April 1853, in *Letters*, vol. III, p. 150.

61. See for instance the famous incident at the Roe Head School, retold by Gaskell, when her friend Mary Taylor told Charlotte that she was 'very ugly'. Mary later regretted this comment but was told by Charlotte: 'You did me a great deal of good, Polly, so don't repent of it', Gaskell, p. 130.

JOAN BELLAMY

The Tenant of Wildfell Hall:
What Anne Brontë Knew and
What Modern Readers Don't

In writing *The Tenant of Wildfell Hall* Anne Brontë was creating not a melodrama and love story remote from the realities of her times as some modern readers may assume but a work which raised serious questions relating, among others, to religious belief, morality, redemption, conjugal relations, and injustice. A particularly interesting aspect of *The Tenant* is the way in which she places Helen Huntingdon's tempestuous story in the real world of the first half of the nineteenth century as it defined, through law and convention, the status of women.

In the 1840s, when Anne Brontë was writing, married women had no property rights. If they owned anything it became their husband's property unless trusts and settlements were set up as part of a marriage contract; a resource generally available only to the rich.

Helen's romantic illusions lead her into a marriage which reduces her to utter dependence on her husband. In the absence of a legal settlement all her fortune becomes the property of Arthur to do with it as he thinks fit. Given Arthur's profligacy this risked the loss of Helen's wealth and the subsequent impoverishment of their son. There were cases in which men actually bequeathed property, acquired through marriage, to their mistresses, which, when challenged in the law courts was ruled to be quite lawful.

Of course, Helen's economic dependence becomes an acute problem, not in the abstract, but when she finds she can no longer co-habit with Arthur in a

Brontë Studies, Volume 30, Number 3 (November 2005): pp. 255–257. © 2005 The Bronte Society.

157

decadent household of heavy drinking, reckless gambling, sexual promiscuity, and corruption of the child.

Factual accounts of the ways of life of sections of the rich in the first three or four decades of the nineteenth century confirm the picture Anne gives in her depiction of Arthur's way of life. Biographies of the Prince Regent, his brothers, and prominent politicians such as Charles James Fox and the Duke and Duchess of Devonshire, are witness to the way of life like that led by Arthur and his friends. This knowledge would be had by contemporary readers of *The Tenant*. The complaints about the coarseness of the novel rested not so much on a denial of the facts of a situation on which her fiction is based as on her temerity in bringing them further out into the open.

It becomes clear that Arthur is committing adultery and, moreover, tries to trap Helen into appearing to do the same. Laws controlling marriage and divorce still had their roots in ecclesiastical law, treating the genders unequally. Divorce required complex legal procedures including a private Act of Parliament, which would be way beyond the means of most people, and the terms on which husbands and wives could sue for divorce were not identical. A man could sue on the grounds of his wife's adultery; women had to establish not only adultery but other misdemeanours such as bestiality. So in seeking to trap Helen into committing adultery, or even the possible appearance of it, Arthur was safe in assuming that she was vulnerable to divorce proceedings while he, for the same transgression, was not.

Helen both defies her husband and risks conflict with the law on several counts. Firstly, when she slams the door on the matrimonial bedroom firmly excluding Arthur. The law gave a husband the right to take action in the courts for the restitution of his conjugal rights; she could be forced back into co-habitation and sexual relations. This is one of the reasons that Helen, having left Arthur, has then to hide away from him. She defies the law secondly, when she takes their son with her into hiding. Women had no legal rights in relation to their children; they were the property of the father. When she runs off with the child, depriving Arthur of access, she is violating his legal rights. Thirdly, she is in breach of the law by retaining the money she earns. Anne Brontë endows her heroine with the skills which so many gentlewomen acquired, that of painter; not because they were intended for a profession but because it was a desirable accomplishment. However, we know that Charlotte had considered the possibility of earning money in the sphere of visual arts and Helen is sufficiently accomplished to earn money by her work. Helen, in retaining the money she earns is acting illegally because a wife's earnings were the property of the husband; they legally belonged to Arthur. So not only has she stolen his son, she has stolen his money too! In light of the legal context in which the book is placed, that of the 1820s and 30s, Helen's actions, which today might appear extreme and melodramatic, can be seen to be a justifiable response to conditions which readers in 1848 could be expected to know about.

Helen's terrible situation is, of course, resolved, not by legal reforms but by Arthur's death, the virtually inevitable outcome of his own profligate conduct. Helen is ennobled by her return to him, motivated by her deep religious convictions. Anne Brontë was here expressing her religious beliefs as well as her conviction of the injustices suffered by women.

To establish the nature of this novel as realist and reformist, we need only refer to one of the most notorious society scandals of the late 1830s and 40s which has some points of connection to the Huntingdon story and serves to illuminate the context of the fiction. Mrs Caroline Norton, granddaughter of the playwright Richard Brinsley Sheridan had, at the age of nineteen, married Ralph Norton, a younger son of the owner of the Norton Conyers estate near Ripon. She was the centre of a brilliant Whig circle of politicians, writers, and artists. The Nortons lived above their income; Ralph pressed Carolyn to use her influence to get him a more lucrative Government post. This she refused to do. He assaulted her. Reconciliations were always succeeded by further quarrels and violence with her taking refuge with relatives. During her absence from their home he removed their three children and placed them out of reach of their mother and, when she discovered where they were, refused her any access to them. He was not in breach of the law.

At the same time he charged Lord Melbourne, the then Prime Minister, with 'criminal conversation,' namely adultery, with Caroline. She discovered that she could not give evidence in the courts to clear her name and support Melbourne's denial because she had, as a married woman, no legal existence. While Melbourne was found not guilty, Caroline remained separated from her children and without means of subsistence. She was quite a good poet and composer but she discovered that Ralph had the right to her earnings which he promptly appropriated. She retaliated with a privately distributed pamphlet outlining the case and the injustice of the denial of access to the little boys, one of whom died. The case was taken up by lawyers and some Members of Parliament. This resulted in the Infant Custody Act of 1838 which, if the mother was innocent of adultery, allowed her to have custody of children under the age of seven and access thereafter. Caroline Norton subsequently made a contribution to the campaign for a Married Women's Property Act, though she never identified with the growing women's rights movement.

So, the novel of the innocent little sister, as Anne has often been seen, is a tough, realist novel. It has structural flaws but can only be fully appreciated if the modern reader is equipped with knowledge of the status of women of Anne's time.

SUSAN OSTROV WEISSER

Charlotte Brontë, Jane Austen, and the Meaning of Love

The text of an Address to the Annual Meeting of the Brontë Society, New York, December 3, 2005

Charlotte Brontë's novels were a clear departure from the romantic novels in vogue in her time, typified in the work of Jane Austen. No longer were manners, appearance and submissive conformity the ideal. Charlotte believed in a heroine's inner strength, her moral integrity, and her intellectual qualities. The nature of this change is analysed.

I would like to begin with a fact that startled me when I first read of it: Charlotte Brontë very much disliked Jane Austen and could not quite comprehend why she was valued so highly by critics in her time. Until I learned this, I had grouped the two together as if they had a natural affinity: both were of primary importance in the British literary tradition as major female novelists; both were influential in inventing the modern novel; and both situated their love stories in frames that engaged these narratives with issues of money, class and social prestige. But, in Charlotte Brontë's view, their similarities were not as significant as their differences. I would like to suggest that the radical gap that Charlotte Brontë perceived between herself and Austen is a key to understanding Charlotte's own work. In fact, I will make a larger claim: that her perception of Jane Austen not only reveals

Brontë Studies, Volume 31 (July 2006): pp. 93–100. © 2006 The Brontë Society.

much about Charlotte, but also highlights an important cultural change in
the Victorian definition of romantic love. Furthermore, this change fore-
shadows our contemporary understanding of that malleable term 'love', a
shift in meaning to which, we might speculate, Charlotte Brontë substan-
tially contributed herself.

We know about Charlotte's opinion of Austen from her correspondence
with the respected critic George Henry Lewes, later the companion of
George Eliot. *Jane Eyre* had received a good review from Lewes and when
he wrote to give Charlotte comments and advice, she took his critique of her
novel seriously. Lewes wanted to underline a fault in *Jane Eyre*, the moments
of melodrama in it that he called 'suited to the circulating library'—not a
compliment, and he held out Austen as a model of calm and balanced wisdom
through a more naturalistic style. When he praised Austen, whom Charlotte
had neglected to read, she went to some trouble to obtain *Pride and Prejudice*.
In her own words to Lewes,

> I got the book and studied it. And what did I find? An accurate
> daguerrotyped portrait of a commonplace face; a carefully fenced,
> highly cultivated garden, with neat borders and delicate flowers; but
> no glance of a bright, vivid physiognomy, no open country, no fresh
> air, no blue hill, no bonny beck. I should hardly like to live with her
> ladies and gentlemen, in their elegant but confined houses. These
> observations will probably irritate you, but I shall run the risk.[1]

For Charlotte, something was lacking, an element she called 'what throbs
fast, full, though hidden, what the blood rushes through'.[2] This of course
is the heart. Lewes's praise of Jane Austen's fiction caused her resentment:
she interpreted his admiration for Austen as a requirement that an author,
to be worthy of esteem, must eliminate the life beneath the surface, the full-
blooded life of experience, including dark experience, while privileging the
carefully worked appearance of social life she saw in Austen.

I am aware that this evaluation of Charlotte's has a particular irony
in view of the recent opening of the filmed version of *Pride and Prejudice*,
starring the beautiful Keira Knightley as Elizabeth Bennett. The irony I
refer to lies in the way the film revises and sells the original love story of
Augustan balance and harmony as a romanticized version of the original: one
prominent television ad screams, 'Romance hasn't looked this sexy in years!'.
In a recent review of the film, *The New Yorker* reviewer put it this way: 'What
has happened is perfectly clear: Jane Austen has been Brontëfied'.

But what exactly does that imply about what Charlotte Brontë, and
the Brontës in general, have contributed to our own definition of love and
romance? And is that modern idea in fact the same as the meaning of

romantic love to Charlotte Brontë? The answer to the latter question, I would say, is not quite. But what I will claim for Charlotte Brontë is that she very deliberately altered the term 'love' as it was understood in her time in a way that has influenced our society far beyond her own expectations or, perhaps, beyond her intentions.

It is now a commonplace to say that there is no one definition of romantic love; that its meaning has been in flux for many centuries. We may begin with what is often called the beginning of the ideology of love in Western society. From the Middle Ages until the late eighteenth and beyond, what we now call 'romance' was associated with passion, which is to say intense sexual longing and erotically charged emotionality. To read about romantic passion was to enter a world of fantasy, magic and idealized eroticism such as that expressed by the twelfth century troubadour poets, or found in the tales of Tristan and Isolde or Lancelot and Guinevere. From the beginning, an association of anti-social rebelliousness clung to traditional romantic love, as the medieval poet expressed intense desire for his usually married lady, or lovers such as Tristan and Lancelot defied the greatest of social prohibitions, the betrayal of the king, risking all for the greater good of love's pleasure. The reaction of the church to a concept of love as close to lust was understandably strong. In a literary work such as Dante's late medieval *Vita Nuova*, in which the narrator feels true love without desiring more than to hear his beloved's greeting, we can see the attempt to detach romantic love from the body in order to Christianise it. As enlightenment comes to the narrator of the *Vita Nuova* after Beatrice's death, we see romance in the old sense discarded for a disembodied sense of adoration, as the spirit of the dead beloved shows him the road to salvation.

By the end of the eighteenth century, when Mary Wollstonecraft and Jane Austen were writing, the term 'romance' was still generally associated with idealized expectations having little to do with real life. 'Love', wrote Wollstonecraft in 1792, 'such as the glowing pen of genius has traced, exists not on earth, or only resides in those exalted, fervid imaginations that have sketched such dangerous pictures. Dangerous [in that they] take from the dignity of virtue.'[3]

At the same time, in the late eighteenth century, there was an increasing acceptance of marriage based on individual choice in the middle class. A marriage based on mutual attraction and affection was commonly known as the 'love-match', to distinguish it from the pragmatic exchange of women's attractiveness and domestic labour for the man's economic provision and social power that was the usual configuration of matrimony. Both Wollstonecraft and Austen favoured love as the basis for marriage, as opposed to marrying for money and social prestige, but their definition of love is *opposed* to 'romantic love', as Wollstonecraft defines it above. Though Wollstonecraft was a radical and Jane Austen arguably conservative in many ways, both devalued 'romantic' views of love as flighty, inimical to the importance of rationality and judgment, companionship, sensible affection and admiration for good character in marriage. In *Pride and Prejudice*, the union of Lydia and Wickham represents selfish lust and the marriage of Elizabeth's friend Charlotte to the odious Mr. Collins is one that exposes the limitations of the purely pragmatic marriage with no real affection at all. In between these stands a relatively new concept of love, one that is defined by a growth into mature self-development as well as sober recognition of and esteem for the other. In the view of both Wollstonecraft and Austen, mutual respect and valuing of character enables women to maintain greater dignity and worth in the social arrangement of courtship and marriage that still ultimately determines their lives.

The Romantic era, as it appeared in Britain in the late eighteenth to early nineteenth century following its philosophical and literary origins in Europe, provided an important alternative definition of romance, entangling romantic love with sexual desire, intense and all-consuming feeling, and longing for a transcendent ideal, as Goethe had illustrated in the wildly popular tale, *The Sorrows of Young Werther*. As admirers of the medieval, the Romantics once again restored to love a deep sense of mystery and the sublime, an admiration for wildness and rule-breaking in passion. Romanticism raised the value of emotion for its own sake, the deeper and more intense the better, explored through plumbing psychological depth and expressed through dreams and fantasy. As opposed to the moderation, balance and calm of rational affection, the sorrow and alienation of unrequited and forbidden love symbolized the rejection of stultifying convention for the sake of primal emotion. Young Werther, for example, committed suicide at the end of the German novel for love of an unattainable married woman.

Jane Austen's own ambivalence about this new and rebellious movement is embodied in the character of Benwick in *Persuasion*, where, under the influence of Romantic reading, he sighs, reads verses aloud all day and cultivates 'a melancholy air', a practice she obviously finds amusingly absurd and pretentious. But we know that Charlotte Brontë was an avid reader of the British Romantic poets, including Byron, an icon of masculine wildness and sexual experience. It is not difficult to trace much of Charlotte's imagery to the Romantic sense of harmony in man and nature, their high valuation of imagination and imaginative freedom, and their admiration for liberty and equality rather than authoritarianism. It is generally agreed that the Brontë sisters were not only interested in and influenced by the Romantic movement, but represent a continuation of it in some form.

In 1840s Britain, when Charlotte Brontë began writing *Jane Eyre*, there were various other traditions concerning romance, literary and popular, on

which she was able to draw, either as model or in protest; each in its way
contributing to her understanding and representation of romantic love:

1. Popular advice books in the Victorian age, often aimed at women,
attempted to enforce the necessity to look to worthiness of character in marriage choice as opposed to matters of feeling. As one mid-century clergyman
intoned, 'There are ideas, romantic, impassioned, immodest, derived from
impure novels and impurer fancies, which you must prayerfully exclude from
the chambers of your soul . . . Learn that your affections are under your
own control; that pure affection is founded upon esteem . . . restrain your
affections, therefore, with vigor'. This may sound like a version of eighteenth
century rational love, but in fact there is a great difference. Because early
Victorian Britain was more explicitly focused on religious matters than was
the freethinker Mary Wollstonecraft or Jane Austen for that matter, this
emphasis on conduct and character as the basis for love in marriage was
strongly associated with Christian spirituality: 'Marriage, properly viewed',
this author writes,

> is a union of kindred minds, a blending of two souls in mutual, holy
> affection. Its physical aspects, pure and necessary as they are, are
> its lowest and least to be desired ones; indeed, they derive all their
> sanctity from the spiritual affinity existing between the parties.[4]

Thus, mainstream advice literature emphasized the distinction between passionate love, whose basis is lust, essentially sinful and selfish, and romantic
love as the spiritualization of sexuality, ennobling the lovers through serving
God's purposes in holy matrimony. This is clearly a descendant of Dante's
idea, though not so extreme, since the body and sexual relations are folded
into the legitimizing arena of marriage.

2. Popular literary depictions of courtship, of which Coventry Patmore's
widely read narrative poem 'The Angel in the House' (1854–62) might
stand as a particularly useful example. Patmore's poem was so well known
that the title later came to stand for the very idea of woman's domestic role in
Victorian culture; the phrase was used by Virginia Woolf when she famously
wrote, 'In those days every house had its Angel', who was 'immensely
charming', 'utterly unselfish', 'sacrificed herself daily', 'never had a mind
or wish of her own', and above all, was 'pure'.[5] Virginia Woolf expressed a
strong desire to 'kill' her, and when we read the Patmore poem, it is easy to
see why. Here is the description of the beloved:

> Her disposition is devout
> Her countenance angelical . . .

How amiable and innocent
Her pleasure in her power to charm. . . .
Her beauty is the genial thought
Which makes the sunshine bright . . .
. . . She grows
More infantine, auroral, mild,
And still the more she lives and knows
The lovelier she's expressed a child.

The pervasive medium of magazine fiction featured a parade of virtuous, modest, sweet, demure and submissive girls, always depicted as beautiful in that particularly virtuous, modest, sweet and demure way, who won the hearts of gallant, handsome, well-placed young men.

3. Popular tales of cross-class seduction of a virtuous young woman by an immoral aristocratic libertine, who tries to take advantage of her or succeeds in the seduction and then abandons her. The extraordinarily popular *Pamela*, an eighteenth century novel by Samuel Richardson, was the first of its kind to achieve wide recognition, but the genre continued until mid-century to be popular with the working class. A subgenre in the early nineteenth century is the cautionary tale of the fallen woman, who is laid low by poverty and sexual exploitation.

4. The popular Gothic literary tradition, a subgenre of Romanticism, which favoured distressed and beset heroines amidst wild and picturesque land-scapes or gloomy, macabre castles, haunted mansions, and supernatural, scary doings inspiring horror and thrills.

I believe we can recognize suggestions of all these in the works of Charlotte Brontë, generally. But I am going to focus now, particularly, on *Jane Eyre*, because I would say that this novel has, perhaps more than others by Charlotte or any other author, especially defined romantic love through a paradigmatic story that has lasted into our contemporary age. That is, as the new filmed version of *Pride and Prejudice* and its reviews imply, we have come to accept the Romantic idea of feeling charged with sexual pas-sion as the very basis for romantic love, but we do not stop there. Instead, we have united this view of romance, as Charlotte does, with the domestic virtues, affectionate intimacy and support, and suitability of temperament that Austen identified as the proper basis for marriage. This improbable union of romantic passion and domestic relationship is now the dominant paradigm. Thus, the necessity for revising Austen, for 'Brontëfying' her: the Hollywood version *must* be the 'Brontëfied' vision of romantic love to sell widely, *not* the Austenian version, which is not as comprehensible to a modern audience.

To see how Charlotte constructed her own interpretation of romance, we may look at the way in which she synthesized some of the elements above. Taking the last of my list first, the Gothic tradition appears in *Jane Eyre* quite seriously, though it is parodied in *Villette*. It's fair to ask what Charlotte's interest in it was. The wildness of the landscape, the field of thorns and knotted trees, and the thrilling risks of the mansion haunted by the mad and apparition-like Bertha, recall the elements of the fantastic in Charlotte Brontë's youthful fantasies, pursued over many years with her siblings. Her first love stories were set in Glasstown and Angria, the lands of dreams she associated with a life of melodrama and passion outside the restrictive confines of the life of a minister's daughter.

For *Jane Eyre*, Charlotte took fundamentals of this emotional landscape and integrated into it the popular story of the lustful aristocrat, who has a shady past and selfishly seduces, or tries to seduce, the poor but virtuous maiden. In Samuel Richardson's version of the seduction tale, the maidservant Pamela eventually marries the master, thus 'reforming the rake' and rising to a social class she sincerely never attempted to reach. In *Pamela* and Richardson's great tragic novel *Clarissa*, the theme of sexual seduction appears in a melodrama in which the mere thrill of action is transformed by a moral perspective, a model Charlotte Brontë adapted to her own purposes, as Rochester is transformed melodramatically and morally.

We know that Charlotte also read and reacted to the magazine fiction that was increasingly available with the spread of print media in the Victorian age. Mrs. Gaskell's famous story has become literary history: during the period when the Brontë sisters were composing their first novels, Charlotte is said to have told Emily and Anne, 'I will prove to you that you are wrong; I will show you a heroine as plain and as small as myself, who shall be as interesting as any of yours'.[6] It has often been remarked, too, that Rochester is not the young, handsome, charmingly elegant and well-mannered hero of these fictions, and still less is Jane Eyre, who though young, is not anything like the lovely, sweet, demure and angelic maiden.

Why did subverting the literary convention appeal so much to Charlotte that she would take this risk of alienating her would-be publishers and readers? It is all too easy to give a psychological motive based on Elizabeth Gaskell's biography, but Jane's low status and lack of beauty are integral to Charlotte's literary vision of romance as well. In *Jane Eyre*, Charlotte dramatically reveals the power structure which placed little value on children, the poor and women in Victorian society: Jane suffers from being all three, a poor and female child at the beginning, a poor female adult till just before the end. It seems fair, then, to view this rebellious gesture, Charlotte's insistence on a plain heroine, as her comment on Victorian notions of romance. I would say this gesture marks her recognition of romantic love as it was defined in her society as an idealized mask for a social game in which female beauty is exchanged for the attention of men and the reward of marriage, with its conferral of economic security and prestige on the woman.

Instead, Charlotte substitutes an alternative view of romance, which is derived from the Romantics. In fact, she insists on it: romantic love entails intense feeling, intimations of erotic pleasure, uncontrollable longing even in the face of almost certain rejection. In the lovers and in the landscape of *Jane Eyre*, we can apprehend the wildness, the appreciation of the imagination and of the power of the dream that is her inheritance from the Romantic era. Just as important, we may see the significance of the *inner* landscape as the lovers reveal themselves to each other, share souls and confidences and tastes, across a barrier that seems at the time insurmountable. He 'dives into her eyes', she is 'his sympathy', she is 'akin' to him, his 'diary', 'assimilated to him', and in sum, 'his second self'.[7]

But Charlotte Brontë is also a moralist, a sincere and devout Christian moralist. Under the pressure of necessity, she produces a framework in which the Gothic elements are displaced onto the story of a lustful and intemperate character, Bertha, as the elements of conventional romance are critiqued and disposed of in the subplot of the triumph of Jane over Blanche Ingram. She anchors the romanticism, as well as these elements, in a plot through which Jane is allowed to manifest and prove a spiritual love for Rochester by rejecting the choice of immoral passion. From the beginning of their love relation, Rochester has looked to Jane to 'save' him, calling her his 'angel'. In this, we can see the strong influence of the Victorian view of marital love as spiritualized, incorporating and controlling the Romantic view of the essential nature of passion to life.

Yet the novel does not end there, and in the last phase, the character of St. John Rivers reverses the trajectory of the novel toward an unexpected, if notably ambivalent, critique of the Christian rejection of sexual passion as foundational for romantic love. In a way, St. John represents the passionless Angel in the House, restraining his feelings as the advice-giving Victorian clergyman advised. Though attracted to his Christian self-sacrifice and moral vision, ultimately Jane is horrified at his view of sexuality: 'As his wife', she says, 'always restrained, always checked, forced to keep the fire of my nature continually low, to compel it to burn inwardly and never utter a cry, though the imprisoned flame consumed . . . *this* would be unendurable' (p. 472). In the end, she rejects him, as we know, crying, 'I scorn *your idea of love*, I scorn the *counterfeit sentiment* you offer' (p. 473, my italics). Though Jane mastered her own actions when loving Rochester was immoral, it is fundamental to her romantic vision that passionate feeling itself is uncontrollable.

Much has been said about the conclusion of *Jane Eyre* in which Rochester, the former master, is reduced to a state of helpless need, leaning on Jane, his nurse and beloved. Some have seen Rochester's mutilation of hand and eye as a reduction of the threatening element of sexuality; some as a religious punishment for his adulterous desire for Jane; and some as a proto-feminist wish-fulfillment, a fantasy of equalization between the soon-to-be married lovers achieved through a plot device. Perhaps, in the way of complex works of the imagination, it is all three.

Charlotte Brontë was fascinated with relations of power; powerlessness and estrangement, a sense of displacement from being at home, is the condition for falling in love, especially for women in her novels. But sexual love is represented as both liberation and oppression. Jane Eyre is powerless and becomes ensnared in helpless love for her master, for example, but she also masters her dominating employer, then goes on to master her own feelings, including anger and desire. Lacking bodily self, small, thin and plain, the heroine's strength is her spirit and desire.

The meaning of romance to Charlotte Brontë, then, is a complex one, combining disparate and indeed contradictory elements of her personal psychology, her private imaginative life, her religious belief, her reading of popular and Romantic literature, and her rebellion against convention. Why, one might ask, did Bronte put so much effort, as her character Jane directs so much energy, into altering the usual definition of romantic love, especially in view of the way it left the author vulnerable to harsh criticism? Again, one might offer a psychological explanation regarding her desire to conciliate opposing elements in conflict: her wish to legitimize sexual passion and incorporate it into romance along with her fearful consciousness of its prohibition. But psychoanalytic analyses of long-dead people are not my business; instead, I would note that one of Charlotte's concerns is social, a rebellious desire to protest the 'keeping down' of women, including their sexual repression, without sacrificing her moral concern that this passionate element of love be sanctified in the eyes of God.

To conclude, I would like to go back to a consideration of the effect of Brontëan romance on the new film version of *Pride and Prejudice*. I have said that Charlotte Bronte, along with her sister Emily, has influenced our contemporary ideas of romantic love so that we now expect elements of uncontrollable feeling, intense passion and the drama of emotion to define romance, integrating these features with courtship and marriage. But, though the film of *Pride and Prejudice* is, in the phrase of *The New Yorker* reviewer, 'Brontë-fied', it is also modern in a very particular way that directly contradicts and undermines one of Charlotte's purposes. That is, in the Austen novel, the heroine Elizabeth Bennet is not the most beautiful girl in the town, the room, or even her family, though very attractive. Instead, the filmed version features an actress who frequently attracts the epithet 'gorgeous', with the result that in the movie the heroine outshines her sister Jane, who is the beauty of the family in the novel. What does this alteration tell us about the way we see romantic love now?

I would say that our celebrity culture, in which a movie can't sell itself to an audience unless it gives star billing to a young, fabulously beautiful actress with sexy looks, embodies the regressive element in the conventional way of looking at women that Charlotte Brontë herself consciously tried to protest through 'plain' heroines like Jane Eyre and Lucy Snowe. In the now-conventional popular ideology of romance, we remember Charlotte's attempt to make sexuality meaningful, but we could care less about her desire to question and revise the system of value that makes women worthy of love only as long as they are the Victorian equivalent of movie stars. This, I would suggest, is the greatest irony of all in considering Charlotte's relation to past and future in defining love.

Notes

1. Letter from Charlotte Brontë to G. H. Lewes, 12 January 1848.

2. Letter from Charlotte Brontë to W. S. Williams, 12 April 1850.

3. Mary Wollstonecraft, *A Vindication of the Rights of Woman* (1792), Penguin, 1975, reprinted 1992, p. 170.

4. Daniel Wise, *The Young Lady's Counsellor; or, Outlines and Illustrations of the Sphere, the Duties, and the Dangers of Young Women*, New York: Carlton & Phillips, 1855, pp. 234–235.

5. Virginia Woolf, 'Professions for Women' in *The Death of the Moth and Other Essays* (1942). Chatto & Windus, 1970.

6. Elizabeth C. Gaskell, *The Life of Charlotte Brontë* (1857), Introduction by Winifred Gérin. New York: Dutton, 1971, p. 215.

7. All quotations are from the Barnes and Noble Classics edition, edited with Introduction and Notes by Susan Ostrov Weisser, New York: Barnes and Noble, 2003.

ANNE LONGMUIR

Anne Lister and Lesbian Desire in
Charlotte Brontë's Shirley

In May 2003, the British network television station, Channel 4, screened a documentary entitled 'Queer as 18th Century Folk' as part of its *Georgian Underworld* series. It offered a revisionist history of homosexuality in the eighteenth (and nineteenth) centuries that tacitly challenged Michel Foucault's assertion that characterization in psychiatric, psychological and medical discourse constituted the modern homosexual in the late-nineteenth-century.[1] Among the stories told was that of Anne Lister (1791–1840), a nineteenth-century Yorkshire landowner, whose extensive diary reveals numerous affairs with women, as well as her 'marriage' to the shy, nervous Ann Walker, a local heiress, in 1834. Watching this documentary, I was struck immediately by the similarities between the story of Anne Lister, and Charlotte Brontë's novel, *Shirley* (1849). Charlotte's novel depicts a Yorkshire heiress and landowner who affects, a little like Anne Lister, a masculine identity. Furthermore, like Anne Lister, Charlotte's heroine has an economic and political standing normally denied to women in the nineteenth century. And, just as Lister sought a life partner in Ann Walker, so Shirley humours the quiet, feminine Caroline Helstone, functioning as her 'alternative "mate"'.[2] A little research revealed, more startlingly, that the connections between Charlotte Brontë's novel and the life of Anne Lister are more than just in subject matter: during the winter

Brontë Studies, Volume 31, Number 2 (July 2006): pp. 146–155. © 2006 The Bronte Society.

171

of 1838–39, Charlotte's sister, Emily, lived within a mile of Anne Lister. Despite the proximity of Emily Brontë to Anne Lister in 1838–39 and the similarity between Anne Lister's life and Charlotte Brontë's plot, neither Channel 4's filmmakers nor literary critics have explored the connection between Charlotte's novel and Anne Lister. This article seeks to rectify this oversight by exploring the parallels between Charlotte's novel and Anne Lister's life, and by examining the significance of this coincidence to our reading of *Shirley*.

Relatively little is known about Emily Brontë's time at Elizabeth Patchett's Law Hill School, principally because Patchett was so offended by the reprinting of Charlotte Brontë's description of life at Law Hill as 'hard labour' and 'slavery' in Elizabeth Gaskell's *Life of Charlotte Brontë* that she refused to give any information about Emily's experiences at Law Hill during her lifetime.[3] However, critics have established that Emily arrived at Law Hill in September 1838, while Anne Lister was visiting the Pyrenees with Ann Walker. Emily's date of departure is also uncertain, though it seems likely to have been in March or early April 1839, around four months after Lister returned to Shibden Hall in November 1838.[4,5]

Unsurprisingly, Lister's proximity to Emily Brontë in the winter of 1838–39 has become the subject of some speculation. As Jill Liddington writes: 'Biographers since Winifred Gerin (1971) have become increasingly fascinated by Law Hill's closeness to Shibden and by any link between Elizabeth Patchett and Anne Lister'.[6] Liddington cites Maureen Peters's romantic novel about Emily Brontë's life, *Child of Earth* (1999), which includes a scene in which Elizabeth Patchett invites Emily to a musical soirée given by Anne Lister, and Glyn Hughes's novel, *Brontë* (1996), in which Emily encounters Anne Lister and Ann Walker kissing. But unfortunately for Glynn Hughes and Maureen Peters, there is no reference to Emily Brontë, Elizabeth Patchett or Law Hill in Anne Lister's diaries during the period from November 1838 to March 1839.[7,8] Jill Liddington argues that the absence of any reference is conclusive proof that Anne and Emily did not know each other socially: 'Given the almost obsessive video-camera detail of the daily journals 1838–39, we can emphatically assert: there was not a single meeting of Anne Lister with Emily Brontë during her Law Hill months'.[9] But Liddington also reminds us that the social mores of the period mean any kind of friendship or relationship between the women was unlikely in any case: 'Would Anne Lister have *known* Emily Brontë? The answer is a categoric 'No': no more than Mrs Ingham 'knew' Anne Brontë, or Blanche Ingram 'knew' Jane Eyre'.[10]

But just as Elliot Vanskike argues in his article 'Consistent Inconsistencies: The Transvestite Actress Madame Vestris and Charlotte Brontë's *Shirley*', that '[w]hile it seems all but impossible to *prove* that Brontë knew of Vestris, it is equally implausible to assert that she did not know of her', so it is equally implausible that Emily Brontë did not know of Anne Lister.[11] Law Hill is less than a mile from Shibden Hall and, according to Edward Chitham, Shibden Hall can be seen from the top windows at Law Hill.[12] Phyllis Bentley even argued that Law Hill and Shibden Hall inspired Wuthering Heights and Thrushcross Grange in *Wuthering Heights* (1847).[13] Anne Lister and Elizabeth Patchett were also acquaintances.[14,15] Even Jill Liddington acknowledges that despite a lack of 'friendship' between Anne Lister and Emily Brontë, Emily would have seen Lister and Ann Walker around the Shibden estate and that she 'would surely puzzle over the tensely transgressive nature of their relationship'.[16]

Anne Lister was a conspicuous figure, who kept her hair short and wore all black bodices, which resembled men's coats.[17] Her masculinity was apparent to locals, who nicknamed her 'Gentleman Jack', and her predilection for women was also an open secret.[18] A mocking advertisement for a husband for Lister appeared in the *Leeds Mercury*,[19] while a mob was rumoured to have burned effigies of Lister and Walker in the spring of 1836.[20] It seems likely therefore that Emily would have heard tales of Anne Lister from her neighbours at Law Hill. Indeed, Jill Liddington even argues that 'bitter inheritance disputes among the extended Walker–Priestly–Lister families' inspired *Wuthering Heights*, as much as the more often cited tale of Jack Sharp. Liddington believes these stories have not been given the same standing as that of Jack Sharp 'because the Anne Walker "marriage" to Anne Lister was deliberately erased, and so the Walker family history suppressed'.[21] Here Liddington makes an important claim for the impact of Anne Lister on Brontë studies, arguing that the taboo nature of Anne Lister's relationship with Ann Walker has had a material impact on critical understanding of the sources of *Wuthering Heights*.

This article is indebted to the work of Jill Liddington and others, who have extensively explored the connection between Emily Brontë and Anne Lister. However, no literary critic or historian has yet examined the connection between Anne Lister and *Charlotte* Brontë. This omission is despite the striking similarities between *Shirley* and Anne Lister's story, and the likelihood that Charlotte Brontë also knew of Anne Lister. This article is an attempt to rectify this oversight.

§

Anne Lister must have been a conspicuous and intriguing figure for any young woman: she had achieved a personal and economic independence enjoyed by few women in the nineteenth century, and had travelled extensively in Europe. What is more, Charlotte may have recognised something of her relationship with Ellen Nussey in Anne Lister's relationship with Ann Walker. Charlotte and Ellen were extremely close and once dreamt of living together themselves: 'Ellen, I wish I could live with you always. I begin to cling to you more fondly than ever I did. If we had but a cottage and a competency of our own, I do think we might live and love on till Death without being dependent on any third person for happiness'.[22] Elaine Miller even claims Charlotte and Ellen's relationship was a lesbian relationship, pointing to the passion of their letters, and to Arthur Nicholls' apparent jealousy of Nussey. Furthermore, Lister would surely have intrigued Charlotte, given the fascination with cross-dressing and androgyny which is apparent throughout her fiction from Rochester's gypsy woman disguise in *Jane Eyre* (1847) to Lucy Snowe's performance of the male lead in the school play in *Villette* (1853).

The thematic similarities between Lister's life and *Shirley* are immediately apparent. Shirley Keeldar and Anne Lister are both local landowners who adopt masculine personas to bolster their power. Shirley refers to herself as 'Captain Keeldar', and explicitly adopts a male identity when dealing with local businessmen and clergy:

> Business! Really the word makes me conscious I am indeed no longer a girl, but quite a woman and something more. I am an esquire: Shirley Keeldar, Esquire ought to be my style and title. They gave me a man's name; I hold a man's position: it is enough to inspire me with a touch of manhood; and when I see such people as that stately Anglo-Belgian — that Gerard Moore before me, gravely talking to me of business, really I feel quite gentlemanlike.[23]

Similarly, Anne Lister discovered that her sexual identity had some business advantages. As Jill Liddington writes: 'Her lesbianism also undoubtedly made a difference; other landowners must have guessed she was there to stay and so had to be taken more seriously'.[24] Both women inherit their property 'for lack of male heirs'.[25] And, as the lack of male heirs prompts Shirley's parents to give her 'the same masculine family cognomen they would have bestowed on a boy, if with a boy they had been blessed',[26] so Anne Lister discovered that adopting a masculine identity helped persuade her uncle to leave Shibden Hall to her, as he knew Lister would never fall into marriage with an unscrupulous fortune hunter.[27] Shirley and Lister are also considered masculine by other men of their acquaintance. The Rev. Helstone assigns the protective power of the male to Shirley, asking her 'as a gentleman—the first gentleman in Briarfield [. . .] to [. . .] be master of the Rectory, and guardian of your niece and maids while you are away?',[28] while an acquaintance of Anne Lister, Mr Lally, ascribes a masculine sexual predator quality to her: 'Mr Lally had been visiting at Moreton last September & said he would as soon turn a man loose in his house as me'.[29]

Both women woo a female companion (or in Lister's case, several female companions). Each takes on a masculine role in such relationships. Shirley explicitly adopts the role of an eligible bachelor when she arrives at Briarfield, bemoaning the fact that 'If she had had the bliss to be really Shirley Keeldar, Esq., Lord of the Manor of Briarfield, there was not a single fair one in this and the two neighbouring parishes, whom she should have felt disposed to request to become Mrs Keeldar, lady of the manor'.[30] When she first meets Caroline Helstone she courts her as a gentleman, presenting her with flowers 'in the attitude and with something of the aspect of a grave but gallant little cavalier'.[31] Lister also saw her relationships through a heterosexual paradigm, believing that 'two Jacks do not go together'.[32] She always characterized herself as male, often fantasizing she had a penis,[33] and even refusing one lover's offer of sexual release on the grounds that 'This is womanizing me too much'.[34] Both Anne Lister and Shirley Keeldar also reject educated or bluestocking women in favour of what they perceive as more feminine companions. Lister states: 'I am not an admirer of learned ladies. They are not the sweet, interesting creatures I should love',[35] while Shirley argues that 'hard labour and learned professions, they say, make women masculine, coarse, unwomanly'.[36] Unsurprisingly, each woman's object of affection is a weaker, more feminine figure.

Both Caroline Helstone and Ann Walker exhibit more fragile personalities than their 'mates'. Crucially it is their acceptance of feminine roles that causes both to suffer physically and mentally. Ann Walker endured for many years what Elizabeth Foyster calls 'the fashionable female afflictions of nervousness and hysteria',[37] which seemed to stem in part at least from her (socially expected) lack of occupation or purpose. As Dr Belcombe suggested to his sister Marianna: 'Is she une malade imaginaire? Because Steph says, in speaking of her to me, "If Miss Walker was poor she would probably not be sick"'.[38] Caroline Helstone also feels her lack of occupation keenly. She frets: 'What was I created for, I wonder? Where is my place in the world?'.[39] But, like Ann Walker, Caroline's class position will not allow her to find purpose through work. Her uncle declares: 'While I live, you shall not turn out as a governess, Caroline. I will not have it said that my niece is a governess'.[40] As an unmarried genteel young woman Caroline is condemned to a life of enforced idleness. Caroline is disturbed by her lack of economic independence, as her conversation with Robert reveals:

'I am making no money–earning nothing.'
'You come to the point, Lina; you too, then, wish to make money?'
'I do: I should like an occupation; and if I were a boy, it would not be so difficult to find one. I see such an easy, pleasant way of learning a business, and making my way in life.'[41]

Just as Walker repeatedly suffered from melancholy, so Caroline's depression at her situation precipitates a life-threatening illness in *Shirley*: 'Winter seemed conquering her spring: the mind's soil and its treasures were freezing gradually to barren stagnation'.[42] But importantly, while Charlotte associates Caroline's malaise with sterility, she does not see its cure in heterosexual relations.

The problem of lack of occupation for middle and upper-class single women in Victorian society, what Charlotte Brontë calls 'the question which most old maids are puzzled to solve',[43] is one of the central issues of *Shirley*. In Chapter 10, entitled 'Old Maids', Caroline visits Miss Mann and Miss Ainley determined to discover what role these spinsters have carved for themselves. But even the most positive model, Miss Ainley, lives a life of stultifying self-sacrifice, prompting Caroline to ask: 'Is this enough? Is it to live? Is there not a terrible hollowness, mockery, want, craving, in that existence which is given away to others, for want of something of your own to bestow it on? I suspect there is. Does virtue lie in abnegation of the self?'[44] Significantly, Charlotte makes a plea to fathers to educate their daughters: 'Keep your girls' minds narrow and fettered—they will still be a plague and a care, sometimes a disgrace to you: cultivate them—give them scope and work—they will be your gayest companions in health; your tenderest nurses in sickness; your most faithful prop in age'.[45] Ann Walker's lack of intellectual resources certainly seems to have contributed to her depression, causing Anne Lister to encourage her to adopt a daily regime of French, drawing and reading.[46] But Charlotte does not see the solution to the problem of single women lying solely in education; she also promotes female relationships.

Charlotte Brontë suggests for much of *Shirley* that male–female relationships are unsuccessful and doomed to failure. The book contains repeated warnings and diatribes against marriage.[47] Rather than promoting heterosexuality, Charlotte instead, as Jin-Ok Kim argues, 'comes quite close to suggesting that the relation of women with other women is the most natural one'.[48] While her relationship with Robert Moore brings pain and disappointment, Caroline's relationship with Shirley is a source of pleasure and comfort: 'Love hurts us so, Shirley: it is so tormenting, so racking, and it burns away our strength with its flame; in affection is no pain and no fire, only sustenance and balm. I am supported and soothed when you—that is, *you only*—are near, Shirley'.[49] Caroline points to the unique nature of her relationship with Shirley, as if they and not Caroline and Robert are soul mates. Furthermore, as Anne Lister recognised the marriage of her lover, Marianna Lawton, as 'legal prostitution',[50] so Charlotte recognises that many heterosexual marriages are prompted by economic needs rather than feeling or affection: 'what is worst of all, reduced to strive, by scarce modest coquetry and debasing artifice, to gain that position and consideration by marriage, which to celibacy is denied'.[51] In *Shirley* and Anne Lister's world, it seems, true emotional closeness is possible only between women.

Indeed, Charlotte Brontë and Anne Lister repeatedly depict female relations as the most natural. Anne Lister described her attraction to women as 'all nature',[52] while she reported proudly in her diary: 'Speaking of my oddity, Mrs Priestley said she always told people I was natural, but she thought that nature was in an odd freak when she made me'.[53] When Anne's lover Marianna Belcombe objects to their relationship on the grounds of the 'horror she had to anything unnatural',[54] Anne responds by arguing that her 'conduct & feelings being surely natural to me inasmuch as they were not taught, not fictitious, but instinctive'.[55]

Similarly, Caroline and Shirley's relationship is repeatedly associated with nature. When planning a trip alone to Nunnwood, Caroline and Shirley discuss whether to invite any gentlemen. They conclude that in the presence of men:

> 'We forget Nature, imprimis.'
> 'And then Nature forgets us; covers her vast, calm brow with a dim veil, conceals her face, and withdraws the peaceful joy with which, if we had been content to worship her only, she would have filled our hearts.'[56]

In other words, Caroline and Shirley argue that female relationships enjoy an affinity with nature that is impossible in the presence of men. Furthermore, as the nunnery that lies at the bottom of the dell indicates, Charlotte also presents the natural environment of Nunnwood as an exclusively female space. But rather than suggesting celibacy, Nunnwood represents a rejection of heterosexuality, in favour of erotic relations between women. The description of the wood abounds with suggestions of female sexuality and fertility, which offer a direct antidote to the 'barren stagnation' of Caroline's depression.[57] As Caroline tells Shirley:

> 'That break is a dell; a deep, hollow cup, lined with turf as green and short as the sod of this Common [. . .] I know where the wild strawberries abound; I know certain lonely, quite untrodden glades, carpeted with strange mosses [. . .] Miss Keeldar, I could guide you'.[58]

Not only are female relationships associated with nature in *Shirley* therefore, there is also a suggestion that these relationships are—paradoxically—more 'fertile' than heterosexual ones.

Besides their adoption of masculine personas, and their wooing of a more feminine, fragile partner, both Lister and Shirley reinterpret masculine

texts, as they attempt to revise patriarchal discourse. Shirley challenges male
narratives, and especially male depictions of women:

> If men could see us as we really are, they would be a little amazed;
> but the cleverest, the acutest men are often under an illusion about
> women: they do not read them in a true light: they misapprehend
> them, both for good and evil: their good woman is a queer thing,
> half doll, half angel; their bad woman almost always a fiend. Then
> to hear them fall into ecstasies with each other's creations, wor-
> shipping the heroine of such a poem — novel — drama, think-
> ing it fine — divine! Fine and divine it may be, but often quite
> artificial — false as the rose in my best bonnet there. If I spoke
> all I think on this point; if I gave my real opinion of some first-
> rate female characters in first rate works, where should I be? Dead
> under a cairn of avenging stones in half an hour.[59]

Shirley rejects the virgin/whore dichotomy that dominates masculine depictions, and argues that no male text can accurately represent women. Lister
was similarly attuned to depictions of women, and she read voraciously,
hunting for any signs of lesbian desire. But as Shirley finds male depictions of women to be inaccurate, so Lister had difficulty recognising herself
in male texts. As Anna Clark writes: 'References to lesbianism were few,
oblique, and usually scornful. Anne therefore had to summon all her considerable scholarly and monetary resources to track down rare editions and read
in French and Latin to find any references to sexuality between women'.[60]
Woman, as recognised by Shirley and Anne Lister, is left unspoken in male-
authored texts.

Sometimes Lister would rework heterosexual relationships, as Lisa
Moore writes: 'Lister (who also crossdressed) skilfully pillages the male-
authored texts available to her in order to authorise her desires, transforming
these masculine accoutrements into something else altogether: the conditions
of production of female homosexual character'.[61] Just as Judith Butler argues
subversion of culturally imposed identities is possible only 'within the terms
of the law',[62] so Lister constructs her lesbian identity from existing masculine
texts. Shirley also attempts such subversion by rewriting male narratives. She
rejects 'Milton's Eve',[63] claiming it 'was his cook that he saw, or it was Mrs
Gill, as I have seen her, making custards'.[64] Instead, Shirley conceives Eve as a
woman whose 'daring could contend with Omnipotence'.[65] Her Eve is a pagan
Eve, 'a woman-Titan'.[66] However, as Anne Lister's construction of her lesbian
identity remains 'within the terms of the law', so Shirley is ultimately unable to
escape patriarchal narratives entirely, and must also be content to rewrite them,
rather than invent fresh narratives.

§

The connections between the story of Anne Lister and Charlotte Brontë's novel *Shirley* are startling. But what are we to do with them? The Brontës have long suffered from a surfeit of biographical criticism. As Pauline Nestor wrote of Charlotte: 'Influential critics such as Leslie Stephens in the 1880s, and Lord David Cecil in the 1930s have used a simple conflation of the life and literature to denigrate Brontë's work as involuntary self-revelation'.[67] The danger of invoking the story of Anne Lister in our interpretation of *Shirley* is that we once more prioritise biography in our reading of a Brontë text. But rather than promoting a crude cause and effect relation between Anne Lister's diary and Charlotte Brontë's novel, it may be more appropriate to read Anne Lister's journals as an intertext.

No text is a self-contained structure and no text is read in isolation. Instead there is, as Jonathan Culler puts it, always a 'general discursive space that makes a text intelligible'.[68] Lister's diary has become part of the general discursive space that makes *Shirley* intelligible. Reading *Shirley* intertextually alongside Lister's diaries allows us to open up Charlotte's novel to interpretations that previously may have been considered historically anachronistic. Lister's diary has been called 'the Rosetta stone' of lesbianism, because, crucially, it contradicts the claims of commentators such as Lillian Faderman, who argue that relationships between women were 'non-genital' before the twentieth century.[69] Similarly, Lister's diaries put pressure on Foucault's postulation that homosexual identity was not forged until it was defined by the medical establishment. While Anne Lister did not identify herself as a 'lesbian', of course, she did construct a self identity based on her romantic and sexual attraction to women. The very existence of the Lister diaries, therefore, allows us to read Shirley and Caroline's relationship as more than a 'romantic friendship' of the kind identified by Lillian Faderman.

Furthermore, reading Lister's diaries intertextually alongside *Shirley* also brings up very specific points of interpretation or contention. Sarah Waters frequently plays upon the meanings of the word 'queer' in her Victorian lesbian pastiche novels, *Tipping the Velvet* (1998), *Affinity* (1999) and *Fingersmith* (2002). When her lesbian heroines describe themselves as 'queer', Waters invokes both our contemporary understanding of the word 'queer' as homosexual, and our awareness that this interpretation is 'out of place' in a supposedly Victorian text. The word itself is common in Victorian fiction, but an interpretation consistent with nineteenth century usage would be something like the *Oxford English Dictionary* definition: 'Strange, odd, peculiar, eccentric, in appearance or character.' And despite post-structuralist arguments that all the semantic 'traces' of a word have an impact on our understanding of a text, be they historically consistent with the date of the text's production or not, critics have traditionally resisted imposing any sexual interpretation on nineteenth century usages of 'queer'. This reluctance is despite instances in which our contemporary understanding of 'queer' would make contextual sense. For example, when Caroline muses on the problems of unmarried women in *Shirley*, she says: 'Queer thoughts these, that surge my mind: are they right thoughts?'.[70] Of her relationship with Shirley, she states: '"Shirley, you are a real enigma", whispered Caroline in her ear. "What queer discoveries I make day by day now!"'.[71] In a Sarah Waters' novel we would recognise a knowing wink behind these uses of 'queer', but in Charlotte Brontë's fiction, we do not usually permit ourselves that interpretation. How then are we to figure Anne Lister's use of 'queer' in our interpretation of Charlotte's novel?

'Queer' had a very specific sexual meaning for Anne Lister; she uses the word to refer to the pudenda. She writes, for example: 'Marianna put me on a new watch riband & then cut the hair from her own queer & I that from mine, which put each into little lockets we got at Bright's this morning, twelve shillings each, for us always to wear under our clothes in mutual remembrance'.[72] Anne Lister's use of the word 'queer' in this way is apparently the only known instance, though Helen Whitbread speculates that it may be a corruption of quim or queme.[73] While it may be reckless to suggest that Anne Lister's usage of 'queer' allows us to read the word as sexual in *Shirley*, Lister's employment of the word does force us to consider why two female writers of the same period would adopt this word to refer implicitly and explicitly to female sexuality. The *Oxford English Dictionary* definition is useful here, because, of course, female sexuality was regarded as 'strange, odd, peculiar, [and] eccentric' at least in public discourse in the mid-nineteenth century. An intertextual reading of *Shirley* alongside Lister's diaries can thus bring the nuances of Charlotte's text into focus.

But there are also some key differences between *Shirley* and Lister's diary. While Charlotte's novel was written as a commercial, public text, Lister's diary is a private document, with a very small intended audience. As Danielle Orr reminds us: 'Our theorizing of these diaries and journals entails an interference into the text, that was most likely not envisioned by these women in the act of writing'.[74] Journal writing is often interpreted as a means of making the self, and Lister's diary has been cited as extremely important in this regard as she forges a prototypical lesbian identity for herself. Critics and historians have also interpreted journal writing as a feminine endeavour, not least because it belongs to the private sphere. In contrast, Charlotte's novel *Shirley* does not only belong to the public sphere, but Charlotte deliberately attempted to adopt a more masculine discourse in this novel. As she wrote to her publisher, James Taylor, shortly after its publication: 'I imagined, mistakenly it now appears, that "Shirley" bore fewer traces of the female hand than "Jane Eyre"'.[75] She abandoned the first person confessional narrative — a style closer to Lister's journal, of course — for the omniscient third person narrative familiar from the works of Charles Dickens and William Makepeace Thackeray. In other words, as Shirley adopts a kind of transvestism to bolster her power, so Charlotte attempts a kind of literary transvestism in this novel in an attempt to bolster her literary reputation. But as Shirley and Lister's failure to move beyond a patriarchal paradigm shows ultimately the limits of their reimagining of the role of women, so Charlotte Brontë's adoption of a masculine discourse ultimately results in the re-enforcement of patriarchal norms. Indeed, it is precisely because Charlotte's text was written for the public sphere that the resolution Anne Lister was able to achieve in her private sphere proved impossible; what Anne Lister's private discourse permitted was literally 'unsayable' in mid-nineteenth century public discourse. Indeed, lesbianism was even outside that most public of discourse in Britain, the law, which criminalised male homosexuality, but remained tellingly silent on the subject of female homosexuality.

So should Anne Lister and her diary be more than a footnote in any reading of *Shirley*? The thematic similarities between Charlotte's novel and Lister's life are remarkable and these should be recorded. This article attempts to rectify this oversight. However, I am not suggesting a simple cause and effect between Lister's life and *Shirley*. Rather, I argue the real significance of the Lister diaries lies in their role as intertexts. These diaries permit us to alter our contemporary conception of the general discursive space that engendered *Shirley*. In this way, Lister's text allows a more explicitly sexual interpretation of female relationships in Bronte's novel than critics could previously have considered. As such, the Lister diaries are more than a footnote, and have a material impact on our understanding of *Shirley*.

Notes

1. Michel Foucault, *The History of Sexuality, Volume 1: An Introduction* (New York: Vintage, 1990), p. 43.

2. Nancy Quick Langer, '"There is no such Ladies Now-a-Days": Capsizing "the Patriarch Bull" in Charlotte Brontë's "Shirley"', *Journal of Narrative Technique*, 27.3 (1997), 276–296, p. 283.

3. Elizabeth Gaskell, *The Life of Charlotte Brontë* (London: J. M. Dent, 1971), p. 96.

4. Juliet Barker, *The Brontës* (London: Phoenix, 1994), p. 306.

5. *The Oxford Companion to the Brontës*, ed. by Christine Alexander and Margaret Smith (Oxford University Press, 2003), p. 291.

6. Jill Liddington, 'Anne Lister and Emily Brontë 1838–39: Landscape with Figures', *Brontë Society Transactions*, 26.1 (2001), 46–67, p. 46.

7. Liddington, 'Anne Lister and Emily Brontë 1838–39', p. 54.

8. Edward Chitham, *A Life of Emily Brontë* (Oxford: Basil Blackwell, 1987), p. 120.

9. Liddington, 'Anne Lister and Emily Brontë 1838–39', p. 54.

10. Liddington, 'Anne Lister and Emily Brontë 1838–39', p. 54.

11. Elliott Vanskike, 'Consistent Inconsistencies: The Transvestite Actress Madame Vestris and Charlotte Brontë's *Shirley*', *Nineteenth Century Literature (NCF)*, 50.4 (1996), 464–488, p. 468.

12. Chitham, *Life*, p. 104.

13. Phyllis Bentley, *The Brontës and their World* (London: Thames & Hudson, 1969), p. 54.

14. Liddington, 'Anne Lister and Emily Brontë 1838–39', p. 53.

15. Edward Chitham, *The Birth of Wuthering Heights: Emily Brontë at Work* (Basingstoke: MacMillan, 1998), p. 188.

16. Liddington, 'Anne Lister and Emily Brontë 1838–39', p. 59.

17. Anna Clark, 'Anne Lister's Construction of Lesbian Identity', *Journal of the History of Sexuality*, 7.1 (1996), 23–50, p. 42.

18. Clark, p. 47.

19. Anne Lister and Helena Whitbread, *I Know My Own Heart: The Diaries of Anne Lister, 1791–1840* (New York: New York University Press, 1992), p. 106.

20. Jill Liddington, 'Gender, Authority and Mining in an Industrial Landscape: Anne Lister 1791–1840', *History Workshop Journal*, 42 (1996), 59–86, p. 73.

21. Liddington, 'Anne Lister and Emily Brontë 1838–39', p. 62.

22. Charlotte Brontë quoted in Elaine Miller, 'Through all Changes and through all Chances: The Relationship of Ellen Nussey and Charlotte Brontë', in *Not a Passing Phase: Reclaiming Lesbians in History 1840–1985*, ed. By Lesbian History Group (London: The Women's Press, 1989), pp. 29–54, p. 36.

23. Charlotte Brontë, *Shirley* (London: Penguin, 1974), p. 213.

24. Jill Liddington, 'Gender, Authority and Mining in an Industrial Landscape: Anne Lister 1791–1840', *History Workshop Journal*, 42 (1996), 59–86, p. 82.

25. Brontë, *Shirley*, p. 208.

26. Brontë, *Shirley*, p. 211.

27. Anne Lister and Jill Liddington, *Female Fortune: Land, Gender, and Authority: The Anne Lister Diaries and Other Writings, 1833–36* (London: Rivers Oram Press, 1998), p. 19.

28. Brontë, *Shirley*, p. 326.

29. Anne Lister, *No Priest but Love: Excerpts from the Diaries of Anne Lister, 1824–1826* (Washington Square, N.Y.: New York University Press, 1992), p. 127.

30. Brontë, *Shirley*, p. 217.

31. Brontë, *Shirley*, p. 212.

32. Lister, *No Priest But Love*, p. 127.

33. Lister, *No Priest But Love*, pp. 42, 153.

34. Lister, *No Priest But Love*, p. 85.

35. Lister, *I Know My Own Heart*, p. 237.

36. Brontë, *Shirley*, p. 235.

37. Elizabeth Foyster, 'Recovering Lives from behind the Gloss of Ideology: Recent Histories of Elite and Middle-Class Women in England and America', *Gender and History*, 12.1 (2000), 237–242, p. 239.

38. Liddington, *Female Fortune*, p. 99.

39. Brontë, *Shirley*, p. 190.

40. Brontë, *Shirley*, p. 204.

41. Brontë, *Shirley*, p. 98.

42. Brontë, *Shirley*, p. 199.

43. Brontë, *Shirley*, p. 190.

44. Brontë, *Shirley*, p. 190.

45. Brontë, *Shirley*, p. 379.

46. Liddington, *Female Fortune*, p. 88.

47. Brontë, *Shirley*, pp. 124, 223, 224.

48. Jin Ok Kim, *Charlotte Brontë and Female Desire* (New York, NY: Peter Lang, 2003), p. 71.

49. Brontë, *Shirley*, p. 265.

50. Lister, *I Know My Own Heart*, p. 104.

51. Brontë, *Shirley*, p. 378.

52. Lister, *No Priest But Love*, p. 49.

53. Lister, *I Know My Own Heart*, p. 347.

54. Lister, *I Know My Own Heart*, p. 297.

55. Lister, *I Know My Own Heart*, p. 297.

56. Brontë, *Shirley*, p. 222.

57. Brontë, *Shirley*, p. 199.

58. Brontë, *Shirley*, p. 221.

59. Brontë, *Shirley*, p. 343.

60. Clark, p. 32.

61. Lisa Moore, '"Something More Tender Still than Friendship": Romantic Friendship in Early-Nineteenth-Century England', *Feminist Studies*, 18.3 (1992), 499–520.

62. Judith Butler, *Gender Trouble* (New York: Routledge, 1999), p. 119.

63. Brontë, *Shirley*, p. 314.

64. Brontë, *Shirley*, p. 315.

65. Brontë, *Shirley*, p. 315.

66. Brontë, *Shirley*, p. 315.

67. *New Casebooks: Villette*, ed. by Pauline Nestor (Basingstoke: MacMillan, 1992), p. 2.

68. Jonathan Culler, *On Deconstruction: Theory and Criticism after Structuralism* (London: Routledge, 1983), p. 106.

69. Lillian Faderman, *Surpassing the Love of Men* (London: The Women's Press, 1985).

70. Brontë, *Shirley*, p. 190.

71. Brontë, *Shirley*, p. 437.

72. Lister, *No Priest But Love*, p. 131.

73. Lister, *No Priest But Love*, p. 55, n.1.

74. Dannielle Orr, '"I Tell Myself to Myself": Homosexual Agency in the Journals of Anne Lister (1791–1840)', *Women's Writing*, 11.2 (2004), pp. 201–222 (p. 203).

75. Charlotte Brontë quoted in Tim Dolin, 'Fictional Territory and a Woman's Place: Regional and Sexual Difference in "Shirley"', *ELH: Journal of English Literary History*, 62.1 (1995), 197–215, p. 201.

PATSY STONEMAN

"Addresses from the Land of the Dead": Emily Brontë and Shelley

'We have seen that [Emily] and Anne read "Epipsychidion", in which the surprising addresses to "Emily" refer to Aemilia Viviani. To Emily Brontë, they may have sounded like direct addresses from the land of the dead.'
(Edward Chitham, *A Life of Emily Brontë*, pp. 133–134)

Emily Brontë's writing suggests that Percy Bysshe Shelley had a wide-ranging influence on her ideas. His atheist attacks on religion, his political attacks on aristocratic privilege and his condemnation of war-mongering are likely to have intrigued a young woman who lived a secluded life in practical terms, but imaginatively engaged on a daily basis with monarchs and republican rebels. Shelley's life-story alone must have been exhilarating. This essay sketches an outline of Shelley's life, suggests how Emily Brontë may have come to know it and his writings, and briefly outlines what previous critics have made of the connection between the two writers. Its focus, however, is an aspect of Shelley's life and writing which I believe had a central influence on *Wuthering Heights*, although it has been consistently overlooked by readers: his views on free love.[1]

The outline of Shelley's life is well-known—he was a rebel in terms of religion, class politics, and the convention of marriage. Born into the rural gentry in Sussex, Percy Bysshe Shelley was the eldest of six children and became a kind of wild hero to his four younger sisters, whom he enthralled

Brontë Studies, Volume 31, Number 2 (July 2006): pp. 121–131. © The Brontë Society 2006.

and terrified with gothic stories and scientific experiments. At Eton School, he learned to hate authority and he was expelled from Oxford for atheism.

At the age of 19 he eloped with, and married, Harriet Westbrook (who was only 16), and they went immediately to Ireland (with Harriet's sister, Eliza) to incite the Irish to revolt against English oppression. At 21 (in 1813) he wrote *Queen Mab*, a long poem opposing conventional religion and social tyranny. In 1814, having tired of Harriet, he eloped with another sixteen-year-old, Mary Wollstonecraft Godwin, the daughter of the radical philosopher William Godwin and the feminist Mary Wollstonecraft. Mary's step-sister, Claire Clairmont, who was also 16, went with them to the continent, where they met and lived close to Byron. In 1816, Shelley wrote his long poem, *Alastor*, about a poet who dies in pursuit of an ideal woman. In the same year, back in London, Harriet Shelley committed suicide and Mary became Mary Shelley. During this time, Mary was working on her novel *Frankenstein*, which contains a scarcely concealed criticism of Shelley's early obsessions with electrical experiments, ghosts, charnel houses and the pursuit of extremes; it was published in 1818.

In 1817, however, Percy Shelley published another long political work, originally entitled *Laon and Cythna*, in which the hero and heroine of the title are both lovers and brother and sister. They are also revolutionary leaders and, interestingly for the Emily Brontë connection, it is Cythna, the sister, who takes the revolutionary initiatives, inciting the women in particular to revolt, and advocating free love. It is also Cythna who arrives on her huge black stallion in the nick of time to rescue Laon from execution. In the event, the publisher took fright at the subject matter, and Shelley had to remove the incestuous relationship, together with explicit references to atheism and republicanism, before the poem was published as *The Revolt of Islam*.

1819 was a productive year for Shelley; he wrote *The Mask of Anarchy*, a vitriolic attack on the repressive British government which had massacred innocent people at Peterloo; he wrote a long verse-drama, *Prometheus Unbound*, foretelling the liberation of the human race from tyranny; and he wrote his *Ode to the West Wind*.

By 1821, the Shelleys were living in Pisa, where Shelley became obsessed with Emilia Viviani, a young Italian woman (19 years old) who was confined in a convent while her father found her a suitable husband. Shelley addressed to her a long poem called *Epipsychidion* — which seems to mean 'a song to the soul outside the soul' — in which he declares that they are like twin souls and invites her to come away with him. This is the poem which has most obvious parallels with *Wuthering Heights*, and I shall come back to this poem later. *Epipsychidion* had no practical outcome — Emilia's father found her a husband and, by 1822, the Shelleys had moved again, this time to Lerici, on the Italian coast, where he was drowned at sea, just short of his thirtieth birthday.

It is difficult nowadays fully to comprehend how shockingly unorthodox Shelley was in his own time, both in his life and in his writing. He professed atheism, he advocated revolution (though not violence) and he not only lived openly with a woman who was not his wife, but also surrounded himself with other young women with whom he was emotionally, and sometimes sexually, involved. His biographer, Richard Holmes, writes that

> At the time of his death his reputation was almost literally unspeakable in England, [. . .] In this he was quite unlike his aristocratic friend and rival Lord Byron [. . .] [W]hile exile had brought Byron fame and the kind of notoriety that is quickly transmuted into fashionable glamour, it brought to Shelley both literary obscurity and personal disrepute. (p. xiv)

Because of Shelley's bad reputation, his friends and relatives at first thought it useless to try to vindicate him, and so kept silent. In later Victorian times, they conspired to produce a sentimentalised figure of 'the gentle, suffering lyric poet' (p. xv) at the expense of the energetic rebel. For similar reasons, Holmes writes, 'there is virtually no literary criticism or critical commentary which is worth reading before 1945' (p. xvi).

This obscurity may explain why scholars were slow to make connections between Shelley and the Brontës. Mrs Chadwick, writing in 1914, did note parallels between *Wuthering Heights* and *Epipsychidion* (p. 340), but the first critics to seriously consider such ideas were John Hewish in 1969 and Winifred Gérin in 1971. Neither of them, however, devotes more than a few pages to this link. The writer who has made most of the Shelley–Brontë connection is Edward Chitham, first in an article in *Brontë Society Transactions* (1978), then in his book, co-authored with Tom Winnifrith, *Brontë Facts and Brontë Problems* (1983), and finally in his biography of Emily Brontë, published in 1987.

Once commentators started looking for the connection between Shelley and the Brontës, it was clearly there to find. There is no doubt that the Brontës had access to Shelley's writing; the only problem is in determining just how early they might have come across him. Chitham argues that Emily and Anne could have been reading Shelley in their early teens (in the early 1830s); it is certain, however, that all the sisters were familiar with his writing by 1838, when Emily was 19 or 20.

It was through Byron that the Brontës came to know Shelley. Between 1830 and 1839, the Irish poet Tom Moore published three different collections of *Byron's Letters, Journals, Works and Life*, although there is no way of knowing which version the Brontës had access to. Because Byron had lived in close proximity with the Shelleys, and was father to Claire Clairmont's child, his letters and journals include much of the Shelley story, and the 1839 edition included an engraved portrait of Shelley by Aemilia Curran. From 1833 onwards, fragments of Shelley's poetry also began to be published and, in 1838, there was a long article on Shelley, including extracts from his work, in *Fraser's Magazine*, to which the Brontës had access. In 1839, Mary Shelley published her edition of Shelley's poems, and it seems certain that the Brontës knew this. Both Hewish and Chitham offer detailed analyses of Emily's poetry from the 1840s showing Shelleyan echoes.

Whether Emily Brontë encountered Shelley in her early teens, as Chitham claims, or whether it was later, the story of Shelley's life and death was recent enough to make a personal impression on her. Although she was only four when Shelley died, his death fixed him forever as a figure of youth. In addition, many of the key events in Shelley's life happened when he and the women he loved were near to Emily's age when she read about him — Shelley was 19 when he eloped with Harriet and she was 16; Mary was also 16 at the time of her elopement, and so was her sister Claire; Emilia Viviani was 19 when Shelley wrote *Epipsychidion* for her. The excitement of these events was, however, crucially reinforced for Emily by the attraction of his ideas and images — his hatred of tyrants and prisons, his impatience with forms and conventions, his love of the imagination and his pursuit of extremes of experience.

Because the area of 'influence' is so wide, different critics have picked up different likenesses between the two writers. Three themes in particular have been noticed: religious scepticism; political revolt; and a Romantic desire for a blending of identities which has come to be called the 'twin-soul' idea. Chitham argues for the atheist influence (1978, p. 195) and both John Hewish and Stevie Davies point out the Shelleyan echoes of one of Emily's last poems, 'Why ask to know the date, the clime?', which combines religious and political scepticism in its bitter message. In this essay, however, I want to focus not on the religious or political relationship between Emily Brontë and Shelley, but on their ideas of Romantic love, and in particular on the relationship between *Wuthering Heights* and Shelley's poem, *Epipsychidion*.

By far the most widely recognised link between Shelley and Emily Brontë has been in the area where human emotion passes into metaphysics — a sense of 'oneness' with something outside the self. Sometimes this takes the form of a union with nature, sometimes with another person. Hewish compares Emily's poem, 'Aye, there it is!' with Shelley's *Ode to the West Wind*, in which the poet implores the wind:

> . . . Be thou, Spirit fierce,
> My spirit! Be thou me, impetuous one!

> Drive my dead thoughts over the universe
> Like withered leaves to quicken a new birth!
> (Shelley, Ode to the West Wind, lines 61–64)

Emily Brontë seems more confident of the wind's omnipresence:

> And thou art now a spirit pouring
> Thy presence into all—
> The essence of the Tempest's roaring
> And of the Tempest's fall—
>
> A universal influence
> From Thine own influence free;
> A principle of life, intense,
> Lost to mortality.
> (from Aye, there it is!: Hatfield No. 148)

In *Epipsychidion*, however, Shelley speaks of the union of two human souls, writing to his beloved:

> How beyond refuge I am thine. Ah me!
> I am not thine: I am a part of *thee*.
> (Epipsychidion, lines 51–52)

and Mrs Chadwick was the first of several critics to set these lines against Catherine's words in *Wuthering Heights*: 'I *am* Heathcliff' and 'He's more myself than I am' (Chadwick p. 340). Mary Visick, in her book, *The Genesis of 'Wuthering Heights'*, does not mention Shelley, but she does combine the ideas of oneness with a universal spirit, and of oneness with another human being, by reading *Wuthering Heights* in terms of Emily's poem, 'No Coward Soul is Mine'. Because the poem refers to a spirit of life in terms so similar to those in which Catherine refers to Heathcliff, Visick argues that the relationship between Catherine and Heathcliff should be read as a metaphor for 'a communion of the individual being with vitality itself' (Visick p. 41).

Visick begins by quoting 'No Coward Soul is Mine':

> O God within my breast
> Almighty ever-present Deity
> Life, that in me hast rest
> As I Undying Life, have power in Thee [. . .]
>
> Though Earth and moon were gone
> And suns and universes ceased to be

And thou wert left alone
Every Existence would exist in thee [. . .]
   'No Coward Soul is Mine' (1846)

                  (Hatfield No. 191)

She sets this against the famous passage from Chapter 9 of *Wuthering Heights*, where Catherine makes a kind of manifesto declaration of her love:

> 'I cannot express it; but surely you and everybody have a notion that there is or should be an existence of yours beyond you. What were the use of my creation, if I were entirely contained here? My great miseries in the world have been Heathcliff's miseries, and I watched and felt each from the beginning: my great thought in living is himself. If all else perished and *he* remained, I should still continue to be; and if all else remained, and he were annihilated, the universe would turn to a mighty stranger: I should not seem a part of it. My love for Linton is like the foliage in the woods. Time will change, it, I'm well aware, as winter changes the trees — my love for Heathcliff resembles the eternal rocks beneath — a source of little visible delight, but necessary. Nelly, I *am* Heathcliff! He's always, always in my mind: not as a pleasure, any more than I am always a pleasure to myself, but as my own being.' (Chapter 9, Oxford World's Classics edition, pp. 81–2)

Visick argues that by comparing this passage with the poem, 'we see what *Wuthering Heights* is "about". Catherine betrays what amounts to a mystical vocation, for social position and romantic love' (p. 9).

This statement is of great importance in relation to Shelley since Shelley also deals in both 'mystical vocations' (for instance, in *Alastor*, where the hero dies in unfulfilled pursuit of an ideal beauty), and in 'romantic love' (as in *Epipsychidion*, where Emilia Viviani is entreated to join him in an idyllic escape). The concept of 'romantic love', however, needs clarification. When Visick links 'social position' with 'romantic love', it becomes clear that what she means by 'romantic love' is the process of love and courtship which leads to marriage, which corresponds to Catherine's relationship with Edgar rather than that with Heathcliff. If we put the word 'romantic' in the context of the Romantic movement, however — Romantic with a capital R — we find that the Romantic poets were very likely to fall in love not with marriageable partners, with whom they could settle down and have a family, but with figures outside normal social structures, sometimes seen as images of beauty or the imagination (as in Shelley's *Alastor*) and sometimes seen as sisters (as in Shelley's *Laon and Cythna*).

In psychoanalytic terms, this kind of Romantic love is very different from the romantic love which provides the plot of Mills and Boon fiction — or, for that matter, *Jane Eyre*. Romantic love with a capital R is by its nature tragic; it is characteristic, therefore, that Emilia Viviani is locked up in a convent, and more like a dream lover than a real woman. Psychoanalysts tell us that this kind of love is not really a relationship with another mature individual, but rather an attempt to recreate the security of childhood, in which the gaze of a mother or a sibling reflects back one's own sense of existence and importance. It is thus interesting that Shelley's childhood was spent in the company of four adoring younger sisters, and that both his marriages included his wives' sisters, as well as other women whom he described as 'sisters of his soul'. In *Wuthering Heights*, Catherine and Heathcliff, we remember, are also brought up as brother and sister.

Shelley, writing to Emilia Viviani, wishes,

> Would we two had been twins of the same mother! (line 45)

and the image of two identical persons gazing at each other is reminiscent of the myth of Narcissus, who died for love of his own image in a pool. Typically, this regressive form of Romantic love does not look forward to social integration but imagines escape from ordinary life, or sometimes from life altogether — Shelley's Laon and Cythna, for instance, die together and are reunited in a kind of visionary heaven.

Shelley's *Epipsychidion* is undoubtedly the most famous and extravagant expression of this kind of love. His appeal to his beloved is couched in terms of the most idyllic escape:

> Emily,
> A ship is floating in the harbour now,
> A wind is hovering o'er the mountain's brow;
> There is a path on the sea's azure floor,
> No keel has ever ploughed that path before;
> The halcyons brood over the foamless isles;
> The treacherous Ocean has forsworn its wiles;
> The merry mariners are bold and free:
> Say, my heart's sister, wilt thou sail with me? (lines 407–415)

His concept of 'oneness' is so overwhelming that he can hardly contain the emotion it arouses:

We shall become the same, we shall be one . . .
In one another's substance finding food,
Like flames too pure and light and unimbued
To nourish their bright lives with baser prey,
Which point to Heaven and cannot pass away:
One hope within two wills, one will beneath
Two overshadowing minds, one life, one death,
One Heaven, one Hell, one immortality,
And one annihilation. Woe is me!
The winged words on which my soul would pierce
Into the height of Love's rare Universe,
Are chains of lead around its flight of fire —
I pant, I sink, I tremble, I expire!

(Epipsychidion, lines 573–591)

If we go back to that famous passage from Chapter 9 of *Wuthering Heights* (skipping a little), we must see that the similarities are remarkable:

> 'I cannot express it; but surely you and everybody have a notion that there is or should be an existence of yours beyond you. What were the use of my creation, if I were entirely contained here? [. . .] If all else perished and *he* remained, I should still continue to be; and if all else remained, and he were annihilated, the universe would turn to a mighty stranger: I should not seem a part of it. [. . .] Nelly I *am* Heathcliff! He's always, always in my mind: not as a pleasure, any more than I am always a pleasure to myself, but as my own being'.
> (*Wuthering Heights*, Ch. 9, pp. 81–82)

One remarkable thing about Shelley's notion of 'oneness', however, is that despite its extravagant expression, it is not conceived as exclusive. His most impassioned expressions of oneness with Emilia — whom he calls 'Emily' — includes a wish to assimilate her into his existing relation with Mary. The expression is not quite straightforward in this passage but the 'name' which the world will apply to his love for Emily is presumably 'adulterous', and 'the name my heart lent to another' is 'wife':

I never thought before my death to see
Youth's vision thus made perfect. Emily,
I love thee; though the world by no thin name
Will hide that love from its unvalued shame.
Would we two had been twins of the same mother!
Or, that the name my heart lent to another

Could be a sister's bond for her and thee,
Blending two beams of one eternity!
Yet were one lawful and the other true,
These names, though dear, could paint not, as is due
How beyond refuge I am thine. Ah me!
I am not thine: I am a part of *thee*.

(*Epipsychidion*, lines 41–52)

Some critics of *Wuthering Heights* have toyed with the idea that, like Shelley, Catherine Earnshaw hopes to keep both her lovers — one as husband, and one as lover. None of them, however, takes the idea seriously. Arnold Kettle, in his *Introduction to the English Novel*, says that she 'kid[s] herself that she can keep them both' (p. 255). Q. D. Leavis says that Catherine's idea 'that she would be able both to have her cake and eat it [is] a childish fallacy'. Edward Chitham entertains the idea most seriously, saying that 'critics who suppose that Emily allows Cathy to *reject* Edgar in favour of Heathcliff, or vice versa, have not read carefully enough. Cathy intends, in different ways, to love both; perhaps Emily obtained this idea from Shelley' (1987, p. 73). This is, however, all he says; he does not develop the idea.

I want to argue, however, not only that Emily got this idea from Shelley, but that the tension it produces is the governing idea of the novel. I find it remarkable that of all the critics who have noticed that the 'twin-soul' idea in *Epipsychidion* relates closely to *Wuthering Heights*, not one has noticed the relevance of the even more famous passage, from the same poem, which contains Shelley's manifesto of free love:

I never was attached to that great sect,
Whose doctrine is, that each one should select
Out of the crowd a mistress or a friend,
And all the rest, though fair and wise, commend
To cold oblivion, though it is in the code
Of modern morals, and the beaten road
Which those poor slaves with weary footsteps tread,
Who travel to their home among the dead
By the broad highway of the world, and so
With one chained friend, perhaps a jealous foe,
The dreariest and the longest journey go.

True Love in this differs from gold and clay,
That to divide is not to take away.
Love is like understanding, that grows bright,

Gazing on many truths; 'tis like thy light,
Imagination! which from earth and sky,
And from the depths of human fantasy,
As from a thousand prisms and mirrors, fills
The Universe with glorious beams, and kills
Error, the worm, with many a sun-like arrow
Of its reverberated lightning. Narrow
The heart that loves, the brain that contemplates,
The life that wears, the spirit that creates
One object, and one form, and builds thereby
A sepulchre for its eternity.

(*Epipsychidion*, lines 149–173)

The passage is notorious in the context of unconventional sexual experiments. Sue Bridehead quotes lines immediately following these in *Jude the Obscure* (IV v) and E. M. Forster took the phrase, 'the longest journey' as the title of his novel exposing the tragedy of conventional marriage. Critics of Emily Brontë, however, have been very reluctant to notice its relevance to *Wuthering Heights*. Yet, just as Shelley's declaration of oneness with Emily is placed in the context of his existing relationship with Mary, so Catherine's declaration of oneness with Heathcliff is prompted by her decision to marry Edgar. The passage I have already quoted twice, beginning 'I cannot express it', is in fact thoroughly embedded in dialogue exposing the practical difficulties of her intention to keep both her lovers. Immediately before Catherine's declaration of oneness, Nelly tries to alert her to the probable impact of her proposed marriage, first on Heathcliff, and then on Catherine herself:

'As soon as you become Mrs. Linton, he loses friend, and love, and all! Have you considered how you'll bear the separation, and how he'll bear to be quite deserted in the world? Because, Miss Catherine—'

'He quite deserted! We separated!' she exclaimed, with an accent of indignation. 'Who is to separate us, pray? They'll meet the fate of Milo! Not as long as I live, Ellen — for no mortal creature. Every Linton on the face of the earth might melt into nothing, before I could consent to forsake Heathcliff. Oh, that's not what I intend — that's not what I mean! I shouldn't be Mrs. Linton were such a price demanded! He'll be as much to me as he has been all his lifetime. Edgar must shake off his antipathy, and tolerate him, at least. He will when he learns my true feelings towards him.

Nelly, I see now, you think me a selfish wretch, but did it never strike you that if Heathcliff and I married, we should be beggars? Whereas, if I marry Linton, I can aid Heathcliff to rise, and place him out of my brother's power.'

'With your husband's money, Miss Catherine?' I asked. 'You'll find him not so pliable as you calculate upon: and, though I'm hardly a judge, I think that's the worst motive you've given yet for being the wife of young Linton.'

'It is not,' retorted she, 'it is the best! The others were the satisfaction of my whims; and for Edgar's sake, too, to satisfy him. This is for the sake of one who comprehends in his person my feelings to Edgar and myself. I cannot express it; but surely you . . .'

(*Wuthering Heights*, Chapter 9, p. 81)

Catherine's attempt to 'express' her oneness with Heathcliff is thus an effort to assert a Shelleyan notion of identity with the loved one which is somehow outside social conventions. She believes that this relationship is so different from that with Edgar that the two will not interfere with one another. The passage usually quoted ends 'He's always, always in my mind: not as a pleasure, any more than I am always a pleasure to myself, but as my own being'. It is less often noticed that Nelly immediately places this in the social context that Catherine is trying to avoid: 'If I can make any sense of your nonsense, Miss, [. . .] it only goes to convince me that you are ignorant of the duties you undertake in marrying; or else, that you are a wicked, unprincipled girl' (*Wuthering Heights*, Ch. 9, p. 82).

One reason why critics and readers have been reluctant to recognise that Emily Brontë may deliberately have been exploring 'wicked, unprincipled' ideas is that the implications of free love are very different for a woman. Men have always been more 'free' in this respect, and feminists were quick to point out that Shelley's practice of 'free love' left the women holding the babies. For a woman to have more than one lover, however, challenges the normal expectation that a man should be able to identify his offspring with certainty. In *Wuthering Heights*, it is impossible to say whether Catherine has, or intends to have, a sexual relation with Heathcliff. What is certain, however, is that Catherine never achieves the kind of *ménage á trois* which Shelley had with Mary and Claire, because the men would not tolerate it. The reason why Kettle and Leavis call Catherine's idea 'childish' is that it ignores traditional masculine reactions. Women, like Mary and Claire, or Mary and Emilia, may co-operate in shared relationships with their man, but men expect to have exclusive possession of their women.

The contrast between Catherine's expectations and those of her menfolk is sharply exposed in *Wuthering Heights* when Heathcliff returns to find Catherine married to Edgar. Surprisingly, Catherine shows no sense of tragic mistiming; she does not lament, 'too late, too late!' Instead, she is wildly happy, and sets about arranging a tea-party to be shared by both her men. It is the men who refuse to co-operate, and Edgar who states the ultimatum: 'Will you give up Heathcliff hereafter, or will you give up me? It is impossible for you to be *my* friend and *his* at the same time; and I absolutely *require* to know which you choose' (p. 118). A careful reading of the novel from here on shows that Catherine is bewildered by their refusal to share her attention. Even on her deathbed, she insists that 'you and Edgar have broken my heart, Heathcliff! And you both come to bewail the deed to me, as if you were the people to be pitied!' (p. 158).

For a detailed working-out of this reading of the novel, I must refer you to my Introduction to the World's Classics edition of *Wuthering Heights*, or to the more extended version which appeared as an article in *The Review of English Studies*. Briefly, here, let me say that it seems to me to make sense of what happens after Catherine's death. It is puzzling, when you consider, that Catherine's ghost begs to be let in even while Heathcliff begs her to return. What keeps them apart? The answer may be that even after Catherine's death, Heathcliff cannot focus directly on their love for one another, but must convert his grief into revenge against Edgar. If my reading is correct, and Catherine hoped to keep both men in relation to her, the plaint of her ghost, 'Let me in — let me in!' (p. 23) could be a plea to Heathcliff to open his heart simply to love for her, instead of diverting it to revenge. In this reading, the crucial change comes when Heathcliff observes young Catherine and Hareton, who are now the objects of his revenge, and sees not only that they love one another, but that they both look like *his* Catherine, so that his revenge is effectively against her. When he gives up revenge, 'rapture' dispels 'anguish' (p. 331), and it is his 'soul's bliss' which 'kills [his] body' (p. 333).

The last paragraphs of *Wuthering Heights* are notoriously ambiguous, since two different accounts are given of the lovers after death: the shepherd boy sees 'Heathcliff and a woman' (p. 336) walking on the moors, but Lockwood looks at the graveyard and wonders 'how any one could ever imagine unquiet slumbers for the sleepers in that quiet earth' (p. 338). Lockwood's 'sleepers', however, are not exactly the same as the boy's 'walkers', because Lockwood describes three headstones, and we know that Catherine, in the middle, wears a locket in which Nelly had twisted the hair of both Edgar and Heathcliff (p. 168). It has been easy for readers to accept that the two 'walkers' are Shelley's twin souls. What I want to argue is that the three 'sleepers' are the tragic remains of Emily Brontë's experiment in reversing the genders of Shelley's free love.

NOTE

1. The main argument of this essay has already appeared twice in print: in Patsy Stoneman, 'Catherine Earnshaw's Journey to Her Home Among the Dead: Fresh Thoughts on *Wuthering Heights* and "Epipsychidion"', *The Review of English Studies*, New Series, Vol XLVII, No. 188 (1996), pp. 521–533; and in the Introduction by Patsy Stoneman in *Wuthering Heights*, Oxford World's Classics, by Emily Bronte (1998). This material is reproduced here by permission of Oxford University Press.

BIBLIOGRAPHY

Christine Alexander and Jane Sellars. *The Art of the Brontës*, Cambridge University Press, 1995, pp. 386–387 [for EB's drawing of 'The North Wind' (Ianthe from Shelley's 'Queen Mab')].

Emily Brontë, *Wuthering Heights*, (1847) Introduction by Patsy Stoneman. Oxford World's Classics. Oxford University Press, (1995) 1998.

Lord David Cecil, 'Emily Brontë and *Wuthering Heights*', in *Early Victorian Novelists*, London: Constable, 1934, pp. 147–193 ['metaphysical' reading of *Wuthering Heights*—no Shelley references].

Mrs Ellis H Chadwick, *In the Footsteps of the Brontës*. London: Pitman, 1914, p. 340 (for the 'twin soul' theme).

Edward Chitham, 'Emily Brontë and Shelley', *Brontë Society Transactions*, 17 (1978), pp. 189–196.

Edward Chitham, *A Life of Emily Brontë*. Oxford: Basil Blackwell, 1987, pp. 72–73, 98–, 133–134.

Edward Chitham and Tom Winnifrith. *Brontë Facts and Brontë Problems*. London: Macmillan, 1983 (especially Chapter 6, 'Emily Brontë and Shelley').

Stevie Davies, *Emily Brontë: Heretic*, London: The Women's Press, 1994, pp. 194–195, 239–242 (for Shelleyan political radicalism).

Winifred Gérin, *Emily Brontë*, (1971) Oxford University Press, 1978, pp. 153–154 (evidence of EB's knowledge of Shelley and parallels in their writing).

C.W. Hatfield (ed), *The Complete Poems of Emily Jane Brontë*, New York: Columbia University Press, 1941.

John Hewish, *Emily Brontë*, London: Macmillan, 1969 (early references to Shelleyan influence).

Richard Holmes, *Shelley: The Pursuit*, (1974) New York Review Books, 1994 (excellent biography).

Percy Bysshe Shelley, *Selected Poetry and Prose*. Introduction by Bruce Woodcock. Wordsworth Editions, 1994 (other editions available).

Patsy Stoneman, 'Introduction', Emily Brontë, *Wuthering Heights*, Oxford World's Classics. Oxford University Press, 1995 (for parallel with Shelley's 'free love' argument in 'Epipsychidion').

———. 'Catherine Earnshaw's Journey to her Home Among the Dead': Fresh Thoughts on *Wuthering Heights* and 'Epipsychidion'. *Review of English Studies*, New Series

Vol. XLVII, No. 188 (1996), pp. 521–533 (extended version of the theory in the 'Introduction' above).

Mary Visick, *The Genesis of 'Wuthering Heights'*, (1958) Hong Kong University Press, 1967 (for 'metaphysical oneness'—no Shelley references).

Chronology

1812   The Reverend Patrick Brontë marries Maria Branwell.

1814   Maria Brontë, their first child, born.

1815   Elizabeth Brontë born.

1816   Charlotte Brontë born on April 21.

1817   Patrick Branwell Brontë, the only son, born in June.

1818   Emily Jane Brontë born on July 30.

1820   Anne Brontë born on January 17. The Brontë family moves to the parsonage at Haworth, near Bradford, Yorkshire.

1821   Mrs. Brontë dies of cancer in September. Her sister, Elizabeth Branwell, takes charge of the household.

1824   Maria and Elizabeth attend the Clergy Daughters' School at Cowan Bridge. Charlotte follows them in August, and Emily in November.

1825   The two oldest girls, Maria and Elizabeth, contract tuberculosis at school. Maria dies on May 6; Elizabeth dies June 15. Charlotte and Emily are withdrawn from the school on June 1. Charlotte and Emily do not return to school until they are in their teens; in the meantime they are educated at home.

1826   Charlotte and Branwell begin the "Angrian" stories and magazines; Emily and Anne work on the "Gondal" saga.

1831   Charlotte attends Miss Wooler's school. She leaves the school
        seven months later, to tend to her sisters' education. In 1835,
        however, she returns as governess. She is accompanied by Emily.

1835   After three months, Emily leaves Miss Wooler's school because
        of homesickness. Anne arrives in January 1836 and remains until
        December 1837.

1837   In September, Emily becomes a governess at Miss Patchett's
        school, near Halifax.

1838   In May, Charlotte leaves her position at Miss Wooler's school.

1839   Anne becomes governess for the Ingram family at Blake Hall,
        Mirfield. She leaves in December. Charlotte becomes governess
        in the Sidwick family, at Stonegappe Hall, near Skipton. She
        leaves after two months (July).

1840   All three sisters live at Haworth.

1841   Anne becomes governess in the Robinson family, near York.
        Charlotte becomes governess in the White family and moves to
        Upperwood House, Rawdon. She leaves in December. The sisters
        plan to start their own school. The scheme, attempted several
        years later, fails for lack of inquiries.

1842   Charlotte and Emily travel to Brussels to study in the Pensionnat
        Heger.

1843   Branwell joins Anne in York as tutor to the Robinson family.
        Charlotte returns to Brussels and remains until January 1844.

1845   Charlotte discovers Emily's poetry and suggests that a selection
        be published along with the poetry of herself and Anne.

1846   *Poems by Currer, Ellis, and Acton Bell* is published by Aylott
        & Jones. During their lifetimes, all works by the Brontës are
        published under these pseudonyms: Charlotte was Currer Bell;
        Emily was Ellis Bell; Anne was Acton Bell.

1847   *Jane Eyre: An Autobiography* (edited by Currer Bell), *Wuthering
        Heights*, and *Agnes Grey* are published.

1848   Anne's *The Tenant of Wildfell Hall* published by T. C. Newby,
        which tries to sell it to an American publisher as a new book
        by Currer Bell, author of the immensely popular *Jane Eyre*.
        Smith, Elder & Co. requests that Charlotte bring her sisters to
        London to prove that there are three Bells. Charlotte and Anne

visit London. Branwell and Emily die of tuberculosis, he on September 24, she on December 19.

1849   Anne dies of tuberculosis May 28. Charlotte's *Shirley* by Currer Bell published by Smith, Elder & Co. Charlotte meets Thackeray and Harriet Martineau in London.

1850   Charlotte meets G. H. Lewes and Mrs. Gaskell in London. Edits her sisters' work. Smith, Elder & Co. publish a new edition of Wuthering Heights and Agnes Grey, along with some of Anne's and Emily's poetry, and a "Biographical Notice" of her sisters' lives by Charlotte.

1852   The Reverend A. B. Nicholls proposes marriage to Charlotte. Her father objects, and Nicholls is rejected. Eventually, Reverend Brontë yields, and Charlotte marries in June 1854.

1853   Charlotte's *Villette* as Currer Bell published in January.

1855   Charlotte dies of toxemia of pregnancy, March 31.

1857   Charlotte's *The Professor* published posthumously with a preface written by her husband. Mrs. Gaskell's *Life of Charlotte Brontë* published in March.

1860   "Emma," a fragment of a story by Charlotte, published in *The Cornhill Magazine* with an introduction by Thackeray.

1861   The Reverend Patrick Brontë dies.

Contributors

HAROLD BLOOM is Sterling Professor of the Humanities at Yale University. He is the author of 30 books, including *Shelley's Mythmaking* (1959), *The Visionary Company* (1961), *Blake's Apocalypse* (1963), *Yeats* (1970), *A Map of Misreading* (1975), *Kabbalah and Criticism* (1975), *Agon: Toward a Theory of Revisionism* (1982), *The American Religion* (1992), *The Western Canon* (1994), and *Omens of Millennium: The Gnosis of Angels, Dreams, and Resurrection* (1996). *The Anxiety of Influence* (1973) sets forth Professor Bloom's provocative theory of the literary relationships between the great writers and their predecessors. His most recent books include *Shakespeare: The Invention of the Human* (1998), a 1998 National Book Award finalist, *How to Read and Why* (2000), *Genius: A Mosaic of One Hundred Exemplary Creative Minds* (2002), *Hamlet: Poem Unlimited* (2003), *Where Shall Wisdom Be Found?* (2004), and *Jesus and Yahweh: The Names Divine* (2005). In 1999, Professor Bloom received the prestigious American Academy of Arts and Letters Gold Medal for Criticism. He has also received the International Prize of Catalonia, the Alfonso Reyes Prize of Mexico, and the Hans Christian Andersen Bicentennial Prize of Denmark.

HUMPHREY GAWTHROP was a contributor to the journal *Brontë Studies*. He died in 2004.

ALEXANDRA LEACH has written about creation myths in children's books.

ESSAKA JOSHUA is a lecturer at the University of Birmingham, U.K. She has written *Pygmalion and Galatea: The History of a Narrative in English Literature* (2001) and *The Romantics and the May-Day Tradition* (2007).

K. C. BELLIAPPA is professor of English at the University of Mysore in India. He wrote *The Image of India in English Fiction* (1991).

REBECCA FRASER, daughter of Antonia Fraser, is past president of the Brontë Society. In addition to illustrating books by her mother, she has written *The Brontës: Charlotte Brontë and Her Family* (1988) and *A People's History of Britain* (2003).

JAMES REANEY was professor of English at the University of Western Ontario from 1963 until his retirement. A prolific and accomplished poet and playwright, he is a two-time winner of the Governor's Award for Poetry (1949 and 1958) and the Governor's Award for Drama (1962). He is a life member of the League of Canadian Poets.

MEGHAN BULLOCK is a contributor to the journal *Brontë Studies*.

PAUL EDMONDSON is Head of Education at the Shakespeare Birthplace Trust in Stratford-Upon-Avon. He is co-supervisory editor of the Penguin Shakespeare and co-author (with Stanley Wells) of *Shakespeare's Sonnets* (2004). His study of Shakespeare's *Twelfth Night* was published in 2005.

BIRGITTA BERGLUND is a senior lecturer in English literature at Lund University, Sweden. She is a member of the Jane Austen Society, the Dorothy L. Sayers Society, and the Brontë Society.

JOAN BELLAMY taught in the U.K. Open University and prepared many study guides for students, including *Mary Taylor: "Strong-Minded" Woman and Friend of the Brontës* (1997). She retired as reviews editor of *Brontë Studies* in 2005.

SUSAN OSTROV WEISSER is a professor of English at Adelphi University. She is the author of *A Craving Vacancy: Women and Sexual Love in the British Novel, 1740–1880* (1997). Among her edited books are *Women and Romance: A Reader* (2001) and *Charlotte Brontë's* Jane Eyre (2003), which reprints the novel with supplementary material for students.

ANNE LONGMUIR is assistant professor of English at Kansas State University. She has published articles on Don DeLillo and Wilkie Collins.

PATSY STONEMAN is an emeritus reader in English at the University of Hull in East Yorkshire, England. She is the author of *Brontë Transformations: The Cultural Dissemination of 'Jane Eyre' and 'Wuthering Heights'* (1996) and has edited the *Macmillan New Casebook on* Wuthering Heights (1993) and *Palgrave's Reader's Guide to Essential Criticism of* Wuthering Heights (2000). Her Jane Eyre *On Stage, 1848-1898* was published in 2005.

Bibliography

Allott, Miriam, ed. *Charlotte Brontë:* Jane Eyre *and* Villette: *A Casebook.* London: Macmillan, 1973.

———. Wuthering Heights: *A Casebook.* London: Macmillan, 1970.

Anderson, Walter E. "The Lyrical Form of *Wuthering Heights." Toronto University Quarterly* 47 (1977–1978): pp. 112–134.

Barnard, Louise, and Robert Barnard. *A Brontë Encyclopedia.* Malden, MA: Blackwell, 2007.

Barker, Judith R. V. *The Brontës.* London: Weidenfeld & Nicolson, 1994.

Beer, Patricia. *Reader, I Married Him: A Study of the Women Characters of Jane Austen, Charlotte Brontë, Elizabeth Gaskell, and George Eliot.* New York: Harper & Row, 1974.

Benvenuto, Richard. *Emily Brontë.* Boston: Twayne, 1982.

Berg, Maggie. Jane Eyre: *Portrait of a Life.* Boston: Twayne, 1987.

Bloom, Harold, ed. *The Brontës.* New York: Chelsea House, 1987.

———, ed. *Charlotte Brontë's* Jane Eyre. New York: Chelsea House, 1987.

———, ed. *Emily Brontë's* Wuthering Heights. New York: Chelsea House, 1987.

———, ed. *Heathcliff.* New York: Chelsea House, 1993.

Bock, Carol. *Charlotte Brontë and the Storyteller's Audience.* Iowa City: University of Iowa Press, 1992.

Brick, Allen R. "*Wuthering Heights:* Narrators, Audience and Message." *College English* 21 (November 1959): pp. 80–86.

Buckley, Vincent. "Passion and Control in *Wuthering Heights." The Southern Review* I (1964): pp. 5–23.

Burkhart, Charles. *Charlotte Brontë: A Psychosexual Study of Her Novels.* London: Gollancz, 1973.

Chase, Richard. "The Brontës, or, Myth Domesticated." In *Forms of Modern Fiction:*

Essays Collected in Honor of Joseph Warren Beach, edited by William Van O'Connor. Bloomington: Indiana University Press, 1968.

Clayton, Jay. *Romantic Vision and the Novel.* Cambridge: Cambridge University Press, 1987.

Daiches, David. Introduction. In *Wuthering Heights.* London: Penguin, 1965.

Davis, Stevie. *Emily Brontë.* Bloomington: Indiana University Press, 1988.

———. *Emily Brontë, Heretic.* London: Women's Press, 1994.

———. *Emily Brontë: The Artist as a Free Woman.* Manchester, England: Carcanet Press, 1983.

De Grazia, Emilio. "The Ethical Dimension of *Wuthering Heights.*" *Midwest Quarterly* 19 (Winter 1978): pp. 178–195.

DeLamotte, Eugenia C. *Perils of the Night: A Feminist Study of Nineteenth-Century Female Gothic.* New York: Oxford University Press, 1990.

Dingle, Herbert. *The Mind of Emily Brontë.* London: Martin, Brian & O'Keefe, 1974.

Donoghue, Denis. "Emily Brontë: On the Latitude of Interpretation." In *The Interpretation of Narrative: Theory and Practice,* edited by Morton W. Bloomfield. Cambridge, MA: Harvard University Press, 1970.

Dry, Florence Swinton. *The Sources of* Wuthering Heights. Cambridge, England: W. Heffer & Sons, 1937.

Duthie, Enid Lowry. *The Brontës and Nature.* New York: St. Martin's Press, 1986.

Eagleton, Terry. *Myths of Power: A Marxist Study of the Brontës.* Basingstoke, England: Palgrave Macmillan, 2005.

Ewbank, Inga-Stina. *Their Proper Sphere: A Study of the Brontë Sisters as Early-Victorian Female Novelists.* Cambridge, MA: Harvard University Press, 1966.

Frank, Katherine. *A Chainless Soul: A Life of Emily Brontë.* Boston: Houghton Mifflin, 1990.

Fraser, Rebecca. *The Brontës: Charlotte Brontë and Her Family.* New York: Crown, 1988.

Gaskell, Elizabeth. *The Life of Charlotte Brontë.* 1857. Ed. Alan Shelston. Harmondsworth: Penguin, 1975.

Gezari, Janet. *Charlotte Brontë and Defensive Conduct: The Author and the Body at Risk.* Philadelphia: University of Pennsylvania Press, 1992.

Ghnassia, Jill Dix. *Metaphysical Rebellion in the Works of Emily Brontë: A Reinterpretation.* New York: St. Martin's Press, 1994.

Gilbert, Sandra M., and Susan Gubar. *The Madwoman in the Attic: The Woman Writer and the Nineteenth-Century Literary Imagination.* New York: Yale University Press, 1979.

Hinkley, Laura L. *The Brontës: Charlotte and Emily.* New York: Hastings House, 1946.

Homans, Margaret. "Dreaming of Children: Literalization in *Jane Eyre* and *Wuthering Heights.*" In *The Female Gothic,* edited by Judith E. Fleenor, pp. 257–279. Montreal: Eden, 1983.

———. "The Name of the Mother in *Wuthering Heights.*" In *Bearing the Word: Language and Female Experience in Nineteenth-Century Women's Writing,* pp. 68–83. Chicago: University of Chicago Press, 1986.

Imlay, Elizabeth. *Charlotte Brontë and the Mysteries of Love: Myth and Allegory in* Jane Eyre. Brighton, UK: Harvester Wheatsheaf, 1989.

Keefe, Robert. *Charlotte Brontë's World of Death.* Austin: University of Texas Press, 1979.

Krupat, Arnold. "The Strangeness of *Wuthering Heights.*" *Nineteenth-Century Fiction* 25 (December 1970): pp. 269–280.

Kucich, John. *Repression in Victorian Fiction: Charlotte Brontë, George Eliot, and Charles Dickens.* Berkeley: University of California Press, 1988.

Lamonica, Drew. *'We Are Three Sisters': Self and Family in the Writing of the Brontës.* Columbia, MO: University of Missouri Press, 2003.

Leavis, Q. D. "A Fresh Approach to *Wuthering Heights.*" In *Lectures in America,* by F. R. Leavis and Q. D. Leavis. New York: Pantheon, 1969.

Linder, Cynthia. *Romantic Imagery in the Novels of Charlotte Brontë.* New York: Barnes & Noble, 1978.

Mathison, John K. "Nelly Dean and the Power of *Wuthering Heights.*" *Nineteenth-Century Fiction* 11 (September 1956): pp. 106–129.

Matthews, John T. "Framing in *Wuthering Heights.*" *Texas Studies in Literature and Language* 27, no. 1 (March 1981): pp. 25–61.

McCarthy, Terrence. "The Incompetent Narrator of *Wuthering Heights.*" *Modern Language Quarterly* 42, no. 1 (March 1981): pp. 48–64.

McKibben, Robert C. "The Image of the Book in *Wuthering Heights.*" *Nineteenth-Century Fiction* 15 (September 1960): pp. 159–169.

Mitchell, Judith. *The Stone and the Scorpion: The Female Subject of Desire in the Novels of Charlotte Brontë, George Eliot, and Thomas Hardy.* Westport, CT: Greenwood Press, 1994.

Moglen, Helene. *Charlotte Brontë: The Self Conceived.* New York: Norton, 1976.

Moser, Thomas. "What Is the Matter with Emily Jane? Conflicting Impulses in *Wuthering Heights.*" *Nineteenth-Century Fiction* 17 (June 1962): pp. 1–19.

Newman, Beth. "'The Situation of the Looker-On': Gender, Narration, and Gaze in *Wuthering Heights.*" *PMLA* 105 (1990): pp. 1029–1041.

Oates, Joyce Carol. "The Magnanimity of *Wuthering Heights.*" *Critical Inquiry* 9, no. 2 (December 1982): pp. 435–449.

Paglia, Camille. *Sexual Personae: Art and Decadence from Nerfertiti to Emily Dickinson.* New Haven: Yale University Press, 1990.

Parkin-Gounelas, Ruth. *Fictions of the Female Self: Charlotte Brontë, Olive Shreiner, Ketherine Mansfield.* London: Macmillan, 1991.

Pratt, Linda Ray. "'I Shall Be Your Father': Heathcliff's Narrative of Paternity." *Victorians Institute Journal* 20 (1992): pp. 13–38.

Showalter, Elaine. *A Literature of Their Own: British Women Novelists from Brontë to Lessing.* Princeton: Princeton University Press, 1977.

Spark, Muriel, and Derek Stanford. *Emily Brontë: Her Life and Work.* New York: Coward-McCann, 1966.

Stevenson, W. H. "*Wuthering Heights:* The Facts." *Essays in Criticism* 35 (1985): pp. 149–166.

Tanner, Tony. "Passion, Narrative and Identity in *Wuthering Heights* and *Jane Eyre*." In *Teaching the Text*, edited by Susanne Kappeler and Norman Bryson. London: Routledge & Kegan Paul, 1983.

Tayler, Irene. *Holy Ghosts: The Male Muses of Emily and Charlotte Brontë*. New York: Columbia University Press, 1990.

Thomas, Ronald R. *Dreams of Authority: Freud and the Fictions of the Unconscious*. Ithaca, NY: Cornell University Press, 1990.

Thormählen. *The Brontës and Education*. Cambridge, England: Cambridge University Press, 2007.

Torgerson, Beth. *Reading the Brontë Body: Disease, Desire, and the Constraints of Culture*. Basingstoke, England: Palgrave Macmillan, 2005.

Visick, Mary. *The Genesis of* Wuthering Heights. 3rd ed. Gloucester, UK: Ian Hodgkins, 1980.

Wallace, Robert K. *Emily Brontë and Beethoven*. Athens: University of Georgia Press, 1986.

Williams, Meg Harris. *A Strange Way of Killing: The Poetic Structure of* Wuthering Heights. Strathtay, UK: Clunie Press, 1987.

Winnifrith, Tom. *The Brontës*. London: Macmillan, 1977.

———. *The Brontës and Their Background: Romance and Reality*. New York: Barnes & Noble, 1973.

———. *Charlotte and Emily Brontë: Literary Lives*. Basingstoke, UK: Macmillan, 1989.

Young, Arlene. "The Monster Within: The Alien Self in *Jane Eyre* and *Frankenstein*." *Studies in the Novel* 23 (1991): pp. 325–338.

Zare, Bonnie. "*Jane Eyre's* Excruciating Ending." *CLA Journal* 37 (1993): pp. 204–220.

Zonana, Joyce. "The Sultan and the Slave: Feminist Orientalism and the Structures of *Jane Eyre*." *Signs* 18 (1992–1993): pp. 592–617.

Acknowledgments

Gawthrop, Humphrey. "Slavery: *Idée Fixe* of Emily and Charlotte Brontë, *Brontë Studies: The Journal of the Brontë Society,* Volume 28, Number 2 (July 2001): 113–121.

Leach, Alexandra. "'Escaping the body's gaol': The Poetry of Anne Bronte." *Victorian Newsletter,* vol. 101, (22 March 2002): 27–31. © 2002 Ward Hellstrom Publishing.

Joshua, Essaka. "Almost my hope of heaven: Idolatry and Messianic Symbolism in Charlotte Brontë's *Jane Eyre.*" *Philological Quarterly,* Volume 81, Number 1 (Winter 2002): 81–101. © 2002 Philological Quarterly, University of Iowa. Permission granted by the copyright holder.

Belliappa, K. C. "Macauley's 'Imperishable Empire' and 'Nelly, I Am Heathcliff' in Emily Bronte's *Wuthering Heights." Journal of Indian Writing in English,* vol. 30, no. 1 (Winter 2002): 38–41.

The following articles are reprinted by permission of Maney Publishing on behalf of *Brontë Studies: The Journal of the Brontë Society* and the Brontë Society. These articles can be found at *http://www.ingentaconnect.com/content/maney/bst* or *www.maney.co.uk/journals/bronte.*

Fraser, Rebecca. "Monsieur Heger: Critic or Catalyst in the Life of Charlotte Brontë?" *Brontë Studies: The Journal of the Brontë Society,* Volume 28, Number 3 (November 2003): 185–194.

Reaney, James. "The Brontës: Gothic Transgressor as Cattle Drover." *Brontë Studies: The Journal of the Brontë Society,* Volume 29, Number 1 (March 2004): 27–35.

Bullock, Meghan. "Abuse, Silence, and Solitude in Anne Brontë's *The Tenant of Wildfell Hall.*" *Brontë Studies: The Journal of the Brontë Society,* Volume 29, Number 2 (July 2004): 135–141.

Edmondson, Paul. "Shakespeare and the Brontës." *Brontë Studies: The Journal of the Brontë Society,* Volume 29, Number 3 (November 2004): 185–198.

Berglund, Birgitta. "In Defence of Madame Beck." *Brontë Studies: The Journal of the Brontë Society,* Volume 30, Number 3 (November 2005): 185–211.

Bellamy, Joan. "*The Tenant of Wildfell Hall:* What Anne Brontë Knew and What Modern Readers Don't." *Brontë Studies: The Journal of the Brontë Society,* Volume 30, Number 3 (November 2005): 255–257.

Weisser, Susan Ostrov. "Charlotte Brontë, Jane Austen, and the Meaning of Love." *Brontë Studies: The Journal of the Brontë Society,* Volume 31, Number 2 (July 2006): 93–100.

Longmuir, Anne. "Anne Lister and Lesbian Desire in Charlotte Brontë's *Shirley.*" *Brontë Studies: The Journal of the Brontë Society,* Volume 31, Number 2 (July 2006): 145–155.

Stoneman, Patsy. "Addresses from the Land of the Dead': Emily Brontë and Shelley." *Brontë Studies: The Journal of the Brontë Society,* Volume 31, Number 2 (July 2006): 121–131.

Every effort has been made to contact the owners of copyrighted material and secure copyright permission. Articles appearing in this volume generally appear much as they did in their original publication—in some cases foreign language text has been removed from the original article. Those interested in locating the original source will find bibliographic information in the bibliography and acknowledgments sections of this volume.

Index